Contents

IV Building a global voice to protect women's rights

Editorial

Joanna Kerr and Caroline Sweetman

'The world's giant transnational corporations, and the governments and multilateral institutions that cling to them, are globalising the wrong things, things that are of benefit to them and no one else. And they're refusing to globalise the right things, which would benefit all of us.'
(Jorquera, 2000)

'Globalise this – women's rights now.'
(AWID Forum, 2002)

This collection of articles comes from the Association for Women's Rights in Development (AWID)'s Ninth International Forum, on Reinventing Globalisation. The Forum was held in Guadalajara, Mexico, from 3–6 October 2002. The collection was a collaborative effort between AWID and Oxfam GB. It has been jointly edited by Joanna Kerr, Executive Director of AWID, and Caroline Sweetman, of Oxfam GB.

The goal of the Forum was to understand globalisation and its impact on women's rights and gender relations better, and to pinpoint ways in which we can mobilise to ensure these complex processes can guarantee human rights, development and peace for all. Obviously, there were many different takes on globalisation, what it is and what it is doing, from different individuals and organisations at the AWID Forum. This range reflects the overall diversity to be found within the feminist/

gender equality movement. Yet there was clear agreement on the major analysis: globalisation processes, in their current form, are a threat to the gains women have made over the past three decades, in struggling for an end to poverty and equal status and rights with men: in their families, the community and the state. As shown in this collection of articles, radical action is needed, if globalisation is to be re-routed down a just and sustainable path.

In this brief editorial we will distinguish between two interpretations of what globalisation actually means: a largely technical process, and one that is inherently political. The phenomenon of globalisation needs to be demystified if we are to work together to challenge its current course. We will go on to outline the connections between globalisation and gender inequality. Finally, we introduce each article in this collection, and consider how its writer addresses the key issue: that is, how should we turn gender analysis of globalisation into action for social change?

But first, here are a few words to introduce AWID.

Introducing AWID

AWID began its life in 1982, as a membership organisation offering support, and a forum for discussion for policymakers, practitioners and academics promoting gender equality in developing countries. Since then, AWID has grown in both size and scope, to become the dynamic network of thousands of women and men working in development research, policy and practice that it is today. More than half of AWID's members live and work in the global South, Eastern Europe and the former Soviet Union. AWID aims to facilitate ongoing debates about fundamental and provocative issues, as well as to build the individual and organisational capacity of those working for women's empowerment and social justice.

The AWID Forum occurs every three years, and is the largest regular international meeting focusing on women and gender equality outside the United Nations system. It has become a key event for feminists in development. In Guadalajara, around 1,300 leaders, scholars, and practitioners gathered to consider not only the economic, but also the political, social, ecological and cultural implications of globalisation. In more than 150 workshops, plenaries, skills-building sessions and debates, they discussed their experiences of current models of globalisation of the economy and the political system, and debated viable alternatives to the unsustainable, undemocratic, and exploitative forms that globalisation has taken so far.

What is globalisation?

Reams of paper and thousands of keystrokes have been expended in theoretical debates about globalisation. But the concerns of the readers – and writers – of this collection of articles are about formulating development policy and practice which promotes gender equality as a part of its vision. Two key points emerge from the debates, which help to clarify what globalisation actually is, and its implications for womens' rights.

Globalisation as a technical process
Some, such as broadcasters on CNN,

mainstream economists, or your local IT provider, use the word 'globalisation' in a technical, rather than a political way, to refer to the increasing ease with which people can communicate and do business internationally. This means that international financial transactions can be executed in a split second, changing the fate of national economies overnight. Events unfolding in Asia can be beamed into living rooms in South America in the course of a few minutes.

Some critics of globalisation see these new technologies as being inherently bad for human rights and the sustainable development of the planet. They decry the way in which global technologies promote an international Western-dominated culture of consumerism and capitalist development. They emphasise that the most appropriate, just and fair economic and political decision-making is made at local level, by women and men who have full knowledge of the realities of the social and cultural context.

In contrast, some opponents of globalisation can see the potential of the new technologies for change that benefits people. For example, they believe that if free trade was genuinely free and protectionism was lifted in the global North, developing countries would potentially be able to challenge global inequality. Women around the world could benefit from buying food, clothing, or computers at cheaper prices. Another example, which is often pointed out by feminists, is that of the potential of the Internet to build a new and genuinely participatory kind of democracy. Using the Internet, global networks of activists can meet up, develop their ideas in real-time chat rooms, and plan political action.

Globalisation as a political process
People who see the technical processes of globalisation as potentially useful often tend to use the word 'globalisation' as a shorthand term for the ways the new

technologies are being used by the current generation of economists and politicians.

Some – the supporters of neo-liberal development strategies – think globalisation in its current form is broadly beneficial to humanity. They argue that speedy global travel and communications enable companies to invest in parts of the world which have hitherto been isolated from international production and world trade, and speak of the level playing field which globalisation can potentially create. Globalisation is 'sold' as apolitical, concerned only with economics; as pro-growth and pro-poor.

However, there is now a vast and weighty body of evidence that proves globalisation to be profoundly political: states play a very significant role in facilitating the activities of transnational corporations. The evidence also shows that globalisation in its current form does not challenge deep-rooted, structural poverty, either for nations or for individuals and their families. Critics decry the present model of globalisation for eroding human rights, and diminishing the ability of individual governments to protect their citizens' rights. Governments are not able to determine their own economic policies to suit the particular context of the country they have been elected to rule, and their ability to address and solve problems of inequality and poverty is therefore dramatically compromised.

Many governments of developing countries, and NGOs involved in development in North and South, argue that globalisation processes are consolidating a new kind of colonialism. Increasingly, power and resources are being held by a relatively small number of global players, who are unaccountable to the vast populations of people in poverty in the global South. These global players are international businesses, states in the global North, and elites in North and South. Antony Giddens has asked: 'Does globalisation mark the increasing ever-expanding tendency of Western countries, economies and capitalism to dominate the rest of the world? ... All formal empires, with the possible exception of the American Empire, if you want to call it that, have disappeared from the world' (Giddens, Lecture 1, Reith Lectures 1999).

Gidden's mention of the U.S.A. here chimes with critics of the current model of world development, who highlight the way in which the global North (that is, both the U.S. and other prosperous countries, including Canada and those of the European Economic Community) is forcing its political convictions and its preferred economic model onto poor countries in the global South and Eastern Europe. The countries of the global South have a history of economic exploitation by richer nations, and many are hugely in debt to international financial institutions (IFIs). This, together with a lack of democracy in IFI decision-making, creates a very weak bargaining position for most of them. Through the 1980s and beyond, Southern countries have been forced to introduce a package of neo-liberal economic policies, which are supposed to encourage economic growth.

Their borders have been forced open to trade and investment. While international regulation of world trade by the World Trade Organisation (WTO) is supposed to create equal opportunities for all economies in a global marketplace, in fact 'free trade' is really a misnomer. International trade rules purport to bring prosperity for all, by enabling all countries to compete on equal terms for shares of the international market. Yet, the rich countries of the global North do not follow the same rules as those in the South: for example, protectionist policies continue to shelter farmers and industrialists in Northern countries. In the global South, transnational corporations offer desperate workers precarious and exploitative employment. Their bargaining position is usually too weak to enable them to attain better conditions, since the international migration of workers is prevented by harsh laws protecting the US and 'Fortress Europe' from immigrants in search of a better life.

Why is globalisation a gender issue?

How is globalisation affecting the power imbalance between women and men, which is a feature of almost all cultures throughout the world? What does it do to women's daily lives? For over 20 years, gender and development and feminist researchers have studied aspects of globalisation, and their impact on women. The economic 'reforms' of the 1980s and 1990s promoted a shift in emphasis from production for domestic consumption, in both industry and agriculture. A wealth of research now exists to show the impact of this supposedly 'gender-neutral' change in emphasis, on women's daily lives and on their status in society.

Much of this research examines the links between ordinary women and their dependents, international rules about trade, and policies imposed on debtor countries by the international financial institutions. Far from being gender-neutral in their impact on communities, international financial policies have a dramatic direct impact on individual women and on gender relations throughout society. Some kinds of impact have been researched more than others, over a longer period of time.

For example, one well-established body of work looks at the effect of structural adjustment on women – in particular, in relation to cutbacks to social services and shifts to cash-crop cultivation for export. In agriculture, pressure from governments to produce cash crops for export has led to a reduction in women's control over the fruits of their labour. This is because there is a correlation in the majority of societies between male domination of women and male control over activities which earn income. Women who used to spend their time cultivating staple crops for family consumption are now obliged to labour on fields of sugar or flowers for export. They rarely see the money earned, and cannot use the new crops they grow to feed their families. Women are overworked and disempowered, and their children can go hungry.

Another strand in the feminist research on globalisation looks at the impact of employment for global markets on individual women and on gender relations more widely. In industry, globalisation has resulted in a profound change in the relationship between factory workers and the companies whose products they make. The propensity of factories to employ a female workforce was first noted by feminist researchers in the 1970s and 1980s. Then, women were directly employed by national companies. Nowadays, local employers are part of an international chain which links vast transnational corporations to individual women workers, turning out garments, toys and other consumer commodities for a US-inspired global market.

Many commentators assert that women's primary responsibility for their dependents makes them more desperate then men for work, willing to accept lower wages, precarious terms of employment, and poor working conditions. Much energy has gone into debating whether employment in industry is, overall, a good or bad thing for individual women's daily lives, and for the status of women more widely. But this is a sterile debate, which is based on a false premise that women's working conditions cannot be challenged. Every worker, male or female, throughout the world, should be able to find a job that offers a fair wage in safe conditions.

More recent analysis in the field has examined the many new challenges that have arisen in the context of a globalised world. At first glance, these challenges seem quite unrelated to each other; yet globalisation connects them. The escalation of trafficking in women is an outcome of globalisation that pushes women into new forms of precarious transnational employment. Drug treatments for HIV/AIDS – a disease which is highly gendered – have become pawns in an international struggle for intellectual property rights, as multinational companies try to control the accessibility of generic drugs through trade laws. And the rise in fundamentalism is also connected to globalisation, as politico-religious movements react to Western-imposed cultural domination. These emerging right-wing movements promote their own interpretations of 'tradition' and 'culture', at the expense of women's rights, and often their lives.

Turning analysis into action

So, we have the analysis of the impact of aspects of globalisation on women and gender relations. Yet, all too often, we have not taken up this analysis and transformed it into action, whether we work in women's organisations or in development organisations working on gender equality. It is easier to pinpoint what is wrong with the world than it is to suggest ways of putting it right. Much analysis of the gendered impact of globalisation has gathered dust on the shelves of resource centres and libraries. It is critical now to ensure that political action is taken, based on women's experience of globalisation – both the considerable losses, and the undeniable gains – to ensure that international laws and regulations work for women in poverty rather than against them. This was the starting-point for AWID's Forum.

Envisioning economic policy which is friendly to women

In her article here, Nilüfer Çağatay traces the impact on women of economic liberalisation policies, imposed on countries in the grip of financial crisis through the 1980s and 1990s. International financial institutions imposed a rigid package of 'reforms', aiming to open up markets and reduce the role of the state. Nilüfer Çağatay outlines the impact on women and gender relations of SAPs and macro-economic stabilisation. She highlights the fact that these have typically led to a fiscal squeeze by putting pressure on public budgets, asserting that 'The fiscal policies of most governments in the last 20 years reflect the increased power of capital vis-à-vis labour, on the one hand, and of foreign and national investors vis-à-vis the rest of the citizenry, on the other' (this issue). State spending on social welfare has reduced, throwing the burden of social welfare provision back into the home. Because, in most societies, the gender division of labour leaves women with chief responsibility for the care of the family, reductions in health, education and sanitation spending challenge them to create an alternative. The article points out that a variety of feminist policy positions have been developed on global taxation, debt cancellation, antimilitarism, and overseas development assistance. These policies can be – and need to be – supported by the advocacy efforts of mainstream development organisations as well as feminist organisations, in order to gain visibility and have a real impact on international policy-making.

Ruth Pearson's article provides an accessible guide to some of the key agreements in world trade, and states why international trade cannot be seen as a 'gender-free zone'. The existence of culturally-condoned gender roles in all human societies leads to seemingly neutral policies having different implications for women and men. In order to challenge policies which lead to greater inequality between women and men, these policies need to be demystified by feminist economists who are committed to rendering them comprehensible and accessible to organisations who want to lobby for change. Pearson devotes the second half of her article to outlining ideas for alternative policies, some currently being activated and others that need energy from activists to be turned from ideas into reality.

Economic policy that is friendly to women needs to be based on accurate data which reflect the nature and scope of women's contribution to global production. Marilyn Waring's article reminds us of the fact that international institutions continue to use outdated, inaccurate and illogical measures of economic activity, which ignore key parts of women's economic activity. These are work within the home, and work in the informal sector. Despite challenges from feminists for the past three decades, worthless statistics are still collected year after year, and used to form national and international economic policy. Waring discusses and critiques some practical alternatives that have been developed. Improved methods of data collection and analysis have potential to involve women, and entire communities, in determining the information relevant to policy-formulation, and reporting it accurately.

Acknowledging globalisation's political dimension

Time and again, at the Forum and again in their articles in this collection, writers highlight the political dimensions of globalisation.

For some, this means challenging the idea that economic development is somehow separate from the political sphere. Zo Randriamaro of the GERA (Gender and Economic Reforms in Africa) network addresses this issue in the context of African women's varied experiences of globalisation. GERA is a pan-African research and advocacy programme, set up in 1996. It aims to increase the participation of African women in the formulation of economic policy. Zo's article focuses on three important issues, which she argues GERA and others need to ensure are placed

high on the agenda of the international institutions responsible for economic reform. These are: the false message that economic policy is apolitical; the pressing need to ensure good governance of international trade; and the need for women in Africa and beyond to speak out against the way in which human security concerns are currently being equated with the security of states and corporations, at the expense of the security of individuals.

For others, thinking about the political dimension of globalisation means considering the implications of the rapidly-changing world order over the past 15 years. Many factors, including the fall of the Communist bloc, the rise of the religious right in many countries, (both Islamic and Christian), continuing turmoil in the Middle East, and the attack on the World Trade Centre, have transformed the world we live in. At the AWID conference, there was much discussion around feminist responses to various forms of restrictions on civil liberties, and in particular those of women. In her article, Fatou Sow, of Women Living Under Muslim Laws and DAWN, highlights the way in which 'the woman is the symbol of ethnic purity for nationalists'. The need to protect the nation often results in curtailing women's freedoms and violations of their human rights.

In her article, Brazilian lawyer and activist Valéria Pandjiarjian explores this theme further. Enormous advances have been made in international human rights law in the past few decades, to ensure it meets the needs and interests of women. This is globalisation working in women's favour. It is essential that the advances of the past few decades are not lost, and that where international law has not yet advanced sufficiently far, it is allowed to do so. Valéria Pandjiarjian's organisation, CLADEM (Latin American and Caribbean Committee for the Defence of Woman's Rights) is part of a network of organisations currently campaigning for an Inter-American Convention on Sexual Rights and Reproductive Rights. The goal is to challenge the laws and social beliefs in Central and Latin American countries, concerning sexual practices and reproductive choices. The campaign has been mounted to raise the awareness of policy makers and the public about the connections between reproductive choice, sexuality, and economic, social and political development.

Moving the focus north to the United States, two US academics, Mona Danner and Gay Young, provide a critique of US domestic and foreign policy at this time of global instability, focusing on the impact on women. Like Zo Randriamaro, they assert that global economic policies exported by US- and European-led IFIs, and the current focus on security, act in the interests of international capital at the expense of the human rights of individuals. They highlight the ways in which the focus on ensuring security from terrorism are threatening civil rights, and encouraging xenophobia against ethnic and religious minorities. They call for feminist analysis to make the links between economic globalisation processes and the growing global political dominance of the US, and for feminist action to challenge the rule of white, Western, heterosexual, wealthy men over international institutions which shape the future of us all.

One restriction on women's civil liberties, which occurs daily in all societies, receives markedly little attention from the public, from feminist organisations, or from development agencies. In her article, Sanya Sarnavka discusses the role of the mainstream media – now global, as well as local – in promoting sexist and stereotypical images of women. These feed the public imagination and present a real threat to progress in promoting women's role in public life and, ultimately, gender equality.

Into the future: specific issues of global concern

In addition to critiques of globalisation, the AWID Forum attracted presenters who are at the cutting edge of analysis and action on specific issues of global concern. Presentations ranged over an extremely wide array of topics, ranging from those which have been a focus for feminist action for years, yet remain on the agenda, to those which are entirely new. They included subjects as various as present and future conflict over water resources, to the future role of the UN in furthering a global women's rights agenda. When we started to plan this collection of articles, we wanted to include articles on both the latter, and many more. However, some writers were not able to contribute due to pressures of time and work, and we also had an obvious physical limit on space. Hence, this collection includes only a small number of articles to give a flavour of the array of different concerns at the Forum.[1]

Maternal mortality and the Millennium Development Goals

Lynn Freedman's article is an example of a Forum presentation on a topic of paramount importance to millions of women, on which much remains to be done. While much progress was made in the mid- to late 1990s on promoting women's reproductive rights, reproductive health was expunged from the Millennium Declaration document which outlines development goals to be reached by 2015. The focus on maternal mortality which is included in the document does, however, offer much scope for advocacy. Lynn Freedman argues that: 'In short, a maternal mortality strategy that focuses on emergency obstetric care (EmOC) gives health and human rights advocacy a *structural* perspective and concrete, do-able agenda that simultaneously addresses some of the most important challenges in the health and human rights fields in an era of globalisation' (this issue).

HIV/AIDS: the globalisation of a disease
HIV/AIDS is clearly an overwhelmingly huge current concern in sub-Saharan Africa. It will be an issue of equal enormity in Asia and Eastern Europe in a few years' time. In her article, based on a plenary presentation delivered at AWID, Sisonke Msimang outlines the process through which HIV infection spreads in situations of poverty and gender inequality. She emphasises that AIDS and death come all the quicker to HIV sufferers who lack good food, water supplies and a safe, comfortable place to stay. In the context of Sisonke's home country, South Africa, colonialism and apartheid, with their extreme exploitation of African workers and destruction of family life, have created a recipe for mass HIV infection. The challenge now is to ensure global action to prevent future infections, and enable those who already have the disease to arrest it, using anti-retroviral drugs which are currently available only to the affluent, due to world trade regulations protecting the interests of international drug companies.

Feminist concerns about new reproductive technologies
Moving from the grim ongoing realities of maternal mortality and AIDS to a health-related issue which is entirely new, a pioneering article in this collection discusses the need for a concerted rejection of new genetic technologies. Lisa Handwerker recognises the great diversity of feminist perspectives towards new reproductive technologies, but argues that we need to unite to oppose human reproductive cloning. Despite the fact that this issue appears only to be relevant to a minority of affluent people in the global North, its relevance to human rights activists all over the world should not be underestimated. All of us need to be aware that women's

reproductive rights discourses can be, and are being, misused by organisations employing whatever means possible in their fight for the right to develop processes such as the cloning of human beings for their own ends. This article argues that such technologies are not one more advance in the fight for 'reproductive choice', but are actually a global threat to the interests of women and children, and to wider humanity.

Trafficking and sexual slavery
A significant strand of the discussions at AWID was concerned with the globalisation of trafficking and sexual slavery – the most abhorrent aspect of the globalisation of labour. One key aspect of the ideal of truly free trade is that people should be free to travel, across state boundaries if necessary, to take up employment opportunities. But the fact that international migration has been clamped down on in the past 50 years has now led to a situation where such migration is limited or non-existent. A key survival strategy on which whole families depend is women migrating for work as domestics or sex workers. For women from poor backgrounds who are uneducated, it can often only take place illegally, via a globalised network of traffickers in human beings. Desperate for a livelihood, some travel in full or partial awareness of the dangers they face, yet they take the gamble in the hope of bridging the extraordinary gap between their lives of poverty and the affluence of life in the US and Europe. This issue, and the need for international action to solve the problem is discussed in this collection by Pamela Shifman and an international panel of activists.

Building a global voice to promote women's rights

It is implicit in all the above that action on the part of the international women's movement and gender and development policymakers and practitioners is needed more than ever. We must protect the gains made over the past three decades and hitherto, and ensure the perspectives of women in poverty are heard in global protests against unjust and unsustainable world development.

The need for women's organisations to work together, and in partnership with feminists in government and NGOs, was very clear at the AWID Forum. Two articles in this collection capture a flavour of the lively debates which were had around the challenges of working in these ways.

Challenges for the international women's movement

The women's movement is currently on its 'third wave'.[2] Having successfully drawn in women who do not have direct experience of the dramatic days of the 1970s and 1980s – those in their thirties, and those a decade or so younger – the women's movement is now challenged by inter-generational issues. Who runs the movement? Whose voices are heard? While some older women feel their experience is undervalued by younger women coming in, some younger women feel their energy and grasp of what makes the new generation tick is consigned to the sidelines. In their article, Andrea Medina Rosas and Shamillah Wilson discuss a workshop held at AWID which facilitated a discussion between the generations, aiming to achieve mutual awareness and appreciation of the age-related tensions within the movement, and to build a commitment to use this diversity as a strength.

Challenges for development organisations working to promote gender equality

Another relationship which is often tense, but of great importance, is that between feminist activists in the wider women's movement, and gender and development policy makers and practitioners working in mainstream organisations concerned with development. It is quite clear from the evidence of the gendered impact of globalisation that international financial institutions, and national and international government bodies, have not taken on key messages regarding gender, poverty, and equality. However, despite the blindness of many of them to these issues, the majority of them are – at the very least – playing lip-service to 'gender mainstreaming' – that is, to ensuring that a gender analysis informs all their work. In many organisations, including multilateral and bilateral development agencies, the work of gender mainstreaming is deemed complete. Yet, if gender mainstreaming *had* occurred, we would see radical transformation of the organisation's work, and the end result would be a very different world. In their article, Aruna Rao and David Kelleher assert the need for development organisations to move up a gear, from a focus on systems, procedures and policies, to a more radical approach. Their own work, in the Gender at Work initiative, offers a strategy for mainstream development organisations to use, to ensure gender equality is the outcome of all their work.

Conclusion

This issue speaks to the many complex and interrelated challenges facing gender equality advocates worldwide that continue to emerge as a result of globalisation. It also contributes to a growing number of concrete strategies needed to 'reinvent globalisation' to ensure human rights for all women and men. For AWID, these ideas emerging from the Forum go well beyond the conference. They become the substance of analysis and organising for AWID's growing membership around the world. By moving a human rights and development agenda forward within the women's/feminist communities that can address globalisation's impacts, more actors will have the tools and analysis to fight for economic justice. Similarly, AWID intends to widen the circle and work with a larger constituency of the 'unconverted' – that is, mainstream economists, policy makers and opinion leaders – on transforming the global economic processes that currently underpin gender inequalities. Ultimately, our analysis has to be more rigorous, our policy solutions compelling, and, of course, our voices stronger. The strong feminist leadership and solidarity discernible in Guadalajara is a clear indication that change is possible – or quite simply that women's rights can be globalised.

Joanna Kerr is Executive Director of The Association for Women's Rights in Development. Postal Address: 96 Spadina Avenue, Suite 401, Toronto, Ontario, Canada, M5V 2J6. jkerr@awid.org

Caroline Sweetman is Editor of Gender and Development, and a member of the International Planning Committee for the Ninth AWID Forum. CSweetman@oxfam.org.uk

Notes

1 Nonetheless, there are many articles available in English, French and Spanish on the AWID website at www.awid.org In addition, AWID has published the Highlights of the Forum including issues discussed in many of the workshops and plenaries. Information on this publication is available through the website.

2 The first wave being the nineteenth and twentieth century movement to obtain civil rights for women in many countries, and the second, dating from the 1970s, focusing on employment and reproductive rights, among other issues.

Reference

Jorquera, J. (2000) 'The choice is clear: globalization for capital, or for people', in *The Age*, September 11 (at www.globalpolicy.org/socecon/movement/jorquera.htm, last checked 31 March 2003)

Part I
The economics of globalisation

Gender budgets and beyond:
feminist fiscal policy in the context of globalisation

Nilüfer Çağatay

Macro-economic theories and macro-economic policies in general, and fiscal policies in particular, are seldom, if ever, gender-neutral. Since the mid-eighties, gender budget analysis, which has been undertaken in many countries, has been a key strategy to challenge macro-economic theorising and policy-making. Such initiatives, along with a variety of pro-poor budget initiatives, constitute the major challenge to the prevailing fiscal policy stance in many countries. The purpose of this paper is to discuss the changes in the fiscal policy stance in the context of liberalisation and globalisation in order to draw out their implications for social inequality, especially gender inequality. The article ends by discussing a variety of policy advocacy positions open to feminist activists, to build on the work of gender budget initiatives.

From the Keynesian consensus to the Washington consensus

In the post-war period, macro-economic policy making reflected the 'Keynesian consensus', which highlighted the role of the state in employment generation, growth and redistribution. In economies of the South, the developmental state took a leading role in promoting growth through investment. It was recognised that the active role of the state was needed to counter the effect of market failures, or the simple absence of markets. The Keynesian approach also recognised that capitalist economies are prone to economic crises, and go through cycles. Fiscal policy, especially in economies of the global North, was designed to counter the ups and downs of the cycle. Some forms of state expenditure, such as unemployment benefits, were called 'automatic stabilisers', in that they kicked in automatically to counter the effects of reductions in economic activity,

and increased employment during economic downturns, and diminished as the economy came out of recession.

In the late 1970s and 1980s, partly as a result of the increase in oil prices and the ensuing debt crisis, budget deficits became unsustainable and inflationary. In the South, macro-economic stabilisation policies were adopted in conjunction with structural adjustment policies (SAPs). These were intended to minimise the role of the state, which had begun to be seen as 'inefficient'. The 'Washington consensus', with its emphasis on market liberalisation, replaced the earlier 'Keynesian consensus'. A variety of market liberalisation policies, such as trade liberalisation, financial liberalisation, labour market 'deregulation' and capital account liberalisation, were put into place. Similar sets of policies were also adopted in the industrialised economics in the 1980s. In the 1990s, the transition economies followed suit, under the rubric of economic restructuring. The immediate objective of these policies was to achieve macro-economic stabilisation, which was viewed as critical for achieving sustained growth. The broader objective was the reduction of the role of the state in economic life.

Fiscal policy[1] was usually reoriented toward combating inflation and reducing current account deficits. Public spending – especially on social sectors – was cut in country after country, in order to achieve fiscal balance. Because the state was seen as crowding out the 'efficient' private sector, employment in the public sector was reduced, and the privatisation of public services became a key policy objective. User fees were adopted in order to increase the efficiency of public service delivery, and raise revenues. To be credible to financial investors, governments had to keep budget deficits low and interest rates high, which introduced a deflationary bias (that is, a bias in favour of deflation) into the world economy. All these policies were expected to produce sustained growth, increased efficiency and benefits that would improve the well-being of all, through the trickle-down of wealth.

The record of the last 20 years shows that market liberalisation policies have failed to deliver on many fronts. While the fiscal balances of many countries did improve, inflation rates did come down, and international trade and investment flows did increase immensely, the promise of higher and sustained growth rates has not materialised. The lower world growth rates in the world economy (compared to its record of the previous decades) reflect the deflationary bias of current economic policies. In many Latin American and sub-Saharan African economies, growth rates over the last two decades were very low, and macro-economic performance was generally characterised by stop-and-go cycles. The East Asian crisis of the late 1990s brought home the point that even the 'miracle' economies of East Asia, which had experienced sustained high growth rates

for three decades, were not immune to deep crises. The world economy became more volatile, as economic crises spread from one country to another with lightning speed. The international integration of national economies through trade and investment flows has made it more difficult for governments to shield their economies against crises that break out in other economies.

The increased mobility of short-term capital flows means that relatively few financial investors could potentially wreak havoc in the world economy by moving funds from one country to another in a short period of time. This vulnerability has caused insecurity. At the same time, in many countries, inequality has worsened across households, between capital (business owners) and labour (their workforce), and among different segments of labour (highly skilled versus unskilled workers). Numbers of people living under poverty have either increased or remained constant in many countries. (van der Hoeven 2000; UNDP 1999, Milanovic 2003).

Double jeopardy: the fiscal squeeze

As outlined above, many of the liberalisation policies implemented as part of SAPs and macro-economic stabilisation programmes have led to a fiscal squeeze by putting pressure on public budgets (Grunberg 1998). On the revenue side, market liberalisation has led to erosion of public revenues, as I explain below. On the expenditure side, it has had the effect of increasing economic insecurity and vulnerability, because increasing volatility of markets leads to a rise in the demand for social protection (Rodrik 1997). The preferred way of closing deficits has been to cut expenditure.

Specifically, the Washington consensus has led to the following effects on the revenue side:

Trade taxes

Trade taxes, which amounted to about one-third of government revenues in many low-income countries, have been steeply reduced under trade liberalisation (Grunberg 1998; UNDP 2003). Competition among governments to attract foreign direct investment has led to a reduction in corporate and capital gains taxes. For example, in the OECD countries,[2] all countries except for two reduced their rates in the top tax bracket in the late 1980s (UNDP 1999, 3). Thus the burden of taxation on owners of capital went down. At the same time, many countries have introduced export-processing zones where businesses are exempt from paying tax. This has meant a shift in the burden of taxation from business owners, whose funds are increasingly mobile, to workers, who are relatively immobile (except for highly skilled people). An implication of these phenomena is that the burden of taxation has also been shifting from men to women, since women own and control much less property compared to men worldwide, although the exact figures are not known.

No increase in official development assistance

Official development assistance (ODA), which is an important source of revenue for some of the poorest countries, has not increased, as many industrialised countries have failed to live up their pledge to channel 0.7 per cent of their GNP to development assistance.

Introduction of indirect taxes and user fees

In an effort to increase revenues, a number of countries have reformed tax collection, instituting value-added taxes or introducing user fees for some public services, which leads to people living in poverty shouldering more of the tax burden.

Privatisation and sales of public assets

Together, privatisation and sales of public assets in order to raise revenues have become an important, but unsustainable, method for governments to close budget deficits.

On the expenditure side, the following can be observed:

Increased demand for public spending, but fewer resources

Increased volatility, insecurity and income inequality has resulted in an increased demand for public spending in the form of social protection. But as many economies have continued to suffer from a high debt burden, debt servicing has left little in the way of resources for the provisioning of health, education and other needs. The HIPC (Highly Indebted Poor Income Countries) initiative has failed to provide much relief to such economies, as debt relief was made contingent upon the implementation of 'sound macro-economic policy'. This means in effect the adoption of the Washington consensus approach, albeit with some recent modifications to put more emphasis on poverty and the reform of institutions. PRSPs (Poverty Reduction Strategy Papers) continue to insist on the same type of macro-economic strategies.

Continuing loss of public resources through corruption

The squandering of public resources through corruption has continued. Privatisation, which was supposed to reduce state expenditures and inefficiency as well as curb corruption, has become a new avenue for corruption.

Continued high levels of military spending

The politics of the Cold War and its continuing legacy of militarism in the North and the South, and the activities of arms dealers, mean that in many countries military expenditure has kept its importance. The peace dividend that it was hoped would accompany the end of the Cold War has not materialised. While many governments have continued to plead poverty, they have resisted reducing military expenditure, and some of the poorest countries have continued to develop nuclear arms.[3]

The implications of fiscal retrenchment for growth, development and equality

These changes in the fiscal stance over the last two decades have many implications for economic growth, and for equality (in terms of class as well as gender relations). These are interconnected to some extent. Cuts in government spending and market liberalisation have had adverse effects on the ability of the state to promote growth and employment, human development, and social equity (ECLAC 1998). This has had profound implications for redistribution of income between classes (to the detriment of workers), and between women and men (to the detriment of women).

The way a government allocates its spending shows its vision and economic priorities, as well as the balance of power among different social groups. The fiscal policies of most governments in the last 20 years reflect the increased power of capital vis-à-vis labour, on the one hand, and of foreign and national investors vis-à-vis the rest of the citizenry, on the other. As men generally own and control a higher proportion of capital compared to women, this also represents the increased economic power of men vis-à-vis women.

However, the social content of macroeconomic policies (Elson and Cağatay 2000) – that is, the fact that they reflect, and affect, the balance of power across different social groups because of the way in which they affect the distribution of resources – has been obscured because fiscal policy-making has been presented as a technical

issue over the last 20 years. Because of this, little public debate has taken place on alternative patterns of taxation and public spending, and their impact on different social groups (ECLAC 1998), leading to a lack of accountability and transparency. While fiscal credibility and accountability vis-à-vis potential foreign investors has been of utmost importance, their significance for the citizenry at large as an aspect of economic democratisation is hardly recognised (Elson and Cagatay 2000).

Effects on growth and stability

1. Anti-deficit radicalism
It is argued that inflation is detrimental to economic growth and works against the interests of people in poverty, and that budgets therefore need to be balanced in order to achieve zero inflation rate. However, this 'anti-deficit radicalism' is misguided: while high levels of inflation do have adverse effects on economic growth, moderate levels of inflation do not have such an effect. (Sen, A.K. 1998; van der Hoeven 2000). As keeping budgets in check is accomplished through cuts in social services, anti-deficit radicalism has jeopardised long-term human development, well-being, social equity and growth (Sen, A.K. 1998, Sen, G. 2000). Limiting public spending on infrastructure, which as a rule encourages private investment, and limiting and/or cutting health and education expenditure, reduces social equity (as poor segments of the population and women are more likely to benefit from these services) and human development. In addition, such limitations also have negative feedback effects on the long-run growth potential of an economy (Sen, A.K. 1998).

At the same time, high interest rates that are intended to attract foreign investment have discouraged domestic investment and employment generation by the private sector. The expected flows of foreign direct investment have materialised in only a few countries, mostly in Asia, while the cost of borrowing has remained high for domestic firms.

2. Failure to stabilise during economic downturns

Another related problem of the last two decades is that the approach to government spending in many countries has heightened the peaks and troughs of the economic cycle, rather than evened them out, as it used to during the Keynesian consensus.

Despite the achievement of low inflation rates and fiscal balances, which were envisioned as important elements in stabilising the economy, there are other sources of instability in the Washington consensus policy package. National economies are potentially less stable due to the liberalisation of capital flows.[4] Governments are unable to take measures to stabilise the economy during downswings, partly because multilateral finance agencies that monitor structural adjustment programmes overemphasise deficit indicators without regard to whether the economy is in the upswing or downswing of a cycle (ECLAC 1998). Budget deficits are likely to change over the course of a cycle, usually increasing during the downswing. This practice of ignoring the impact of the cycle in the monitoring of deficits has led to drastic adjustments, with adverse consequences for the economy. For example, one of the initial policy positions, formulated by the IMF in response to the East Asian crisis (despite opposition from the World Bank), was to cut public expenditure (Stiglitz 2002). Increased restraint in government spending during a crisis only exacerbates the economic downturn. In economies with little or no social protection to speak of, the adverse distributive consequences for poor people and poor women, in particular, are immense.

The gender implications of liberalisation
1. Cutbacks in social spending

Gender equality and pro-poor budget initiatives undertaken in the last two decades have shown that the impact of public spending and various revenue-raising methods are seldom, if ever, gender or class-neutral. Excessive reductions in social programmes that directly enhance human capabilities are harmful for all living in poverty. However, social programmes ameliorate the impact of gender inequality within households, and cutbacks in these services therefore affect women and girls disproportionately. In extreme situations, gender inequality results in female deaths. For example, gender inequality means that in many societies, women and girls are less likely than men and boys to be well-nourished, or to have access to health care. There are an estimated up to 100 million 'missing women' worldwide (Sen, A.K. 2001). Given these facts, the state has an extremely important role to play in order to offset this gender bias, through social provisioning.

In most countries, poor or otherwise, the major responsibility for caring for the sick (as well as other forms of unpaid caring labour) at home falls on the shoulders of women. This results in another type of gender bias that can be seen in the unequal labour burden borne by women, which is largely invisible in traditional macro-economic analysis and policy making, since the latter focuses on the monetised economy. Cutbacks in state spending on social provisioning affect women disproportionately because of this unpaid labour. An example is state cutbacks in the provision of clean water. Lack of clean water is a major cause of disease and ill health for women and men alike. However, there are additional consequences for women and girls, as in poor countries it is their responsibility to fetch water.

2. Other spending and revenue-raising

Many other types of expenditure and revenue-raising also have implications for women, aggravating unequal gender relations. Cutbacks in the public sector have particular implications because of gender segregation in labour markets. In some economies, the public sector has in the past given greater employment opportunities to women compared to men. Outside the public sphere, there may be relatively few opportunities of employment that offer comparably good work conditions. Privatisation has led to large employment losses, and to cuts in the number of formal sector jobs, for example in Africa and Latin America (van der Hoeven 2000).

Revenue generation methods, such as user fees or indirect taxation such as consumption taxes (which are less progressive than income taxes) are class-biased against segments of the population with lower incomes, but they are also often gender-biased. This can result from the higher incidence of 'income poverty' among women and girls in some countries. It is also because women earn lower incomes compared to men.

Gender bias in economic crises: the impact on women

The impact of economic crises and volatility is often more severe for women. There are a variety of reasons for this. First is the gender-biased nature of social protection systems. Such systems are very inadequate for both women and men in the global South, partly because women's paid work conditions are inferior and more insecure compared to those of men. It is also because social insurance systems are almost invariably designed on the assumption that families have a male breadwinner in a formal sector job (Elson and Cağatay 2000). Women's work is much more likely to be in the informal sector, and

is therefore often outside the realm of existing social insurance systems. It is also assumed that women whose work consists of unpaid domestic labour will be the beneficiaries of social protection provided to the male breadwinners in the family. Thus, fewer women are recipients of social protection than men (United Nations 1999). This is one of the reasons why they are more vulnerable to poverty, and more insecure economically.

While this bias dates from the Keynesian consensus, the Washington consensus has added another: commodification bias (Elson and Cağatay 2000). This refers to the trend towards the private ownership of knowledge, life forms, and goods that were previously publicly provided or held in common. This works to the detriment of poor people, and especially of women and girls.

Economic crises and instability result in a huge additional work burden for women. In the last resort, women provide social protection in most developing countries, where social safety nets are few. They buffer their families from the ill-effects of economic crisis by working harder both within and outside the household, to make up for reduced private incomes and reduced public services. Their paid and unpaid workload often increases in absolute and relative terms compared to that of men.

Women's role as primary carers for their families means that crisis makes disproportionate demands on their time and energy. Their work in the home (and sometimes in the wider community) increases, as they spend more time shopping trying to stretch their family budgets further, or working at home to substitute home-produced goods for those purchased outside. They may also sometimes respond to crisis by setting up 'communal kitchens', where economies of scale can be gained, or engaging in other types of communal (or volunteer) labour.

A third gender bias may result from the fact that income disparities may increase between men and women, as women crowd further into female-stereotyped work, which is often informal. A fourth gender bias may come about when girls, rather than boys, are pulled from schooling during periods of economic distress to care for younger siblings or other family members when their mothers seek paid work. They may also be pulled out disproportionately from schooling when family incomes go down, even if the cost of schooling remains the same (i.e. no new fees are imposed). Even if family incomes are restored after the economy enters a period of macro-economic recovery, the educational losses incurred are not easily remedied, and translate into permanent gender inequalities.

A fifth problem is that crises and instability may lead to increased social violence and domestic violence, as some dimensions of the ideologies of masculinity, such as the male breadwinner ideology, are challenged. This may result in more violence against women, as men attempt to regain a sense of power and agency.

Democratising fiscal policy and increasing accountability to women

However, during the last two decades, there have also been a wide range of efforts around the world to democratise fiscal policy in the form of pro- poor and gender-sensitive budget initiatives (Cağatay, Keklik, Lal and Lang 2000). The latter focus mostly on the expenditure side, and analyse not only government allocations specifically targeted at women, but rather all allocations. The purpose is to uncover the differential impacts of allocations on women and men; boys and girls (Budlender, Sharp and Allen 1998; Commonwealth Secretariat 1999). Such analyses, which are sometimes accompanied by broader analyses of the macro-economic framework, then serve as the basis for the formulation of gender-equitable budgets. These initiatives have far-reaching political and economic implications, and are very important tools for women and poor people to make governments accountable, and for them to make claims on public resources.

However, in the context of globalisation, fiscal policy cannot be rendered gender-equitable or broadly equitable at the national or local levels alone. It is also necessary to address these concerns at the international level, and to ensure that there is coherence among the international dimensions of policy and advocacy and the national and local ones. A variety of policy positions (for example, on global taxation, debt cancellation, anti-militarism, and overseas development assistance) are taken by civil society organisations, including feminist ones, and these need to be supported by broader constituents of feminists with greater focus and visibility. There also needs to be more debate and dialogue on how to shape these positions in ways that are more gender-equitable.

A number of feminist groups, such as DAWN (Development Alternatives with Women for a New era) have been involved in these debates for a long time. The point here is not the absence of feminist analysis, but rather the strengthening of advocacy based on it. This can be accomplished through greater dialogue between a) feminists who are involved in national or local budget initiatives and those who do advocacy at the international level; b) between feminists and other groups who focus on democratising macro-economic policies (such as those who focus on pro-poor budgets or other types of progressive macro-economic policy making at the national and global levels and c) between feminists involved in budget initiatives in the South and the North. Some of these areas are briefly outlined below.

Global taxation and redistribution schemes

Schemes like the Tobin tax,[5] or the institution of a global taxation authority, need to receive more attention from feminist activists. Revenue generated by such taxation could be an important source of universal public provisioning of basic social services, including healthcare, education, nutrition, sanitation and water, and funding to realise country-specific gender equity goals. A portion of the revenues could be awarded to governments for the design of gender-equitable social protection systems. A Tobin tax would be likely to reduce market volatility (Erturk 2002), a phenomenon which, as we have seen above, has disproportionately detrimental effects on women.

Debt cancellation campaigns

Many feminists from the South support unconditional debt cancellation. Others advocate attaching conditions relating to gender equality to such efforts. Even without specific gender-related conditions, debt cancellation would benefit women, as long as this was accompanied by a parallel demand for universal provisioning of social services. Women have more to gain than men from universal provisioning, as they are the ones who suffer more from a lack of such services, as outlined earlier.

Reallocation of military spending toward poverty reduction and social equity in North and South

This is another important demand, which was put forward recently in Brazil. Feminist activists working on gender budget initiatives in the North can demand from their governments a reallocation of their own military expenditures toward increased overseas development assistance.

Opposition to anti-deficit radicalism

Feminist activists need to oppose anti-deficit radicalism more forcefully, in company with others. More than ever before, the current danger in the world economy is not inflation, but deflation. Assessments of social equity, more specifically, the gender equity and growth implications of alternative fiscal policy scenarios (including scenarios with alternative budget deficit assumptions) can be important feminist tools in opposing anti-deficit radicalism (Sen, G. 2000). These would require integrating gender analysis into macro-economic modelling.

Demand for increased international mobility of labour

As pointed out above, a major reason behind the shift in the burden of taxation between labour and capital stems from the relative immobility of labour compared to capital. Such an asymmetry has also led to the erosion of workers' rights. Feminist advocacy should include demands for increased international mobility of labour, as well as demands for increased national and international resources for the protection of workers' rights (for example, from global taxation schemes). These are not only important as demands in themselves, but also because they have implications for taxation patterns. Campaigns to eliminate tax havens, which allow corporations to reduce their taxes, could also constitute another venue for feminist activism on gender-equitable taxation.

Conclusion

Feminist advocacy in these policy contexts would further the efforts toward democratisation of macro-economic policy making at all levels, from the local to the national and the international. They would help render gender budget initiatives, which have been the most important feminist macro-economic policy challenge so far, more effective by helping build greater solidarity within the global justice movement.

Nilüfer Çağatay teaches at the Department of Economics, 1645 Campus Center Dr., Room 308, BUC, University of Utah, USA 84112. Cagatay@economics.utah.edu

Notes

1 Fiscal policy means policy relating to government revenue, particularly taxation and spending.
2 The OECD (Organisation for Economic Co-operation and Development) is an international organisation helping 30 member governments (mostly of the global North) to tackle the economic, social and governance challenges of a globalised economy.
3 The continued primacy of military expenditures may be one aspect of fiscal policy that has remained 'Keynesian', a feature that is called military Keynesianism.
4 A recent paper by IMF economists, including the chief economist, argues that in poor countries financial integration to the world economy does not result in growth and leads to greater volatility in consumption and output. Although many economists have repeatedly made these arguments, this is the first time IMF economists have done so. See Prasad, Rogoff, and Kose (2003).
5 The Tobin tax, initially proposed by the Nobel prize-winner James Tobin, seeks to reduce volatility in the world economy by imposing a small international tax on foreign exchange transactions. It would be a significant source of revenue that could be used for human development purposes. See Haq, Kaul and Grunberg (1996).

References

Budlender, D. (2000) 'The political economy of women's budgets in the South', *World Development* 28(7)
Budlender, D. and R. Sharp with K. Allen (1998) 'How to Do a Gender-Sensitive Budget Analysis: Contemporary Research and Practice', London: Commonwealth Secretariat
Çağatay, N., D. Elson and C. Grown (1995) 'Introduction', *World Development* 23 (11)
Çağatay, N., M. Keklik, R. Lal and J. Lang (2000) 'Budgets as if People Mattered: Democratizing Macroeconomic Policies', New York: UNDP, SEPED, Bureau for Development Policy
Commonwealth Secretariat (1999) 'Gender Budget Initiative', London: Commonwealth Secretariat
ECLAC, (1998) *The Fiscal Covenant: Strengths, Weaknesses and Challenges*, Santiago: ECLAC, eclac.org/English/aruba/lcg2024/sum.htm
Elson, D. (1998) 'Integrating gender issues into national budgetary policies and procedures: some policy options', *Journal of International Development* 10
Elson, D. and N. Çağatay (2000) 'The social content of macroeconomic policies', *World Development* 28(7)
Erturk, K. (2002) *Why the Tobin Tax Can Be Stabilising*, Levy Institute of Economics, Working Paper 366, available at www.levy.org
Grunberg, I. (1998) 'Double jeopardy: globalization, liberalization and the fiscal squeeze', *World Development* 26(4)
Haq, M., I. Kaul and I. Grunberg (1996) (eds.), *The Tobin Tax: Coping With Financial Volatility*, Oxford: Oxford University Press
Milanovic, B. (2003) 'The two faces of globalization: against globalization as we know it', World Development 31(4)
Prasad, E., K. Rogoff, S.Wei and M.A. Kose (2003) *Effects of Financial Globalisation on Developing Countries: Some Empirical Evidence*, March 17, www.imf.org/external/np/res/docs/2003/031703.htm
Rodrik, D. (1997) 'Has Globalization Gone Too Far?', Washington D.C.: IIE
Sen, A. K. (1998) 'Human development and financial conservatism', *World Development* 26(4)

Sen, A.K. (2001) 'Many Faces of Gender Inequality', *Frontline*, 18 (22).

Sen, G. (2000) 'Gender mainstreaming in finance ministries', *World Development* 28(7)

Stiglitz, J. (2002) Globalization and Its Discontents New York: WW Norton

UNCTAD (1997) 'Trade and Development Report, 1997', New York and Geneva: United Nations

United Nations (1999) 'World Survey on the Role of Women in Development: Globalization, Gender and Work', New York: Division for the Advancement of Women, DESA

UNDP (1999) *Human Development Report*, Oxford: Oxford University Press

UNDP (2003) *Making Global Trade Work for People*, London: Earthscan Publications

UNIFEM (2000) 'Progress of the World's Women 2000', New York: UNIFEM

van der Hoeven, R. (2000) 'Poverty and Structural Adjustment: Some Remarks on the Trade-off Between Equity and Growth', Geneva: ILO, Employment Paper

Feminist responses to economic globalisation:
some examples of past and future practice

Ruth Pearson

In order to challenge unfair international trade rules, it is essential to understand how each of them works. This article presents an overview of the various agreements concerning different kinds of economic activity, which are enforced by the World Trade Organisation (WTO). It aims to make these agreements comprehensible to non-economists, so that proposals to make international trade more gender equitable can be understood. The argument goes beyond the usual rhetoric that women's concerns must be central to international trade regulation, and reviews some existing and new initiatives which seek to do just that.

The world of economic globalisation is confusing. International regulation of world trade by the World Trade Organisation purports to offer a level playing field to rich and poor countries alike; but often in the name of regulation the WTO imposes rules which prevent developing countries from supporting industrial activity for domestic consumption, for example, garment production or food production. Under the new regime, all economies are being moved towards a unitary system, whereby investment can move freely between countries, and enterprises will meet no obstacle in sourcing or marketing their produce from anywhere in the world. While this is the theory, in practice the level of protectionism in the North (in terms of ongoing subsidies to local producers, or tariff barriers against imports) remains extremely high. In spite of the apparent 'level playing field' that the new rules offer all parties, developing countries continue to face difficulties in accessing markets in the global North, and earning sufficient foreign exchange to meet their import requirements.

Different agreements within the WTO structure – such as TRIPS and GATS – all refer to specific parts of the new rules concerning different kinds of international economic activity.

TRIPS

TRIPS stands for Trade Related Intellectual Property. The TRIPS agreement is concerned with the freedom of transnational corporations (TNCs) to protect their brand names and production know-how from copying or adaptation by others without agreement (and payment). Well-known examples of companies that have been protected under TRIPS are the pharmaceutical companies, which have developed effective drugs to treat malaria or to delay the onset of AIDS and to prevent mother-to-child transmission of the virus. TRIPS prevents other companies from copying the basic (generic) form of a drug and marketing it under a different name (and often at a much lower price). Already there have been 'trade disputes' at the WTO about TRIPS – with Brazil successfully challenging the pharmaceutical companies to allow it to manufacture anti-HIV drugs relatively cheaply. However, so far the TNCs have resisted allowing generically produced drugs to be exported to other countries by their producers.

GATS

GATS refers to the General Agreement on Trade and Services. Trade in services was always a difficult area for international negotiation. The new agreement does not only regulate trade in services, it is also about systematising the markets for investment in service sectors. Ultimately, this means that developing countries' service sectors – which include health, education, sanitation, water, transport, communications, tourism, and so on – have to be opened up to competition from international investors. This move is considered to offer the prospect of ongoing investment and improvements in efficiency. There is a relatively long lead-in period over which countries can sign up to the GATS agreement, and decide which of their economic sectors they wish to open up to international investment and competition. But many NGOs and campaigners have warned of its implications for developing countries, particularly since once a country agrees to be bound by GATS it cannot withdraw, even if its economic circumstances or political rule have changed since the original agreement was signed.

The impact of new trade rules on women, men and gender relations

New multilateral trade systems are the institutional face of economic globalisation. As with most economic policies and structures, they are considered by mainstream orthodox economists to be 'gender-free' – that is, to have no special implications for women or men, or for power relations between them. Rather, they are believed to be concerned with flows of factors of production – finance, investment, and trade. The new institutions have gone so far as to categorically exclude considerations about labour from their remit, even though labour is clearly a requisite for any production or trading system. Discussions over the new international economic order have been conducted at a level of abstraction where it is assumed gender analysis is irrelevant. But of course the agreements outlined above – like other economic structures, such as government budgets or tax systems – are deeply gendered. Changing trade rules means changes to the structure of incentives and rewards to different people.

For example, in agriculture, the effect of taking away subsidies for food production, and encouraging farmers to switch to export production is very different for men and women. Women generally control the production of food crops for family consumption and local markets. In contrast, men tend to control larger-scale agriculture undertaken for national and international sale. If control over export production does remain in the hands of women producers, reaching distant markets tends to be harder for women since they face obstacles in accessing financial assets, information, transport and storage networks (Harriss-White 1998).

If you turn land over to cultivation of export crops, women may be the major source of labour for the new NTAEs (non-traditional agricultural exports) such as seasonal fruit (grapes and kiwi fruits) and vegetables (beans and mangetouts) (Barrientos 1999, Dolan 2001). However, even if such production is carried out by smallholders, male heads of household generally have control over production and the income from it. If production is organised in large-scale estates or commercial farms, women tend to carry out onerous work for low pay and under bad conditions, seeing little benefit from their involvement in production for global markets.

When the WTO insists on governments dismantling structures of protection like subsidies to local producers, and taxes on imports, it not only changes the ways in which resources for production are allocated, but also deprives governments of important sources of revenue; trade taxes account for about 10 per cent of total tax revenue in developing countries. This in turn means that money available for the government to spend on social services like health and education is reduced. If the state stops providing social services, people have to look elsewhere for them. In the vast majority of contexts, women are the primary care-givers for their families, assisted by their daughters. If state services are no longer available, women attempt to provide home-based alternatives. This gives them a higher burden of work within the household, and may reduce girls' access to education, in situations where they already face discrimination (Evers 2002, 7-8).

The TRIPS agreement is not a gender-free zone, either. To return to the example of pharmaceuticals, poor governments cannot afford to import essential drugs while the intellectual property rights of TNCs are protected. The effect on nations, communities and individuals is devastating. Unequal gender relations, and poverty, mean millions of women and girls through-out sub-Saharan Africa and elsewhere are particularly vulnerable to HIV infection in a context of grossly inadequate public health facilities, sanitation and nutrition, and general living conditions. Moreover, women are the ones responsible for the care of children, and other family members, who fall sick. There are whole generations of 'grannies' who are currently having to support children orphaned by the pandemic – and many of those children are themselves likely to suffer from HIV/Aids

in the future. But, short of declaring a national emergency in order to import generic drugs, which governments for various reasons have been reluctant to do, access to the anti-retrovirals, which could in some part mitigate this situation by ensuring a much longer life expectancy for HIV-positive adults and children, remain beyond the reach of most developing states.

Under the GATS agreement, the prospect offered is one of commercial companies buying and running essential services in poor countries. Governments will have little control over the cost to the service users, and there is little prospect of the profits being reinvested in the physical and social infrastructure of the country (World Development Movement 2002). Given existing gender power relations, the fact that poor households have to pay cash for basic health or education supplies can produce additional problems for women. Women are likely to have less access to and control over cash, but their household and caring responsibilities means they have the most direct need for supplies to meet their families' requirements. Women's access to clean water, for example, is central to their responsibilities for household reproduction – what Molyneux called their practical gender interests. If women lack cash which they need for health and education services, this will affect their strategic gender interests as well (Molyneux 1985). Yet, as stated above, in the rarified world of international trade and financial negoti-ations, gender issues are rarely taken into account.

Economic globalisation and the international regulation of labour

Significantly, the one area which is not included in the new trade rules is the international regulation of labour. There has been endless discussion about whether the WTO should include a 'social clause' which would require members to demonstrate a certain level of protection for the labour force involved in production for international trade. For example, the social clause would involve adherence to the ILO Core Labour Standards which oblige states to guarantee freedom of association and the right to collective bargaining, the elimination of all forms of forced or compulsory labour, the effective abolition of child labour and the elimination of discrimination in employment and occupation (Murray 2002).

Developing countries have responded that a social clause could be a disguised form of protectionism; that is, a means by which developed countries could refuse entry of goods and services exported from the global South to their domestic markets. This would constitute a new form of non-tariff barrier. Since many people complain about the high level of protectionism that remains in the North, in spite of the existence of the new international frameworks, it is argued that the introduction of a social clause would produce further obstacles to the growth of trade, and therefore the possibilities of development in poor countries. Instead, it is argued, international regulation about labour force conditions and protection should be the preserve of the International Labour Organisation (ILO), which is organised along tripartite representation – that is, governments, employers and trade unions participate in it, thereby dealing with labour-related issues in a labour-related, rather than trade-related, context.

However, economic globalisation has also wrought huge changes in the ways in which both production and the labour force in internationally traded sectors are organised. In the 1970s and 1980s, we were told we were operating under a New International Division of Labour (Frobel et al. 1980). The model for this new way of producing for international markets was to relocate the labour-intensive parts of production processes to 'cheap' labour countries. Here, the workers were mostly young, relatively educated, manually dexterous, single, childless women. They were employed to assemble electronics components, or sew fashion clothing, to provide Northern consumers with cheap goods. Most of the investment came from North America or Europe, a lot of it was located in Free Trade Zones, and the dominant mode of investment was direct investment by the multinational company.

But today, things have changed considerably. Now, there is little direct investment in so-called 'off-shore production'. Instead, transnational 'brand' companies, such as The Gap or Nike, are involved in a whole series of sub-contracting links to produce fashion clothing, sports goods, jewellery, electronics, or computer goods. They do not invest directly in the countries where the production is taking place, instead contracting local producers to manufacture products according to their specifications, using their materials, designs and logos. Often, a particular contractor – say, a company making trainers in Indonesia – will be contracted by several companies to produce shoes in the same factory, to be sold under different brand names in North America or Europe. In some cases, parts of the production process will be sub-contracted to informal workshops, or even home-based workers who do not enter the factory at all. Many of the subcontracted enterprises are owned by Japanese, South Korean, Taiwanese and (overseas) Chinese entrepreneurs, as these countries have developed experience in export production and their successful industrialisation has generated surpluses to invest in the global economy. In China itself, on the other hand, production is contracted to national companies, often in joint ventures with local or state government, who produce under licence for the overseas buyers.

This pattern of production – or 'global value chain' – is also present in the growing, harvesting and marketing of non-traditional agricultural exports. A given buyer – for example, a UK supermarket – will contract suppliers in Kenya or South Africa or Chile, who will then either subcontract to small-holders or will organise estate production using temporary contract labour.

However, two factors have remained constant. First, women still comprise the bulk of the labour employed in both export manufacture and agriculture for consumer markets. Second, although the growth of export production has certainly provided growing employment opportunities for women in many parts of the world, the jobs themselves are low-paid, often insecure and temporary, offer no skills training, frequently involve forced overtime, and the workforce typically has little access to non-wage benefits such as health services and insurance, pension rights, and unemployment benefits. Moreover, many women are subject to health and safety problems, often causing reproductive and other hazards. There are reports of increasing incidences of verbal, physical and sexual abuse as the management of different establishments in the production chains has diversified and women from more and more countries are being pulled into the global value chains (Pearson and Seyfang 2002, Canos 1998). Whilst the global economy has demanded flexibility from the economies of the developing world, it often seems as though much of that flexibility is derived from the extraordinary energy and industry with which women in factories, workshops, vineyards and farms apply themselves to the production of the commodities which form the basis of increasingly extravagant global consumption patterns. With international advertising creating a non-stop demand for sneakers and sweatshirts, cell phones and CD players, apparently identical and standardised products are manufactured by women workers employed under contracts and conditions which differ dramatically according to their location.

Feminist responses – what do they look like?

What if we were to insist not just on conducting a gender analysis of the impact of trade reform and financial liberalisation, but to construct feminist responses and initiatives which would take into account the results of such analyses? Doing this would require us to move beyond recording the different ways in which women are (adversely) incorporated into global production, to learn from the ways in which women workers and others have responded to their experiences.

Codes of conduct

One example of this is the effort which women who work in factories, informal workshops and at home have put into participating in efforts to develop and implement Voluntary Codes of Conduct (VCCs). These are voluntary codes, which are concerned with labour conditions along the value chain involved in production. A VCC requires the main contractor to take responsibility for the pay and conditions of all workers at every stage of production.

Many women workers' organisations have welcomed the opportunity to negotiate with management over VCCs. Because the workforces at different links in the chain have different employers and contractual arrangements, it has been hard in the past to organise the workforce in order to improve pay and conditions for women workers. Traditional forms of organisation by trade unions have not achieved women's objectives: they have little bargaining power, and very often they are not allowed to organise in unions in any case. In addition, experience has shown that mainstream trade unions are not very amenable to listening to women's specific demands, and prioritising them in their negotiating strategies. Even in situations in which trade unions are permitted to operate, they may deal directly with company management, but women workers rarely get a seat at the negotiating table.

Also, as many people are swift to point out, however hard and exploitative the conditions of work might be, most of the women have no better alternative. They are therefore concerned to keep their jobs, rather than forcing companies to take their contracting business elsewhere. Given the flexible and cross-border nature of global production, it is easy to understand that the buying companies do have alternative sources for their manufactures. What the women workers want is 'Trabajo – si pero con dignidad' ('Work, yes – with dignity') (Red CentroAmericana de Mujeres en Solidaridad con las Trabajadoras de la Maquilas, cawn@gn.apc.org).

In many instances, a much wider range of stakeholders has been involved in drawing up VCCs, including community-based NGOs, women's organisations, and coalitions of groups representing women workers. Whilst the idea of this kind of voluntary regulation has been dismissed by some as a public relations gimmick, it is also the case that companies are very vulnerable to changes in consumer prefer-ences, and the young affluent consumers who are the main purchasers of branded clothing and sportswear are also very attuned to information available on the Internet about conditions of production all over the world. It is for this reason that some companies have been willing to co-operate with VCC initiatives.

Although it is cannot be claimed that VCC initiatives have changed the situation of women involved in export production overnight, one thing that they have done is bring into the public domain women's priorities which have often been over-looked by male labour representatives. In many instances, women have stressed not just their rights to appropriate pay for the job which amounts to a living wage, and the right to collective organising and bargaining; they have also made a series of demands which reflect their position vis-à-vis men, and their responsibilities according to the gender division of labour.

For example, the VCC drawn up by the members of the Central American Women's Network (CAWN) included organisations of women workers in Nicaragua and Honduras. They committed their signatures to a policy of no discrimination, job security for all, but in particular for pregnant and post-natal women, consideration in the work place (no verbal, physical, or mental abuse), working conditions which guarantee workers' physical integrity (relating to health and safety, sanitary facilities and so on), access to national social security benefits, a minimum wage, limits to the length of the working day, pay for over-time, freedom to organise and to conduct collective bargaining, and a ban on child labour.

Although there is little concrete evidence that VCCs have the power to coerce TNCs to treat their workforce with dignity and fairness, they have provided a voice for women's groups, so they can publicise the reality of their work situation and connect with international systems of solidarity, monitoring and verification of the imple-mentation of VCCs. They have also challenged the assumption that TNCs can operate in a borderless global economy, accountable to no one, and that the right to exploit cheap labour in the pursuit of economic efficiency is to be tolerated in the global market.[1]

A gender equity clause in the WTO

Although, as explained above, many developing country governments have objected to the introduction of a social clause in WTO negotiations on the grounds that it would constitute a disguised form of protectionism, the idea of proposing a gender equity clause could also be explored.

By 2005, the existing Multi-Fibre Agreement (MFA) will have been phased out in order to bring world trade in textiles and garments in line with WTO rules. It will be replaced by the ATC (Agreement on Textile and Clothing). The MFA regulated imports from developing countries in order to protect the domestic producers in North America and Europe. In theory, ending the MFA should benefit developing countries wishing to export these goods.

However, gender analysts fear that it is the transnational companies which will be able to take advantage of the open markets and deregulated labour forces which will be the result of ending the MFA. In contrast, the mainly female workforce in textile and garment manufacturing in developing countries will suffer increased insecurity and deteriorating conditions of work. Many developed countries no longer see any advantage in continuing the old system which regulated exports of textiles and garments from producers in North America and Europe. However, its demise will put further pressure on the unprotected, predominantly immigrant industrial workforce in the North. It will also pressurise Southern governments into further reductions in their own trade barriers, in exchange for 'concessions' on reducing protection of garments markets in the North (Hale and Hurley, downloaded 10/03/2003).

It is probably right to assume that the phasing-out of the MFA will not directly improve employment opportunities or conditions for women workers supplying the global industry in textiles and garments. However, a gender-equity ethical clause in the new ATC might be a good opportunity to raise issues of gender equity in terms of both opening markets to competitive international sourcing (that is, buyers will be able to get textiles/garments from anywhere in the world), and reducing protection of local industries, in both the North and the South. It could commit importers and exporters alike to adherence to minimum conditions and rights of workers in this sector.

While a gender clause like this would be open to the same kinds of criticisms that developing countries have raised about the social clause and conditionality in general, a focused sector-based demand for gender equity might provide an important factor in ensuring women workers' interests are met in agreements governing this part of international trade.

From the Tobin Tax to the Maria Tax

The Tobin tax (named after the Nobel prize-winning economist James Tobin) is a radical proposal to use the current trading in the international financial markets for the benefit of developing countries. The Tobin tax advocates a tax on foreign currency trading, which is currently estimated at some three hundred thousand billion dollars per year (over 50 times greater than global spending on goods and services including food, housing and transport). Such a tax, even if it were set as low as a fraction of one per cent, would raise between 50 and 100 billion dollars a year. This money would effectively double the current aid budget available for development and poverty elimination activities (see www.tobintax. org.uk). This proposal, which was once dismissed by many as unrealistic, is now garnering increasing political support. The governments of Canada, France, Belgium, Germany and the UK have either declared their support, or are actively considering it.

Whilst the Tobin tax proposal is for the proceeds to be spent on unspecified development activities, the idea can also be adapted to argue for a tax which could be directed at the promotion of gender equality. Given the importance of the foreign exchange earnings of the export sectors to many developing countries it is important to publicly acknowledge the extent to which this rests on the efforts of women who still suffer disadvantages in terms of access to non-wage benefits and development initiatives. A tax could be imposed on the foreign exchange value of exports of manufacturers, agricultural products and services, which could reflect the proportion of women in the export labour force. Such a tax – which I have dubbed a 'Maria tax' – could be levied by governments, and re-invested in initiatives to achieve gender equity for women workers. For example, money could be spent on child-care facilities, reproductive and occupational health facilities, educational programmes, health insurance, and pension schemes. And, just as the Tobin proposal has served to focus attention on the destabilising effects of international currency speculation, the Maria tax could also be used both to highlight the particular contribution of women workers in economies participating in the global economy and to argue for gender equity and justice.

Of course, many will argue that such an initiative would impose extra costs on the employment of women, and that it would result in a decrease in women's job opportunities. However, this would not be the case if the tax were to be imposed on the governments and the importers, rather than on the producers. If such a tax were universally applied worldwide, the incentive for re-location to another country would also be undermined.

Gender budgets as feminist tools

Finally, gender budgets are another recent initiative which have sought to mainstream a concern for gender equity and justice within the process of economic policy formulation and execution and of holding governments to account for their international and national commitments to the advancement of women (Budlender et al. 2002).

Initially devised as a way of analysing budgets from women's perspectives, allowing women to 'follow the money', gender-sensitive budget initiatives start from the premise that national budgets may appear to be gender-neutral policy instruments dealing with financial aggregates, expenditures and revenues, surpluses and deficits rather than with real men and women. But, from the perspective of gender analysis, it is clear that women's gendered responsibilities coupled with inferior economic power and political voice means that government expenditure is frequently allocated in a way that entrenches women's subordination rather than reduces it. For example, apparently gender-neutral expenditure on children's education frequently results in more boys attending school and higher education; a gender-sensitive response would be to build in mechanisms to promote girls and women's access to education and to overcome the current obstacles to their participation.

Different initiatives are currently underway in over 20 countries in four regions. Although fiscal and public expenditure matters are often seen to be dry and boring, feminist activists all over the world have welcomed this new tool as a way of forcing gender issues into the centre of political debate. According to Colleen Lowe-Marna, former CEO, Commission on Gender Equality, South Africa: 'Money talks. Men listen to money talk. These truisms are at the heart of the enthusiasm with which the idea of the women's budget has been embraced by gender activists. When we talk budget, we finally have a sense that we are getting to the heart of the matter...and that men will sit up and listen' (cited in Elson 2000, 114).

The proposals and initiatives outlined above illustrate the ways in which the interests of women can be articulated in the negotiations and agreements concerning international trade and investment within the global economy. For a number of years, many advocates have argued that it is necessary for gender issues to be considered by the international organisations that shape the global economy, and for women's interests to be represented in the new systems. The gender budget initiatives illustrate a number of examples of how gender interests can be mainstreamed within national fiscal and monetary policies. Similar processes also need to be undertaken with respect to international economic systems. The proposals for a gender equity clause in the WTO, and a 'Maria tax', are not yet detailed concrete proposals. Rather, they are ideas which are intended to stimulate debate about how to mainstream gender issues in international trade, and to help focus attention on the contribution women continue to make in the production of goods and services within the global economy.

Ruth Pearson works at the Centre for Development Studies, University of Leeds, LS2 9JT. r.pearson@leeds.ac.uk

Notes

1 For a review of VCCs and the views of different stakeholders see Jenkins et al. (2002).

References

Barrientos, S., A. Bee, A. Matear and I. Vogel (1999) *Women and Agribusiness: Working Miracles in the Chilean Fruit Export Sector*, Basingstoke: Macmillan

Budlender D, D. Elson, G. Hewitt and T. Mukhopadhyay (eds) (2002) 'Gender Budgets Make Cents: understanding gender responsive budgets' London: Commonwealth Secretariat

Canas, M., Y. Martinez, M. Pastora Sandino, J. T. Cortez Magana (1998) *Los derochos hjumanos y la maquila en El Salvador*, Procuraduria Adjunta para la Defensa de los Deroechos Humanos de la Muhr, San Salvador, El Salvador C.A.

Dolan, Catherine (2001) 'The good wife: struggles over land and labour allocation in the Kenyan horticultural sector', in *Journal of Development Studies* 27:3.

Elson, D (2000) *Progress of the World's Women*, UNIFEM Biennial Report, NewYork, United Nation Development Programme (UNDP); full text available, in English, French and Spanish at www.undp.org/unifem/progressww

Evers, Barbara (2002) 'Gender, International Trade and the Trade Policy Review Mechanism: Conceptual Reference Points for UNCTAD'. Available on: http://www.gapresearch.org/governance/wto.html (downloaded 20/03/2003)

Frobel, Heinrichs and Kreye (1980) *The New International Division of Labour*, Cambridge University Press, Cambridge

Hale, A. and J. Hurley 'What does the phase out of the MFA quota system mean for garment workers?' in *Gender Trade and the World Trade Organisation*, www.poptel.org.uk/women-ww/gender_trade_and_the_wto (downloaded 10/03/2003)

Harriss-White, B. (1998) 'Female and male grain marketing systems: analytical and policy issues for West Africa and India', in Jackson, C. and R. Pearson (eds.) *Feminist Visions of Development : Gender Analysis and Policy*, London: Routledge

Jenkins, R. R. Pearson and G. Seyfang (eds.) (2002) *Corporate Responsibility and Labour Rights: Codes of Conduct in the Global Economy*, London: Earthscan

Molyneux, M. (1985) 'Mobilization without emancipation? Women's interests, the state and revolution in Nicaragua', in *Feminist Studies* 11, Summer

Murray, J. (2002) 'Labour rights/corporate responsibilities: the role of ILO labour standards', in Jenkins, R. R. Pearson and G. Seyfang (eds.) (2002) *Corporate Responsibility and Labour Rights: Codes of Conduct in the Global Economy*, London: Earthscan

Oxfam (2002) *Make Trade Fair: Rigged Rules and Double Standards: Trade, Globalisation and the Fight Against Poverty*, available from Policy Department, Oxfam GB, 274 Banbury Road, Oxford OX2 7DZ, or www.maketradefair.org/assets/english/Report_English.pdf

Pearson, R. and G. Seyfang (2002) '"I'll tell you what I want…..": women workers and codes of conduct' in Jenkins, R. R. Pearson and G. Seyfang (eds.) (2002) *Corporate Responsibility and Labour Rights: Codes of Conduct in the Global Economy*, London: Earthscan

World Development Movement (2002) '*GATS: A Disservice to the Poor*', WDM, January, London or:
www.wdm.org.uk/campaign/GATS.htm

Counting for something!

Recognising women's contribution to the global economy through alternative accounting systems

Marilyn Waring

As a political economist, the focus of my research and activism has always been how economic data can be used to influence public policy. I am very familiar with the technical, logistical and measurement arguments traditionally raised by statisticians or economists in the debates on the collection, presentation and imputations related to gender disaggregated statistics. I also have very little patience with them. This article explains why, in the context of a critique of the United Nations System of National Accounts (UNSNA). It also surveys some alternative methods of accounting, which better capture the realities of women's contribution to the global economy.[1] The new feminist challenge is to identify and use these models in public policy making and in advocacy for change.

Since the Second United Nations Women's Conference in Copenhagen in 1980,[2] feminists have strategised to force global and national accounting bodies to make women's economic contribution visible in their data. A main focus for attention has been the United Nations System of National Accounts (UNSNA). UNSNA was instigated in 1953, with the aim of enabling comparisons to be made between national economies, and serving as a guide to countries developing their own accounting systems. In the UNSNA, national economies are defined in terms of market transactions; consumption, investment, and saving measures are given in addition to income and production totals. A vast amount of work performed by women is for household consumption or unpaid work in the informal economy. This work is not counted in UNSNA. The lack of visibility of women's contribution to the economy results in policies which perpetuate economic, social and political inequality between women and men. There is a very simple equation operating here: if you are invisible as a producer in a nation's economy, you are invisible in the distribution of benefits (unless they label you a welfare 'problem' or 'burden').

In 1993, the rules of the UNSNA (United Nations 1993) were changed. This was an opportunity to address feminist concerns, and incorporate essential work performed for home consumption into the accounting system. However, this chance was missed. Paragraph 1.25 of the 1993 UNSNA establishes the 'consumption boundary', enumerating the many domestic and personal services which do not 'count' when they are produced and consumed within the same household. Women all over the planet perform the bulk of these tasks. They are the cleaning, decoration and maintenance of the dwelling occupied by the household; cleaning, servicing and repair of household goods; the preparation and serving of meals; the care, training and instruction of children; the care of the sick, infirm or old people; and the transportation of members of the household or their goods. These services do count in the UNSNA when they are supplied by government or voluntary agencies, and when they are paid for. The 'uncounted' tasks are termed 'indicators of welfare'.

Out of a breathtaking conceptual ignorance, and undoubted Western bias, the UNSNA fails to grasp there is no demarcation for women in the subsistence household between production inside or outside the consumption boundaries. Just picture the following. A woman wakes; she breastfeeds her four-month-old child (unproductive inactive primary production, consumed by a member of the household). There is no accurate way of ascribing value to this activity, even in the proposed 'satellite accounts'. (The satellite accounts are the 'add on' compromise that will include unpaid work. They have to be separate so as not to disturb what the experts call the 'internal integrity and international comparability of the current accounting framework'.) There is no market price for breast milk, so the satellite accounts will price that food at its nearest replacement equivalent. But infant formula, whatever cost is ascribed to it, cannot compete with the quality of breast milk, which means that its use will have a cost impact on the future health and education of the child.

Let's continue with the picture. The woman goes to collect water. She uses some to wash dishes from the family evening meal (unproductive work) and the pots in which she previously cooked a little food for sale (informal work). Next, she goes to the nearby grove to collect bark for dye for materials to be woven for sale (informal work), which she mixes with half a bucket of water (informal work). She also collects some roots and leaves to make a herbal medicine for her child (inactivity). She uses the other half of the bucket of water to make this concoction (inactivity). She will also collect some dry wood to build the fire to boil the water to make both the medicine

and the dye (active and inactive labour). All this time she will carry the baby on her back (inactive work).

Of particular importance to feminists is paragraph 1.22 of the 1993 UNSNA, which describes the UNSNA as a 'multi-purpose system ... designed to meet a wide range of analytical and policy needs'. It states that 'a balance has to be struck between the desire for the accounts to be as comprehensive as possible', and their being swamped with non-monetary values. The revised system excludes all 'production of services for own final consumption within households ... The location of the production boundary ... *is a compromise, but a deliberate one that takes account of most users* [my emphasis - it is difficult to make extensive use of statistics in which you are invisible] ... If the production boundary were extended to include production of personal and domestic services by members of households for their own final consumption, all persons engaged in such activities would become self-employed, making unemployment virtually impossible by definition.' Rather than justifying leaving most of the work done by most women out of the equation, this statement surely demonstrates that the current definition of unemployment is inappropriate.

The International Labour Organisation (ILO) specifies that the production of economic goods and services includes all production and processing of primary products, including that for home consumption, with the proviso that such production must be 'an important contribution' to the total consumption of the household (ILO 1982). In a 1993 resolution concerning the international classification of status in employment, the International Conference of Labour Statisticians defined subsistence workers as those 'who hold a self-employment' job and in this capacity 'produce goods and services which are predominantly consumed by their own household and constitute an important basis for its livelihood.' (ILO 1993).

Compare the concepts of 'an important basis for livelihood', and 'an important contribution' to the total consumption of the household, with the specific exclusions from production in the 1993 UNSNA.

The distinctions made in terms of the boundary of production and consumption, and the definitions of the informal sector worked on so earnestly for the last ten years, are in these few sentences revealed as a load of patriarchal nonsense. As the example above shows, women's lives are not so meaninglessly divided. All tasks of survival in such circumstances are related. The Statistical Commission reported: 'As far as household production is concerned, the central framework includes for the first time all production of goods in households, whether sold or not, and services *if they are supplied to units other than their producers'* (my emphasis) (UN Statistical Commission, www.un.org/Depts/unsd/sna/sna2-en. htm). As concerned as they have been with conceptual and measurement difficulties, and boundaries of consumption or production, the designers of the new UNSNA just miss the point, and in so doing fail to reflect the reality of the majority of women on the planet.

The problem is systemic, and encompasses issues other than gender inequality. There are other significant measurement problems in the current UNSNA framework. Among the research topics of the Inter-Secretarial Working Group on national accounts, co-ordinated by the UN Statistical Commission, have been the indirect measurement of financial intermediation services; services in the informal sector; the classification of the purposes of non-profit institutions serving households; a workshop on intangible assets; the issue of measuring e-commerce; and more on counting the hidden economy. All of these pose significant technical, measurement and valuation problems. Wild, speculative abstractions regarding these concerns have resulted in the figures produced being absolutely meaningless for the purposes of public policy, yet the framework of the UNSNA remains intact. However far removed from reality the UNSNA becomes, governments, business and multilaterals are committed to it, in the misguided conception that it accurately measures the thing which matters most: economic 'growth'.

John Ralston Saul opined in his CBC Massey Lecture Series: 'I would suggest that we are in desperate need of a reformulation of the idea of growth...It is difficult to imagine how we might escape our ongoing economic crisis unless we can reconsider [its] nature... By reconsideration, I mean that we must attempt to draw back far enough to see where value lies in society' (Ralston Saul 1997, 156–7). In the next section, I look at some work which has resulted from such attempts.

Information on real life: alternative models

In the past 12 years, some very fine work has resulted from the consideration of such issues. The figures feminists needed, to ensure that the realities of women's and children's lives are made visible to economists and politicians, are finally starting to be produced. Data on the ways in which we survive in a context of resource exploitation and environmental degradation are emerging. What alternative models have been developed which yield such material, and render it useful for public policy purposes? The new feminist challenge is to identify and use these models.

The Index of Sustainable Welfare (ISEW)
The authors of this model, Herman Daly and John Cobb, share a concern that 'what is needed is *a* new measure.' (Daly and Cobb 1994, 378). They are particularly concerned that 'costs' should be registered as deficits or depletions, not as 'goods' or 'benefits' in production and consumption, as in the UNSNA .

Daly and Cobb propose the Index of Sustainable Economic Welfare (ISEW).

In this method of data collection and analysis, growth is no longer God; the emphasis is now on sustainability. The characteristics used in the ISEW are personal consumption, distributional inequality, household labour services, consumer durables, services provided by highways and streets, improvement in health and education by way of public expenditures, expenditures on consumer durables and defensive private expenditures on health and education. Costs included are the costs of commuting, the costs of personal pollution control, costs of automobile accidents, costs of water pollution, air pollution, noise pollution, losses of wetlands, losses of farm land, depletion of non-renewable resources, long-term environmental damage, cost of ozone depletion, net capital growth, (that is, the growth in the stock of goods used to produce other goods) and a change in net international position (indebtedness).

Attempts to ascribe a value to leisure were omitted from the ISEW, because 'the rather arbitrary assumptions upon which such a calculation is based ... are particularly problematic'(ibid., 455). However, Daly and Cobb include 'a rather speculative estimate of long-term environmental damage, particularly from climate modification' (ibid.). They admit to being forced to make 'heroic assumptions' in compiling the ISEW, such as the cost imposed on future generations by the depletion of natural resources (ibid.).

The ISEW falls down on the issue of unpaid work. While it shows evidence of new thinking, it remains patronising. 'Which of the activities within the household should be classified as work as opposed to leisure or an intrinsically satisfying activity?' (ibid., 457), they ask. There is an easy response to this point: members of the paid workforce also take time for leisure in paid time, and find elements of their employment intrinsically satisfying. We still count all their activities as work.

In addition, Daly and Cobb's valuations are based on old inequalities. In ascribing a value to unpaid work, they adopt Robert Eisner's method of estimating the value of time spent on unpaid household work on the basis of the average wage rate for household domestic workers (Eisner 1989). This, they say, avoids the problem of using differential market wage rates for men and women. However, this does not avoid the problems thrown up by using traditional low wage rates from a female occupation to estimate the value of the work of domestic workers, especially when much of that work is in the management of a small business, even if there is no market exchange!

The results of the ISEW are measured in per capita dollars. They have been calculated in the USA for the years 1950–1990, and show variations when measured against the GDP in each of the four decades, and a decline in the 1980s. In retrospect, these studies can demonstrate that improvements in car safety and reductions in air pollution have made contributions to raising the level of economic welfare. So have social policies to reduce income inequality (ibid., 507). The categories included in the ISEW make this method of data collection yield a far more recognisable picture of reality. But the ISEW still remains one conglomerate, a single new measure, and the dollar is the measurement tool.

The Human Development Index (HDI)

Since its inception in 1990, the United Nations Human Development Report series has been dedicated to ending the mis-measurement of human progress by economic growth alone. 'To be valuable and legitimate, development progress, both nationally and internationally, must be people-centred, equitably distributed and environmentally and socially sustainable ... If present trends continue economic disparities between the industrial and developing nations will move from inequitable to inhumane'(United Nations 1996, iii).

To make the HDI capture gender-related inequalities, life expectancy, adult literacy and education are disaggregated by sex, as are data on share of earned income. A 'Gender Empowerment Measure' (GEM) includes data on the proportion of seats in parliament occupied by women, data on women as a percentage of administrators and managers, professional and technical workers, and women's percentage of earned income. The Human Development Reports are augmented with other data relevant to gender-based poverty and inequality. Despite the data limitations of timeliness and availability, the problems of currency conversions to the USD baseline, differing concepts, classifications and methods, and charges that there are too many data with too many different indicators, the HDI begins to approach approximate accurate input for the purpose of policy making.

Genuine Progress Indicators

One key indicator that is missing from the UN HDI is time-use. Time-use has figured prominently in the work to establish Genuine Progress Indicators (GPI) in Nova Scotia. Prepared by Dr Ronald Coleman, the Nova Scotia GPI project has been designated as a pilot with Statistics Canada, which is providing ongoing assistance in data collection and analysis, and staff support. In addition to the national census, the GPI uses data from the Canadian System of Environmental and Resource Accounts. The index consists of twenty components with a sectoral approach and an emphasis on policy relevance.

The GPI indices distinguish direct contributions to economic welfare from defensive and intermediate expenditures, and from activities that produce an actual decline in well-being. Natural resource accounts include fisheries, soil and agriculture, forestry, wildlife, and greenhouse gas emissions. There are data on the costs of crime, income distribution, and transportation cost analysis. Monetary values are estimated where possible, but in the GPI it is not necessary that all components should have a financial value attributed to them.

The indicators of the GPI include statistics on unpaid work, divided into voluntary and community work, unpaid housework and parenting, and the value of unpaid overtime and underemployment. These figures can be gender-disaggregated. The monetary valuation method used in this study for calculating the economic value of unpaid work is the replacement cost (specialist) method. This reflects the hourly wage rate that would be paid in Nova Scotia to replace existing activities at market prices for the same kind of work. While this financial valuation is used to demonstrate linkages between the market and non-market sectors of the economy, a clear focus of the analysis is on time. In 1997 Nova Scotians contributed an estimated 134 million hours of their time to civic and voluntary work, and more than 940 million hours to unpaid household work. Their unpaid work in these two categories was the equivalent of 571,000 full-year full-time jobs!

The GPI work in Nova Scotia is the most sophisticated measurement work for policy outcomes anywhere. I recommend it to you. Of particular use are the cross-cutting sectoral work in the forestry accounts, the water accounts, and the unpaid work accounts in both the household, and voluntary and community sectors. Only the key points and press statements in each area appear on the website at www.gpiatlantic.org, but full reports can be purchased.

The original aim of the GPI for Nova Scotia was to create an economic data set in which all activities had an estimated monetary value – obviously, the involvement of Stats Canada and the Nova Scotia Provincial Government had to be appeased. But it is the ground-breaking work in the policy field that has saved this from being just another data set, and moved it on inestimably from Cobb and Daly´s work, which continued to 'Redefine Progress'.[3] Rather than producing pages of retrospective alternative data sets with alternative explanations for policy outcomes, GPI Nova Scotia's publications look forward to raising the key questions for policy decisions today and tomorrow, and with cross-sectoral trade-offs explicit in the equations. It is superb work. It is also written in totally accessible language, for non-economists. The ongoing engagement of the Nova Scotia community in the analysis of the GPI has also been a breakthrough in all the projects on alternative indicator sets of which I am aware.

Key challenges remaining

The process in Nova Scotia partially solves two of the key problems that remained (at that point) with the GPI approach (which was originally Daly and Cobb's successor to the ISEW).

Asking people to set their own indicators of well-being

The first of these partial solutions is that while the indices seek to measure the well-being or development of a people or peoples, community, nation state or region, it is not usual for anyone to ask people themselves what indicators they would use to describe their well-being, and how they would measure outcomes of policies based on this data. Instead, the indicator sets are either what the authorities determine as being the figures they will collect (because the World Bank or IMF says so; because you can get a lot of software and hardware and vehicles if you collect particular data in a development assistance programme; because they support a corrupt government and can be easily manipulated; or just because they are the ones that have always been collected and there is comparability over time), or the figures that can be collected, from a logistical and technical standpoint, with a so-called reasonable degree of accuracy. Sometimes the choice of what data to collect depends simply on what is on the UN agenda for that year.

Presenting and interpreting data in non-monetary terms

The fine policy work in Nova Scotia also mitigates the second problem of data which cannot be presented and interpreted other than in monetary terms. This means that all sections of the population – not just academic statisticians and economists, can participate in debates about the research. It is expressed in the way that people might talk about it in a community meeting, in 'real world' terms. It is also important that data can be debated in terms of its own integrity, instead of the somewhat far-fetched abstractions that result when everything is given a monetary value. For example, if we think of gender inequality and the potential users and objectives of time-use data relating to women's and men's workloads, we know that it is not necessary for policy discussions to ascribe monetary values to that work. For example, awareness of unequal time-use may spark off discussions about the need for day nurseries to offer more flexible services so that women's need for child-care can be met. These discussions do not require information about the value of the work which women are undertaking for such long hours. Nor do debates about policy regarding assistance to private businesses, or the planning and production of goods and services for home care. The need for monetary values to be ascribed occasionally is not a reason to abstract all time-use data to the economic model. Far more rigorous planning can be achieved by retaining the time-use framework, and it makes much more sense.

Ascribing monetary values to labour results in a loss of detail and specificity in policy analysis. Nowhere can the consequences of this be more starkly seen than in the case of children who work. Stories in the *State of the World's Children 1997* illustrate this. The ILO Minimum Age Convention allows light work at age 12 or 13, but prohibits hazardous work before 18. It also establishes a general minimum age of 15 years for paid work, provided 15 is not less than the age of completion of compulsory schooling. Yet, of the projected 190 million working children in the 10–14 age group in the developing world, three-quarters work six days a week or more, and one half work nine hours a day or more (UNICEF 1997, 25). In a 1993 study in Malawi, 78 per cent of the 10–14 year olds, and 55 per cent of the 7–9 year olds living on tobacco estates were working full- or part-time (ibid., 38). One quarter of the work force – around 50,000 – in the glass bangle industry of Firozabad in India are children under 14, working in indescribably unsafe and inhumane conditions (ibid., 37). Haiti has an estimated 25,000 child domestics, 20 per cent of whom are 7–10 years old (ibid., 30). In the United States, at least 100,000 children are believed to be involved in child prostitution (ibid., 26). As many as 3 million children aged 10–14 are estimated to work in Brazil's sisal, tea, sugar cane and tobacco plantations (ibid., 38). The most reliable estimates available for the United Kingdom show that between 15–26 per cent of 11 year olds are working (ibid., 20).

Do we want to lose the detail of what we do to children by ascribing monetary values to their production? I certainly do not, but that would be the result of including their labour and its outcome under a generic 'producer' category. Similarly, I do not want to lose the complexity of the impact of human activity on our eco-system behind dollar signs. Yet that is the direction being pursued to give 'visibility' to environmental issues. To establish the United Nations satellite system of integrated economic and environmental accounting, the first step for each country is to draw up a comprehensive balance sheet of natural resources, measured in physical quantities.

That ought to be sufficient for effective policy planning. Different units yes, but with judgement exercised. But the economists want one baseline, so that depletion of capital could include not just depreciation of physical capital, but depletion of natural resources along with deterioration of environmental quality. The problem is, they say, that so much expenditure for environmental protection compensates for the negative impact of economic growth, so it should be a cost to be deducted from national income.

There's an attractive logic here, and it parallels the 'costs' component of Daly and Cobb's ISEW system. The UN satellite system has been tested in several countries. For Mexico between 1986 and 1990, it was found that the environmentally-adjusted domestic product was 13 per cent less than the conventionally measured net domestic product. The new accounting measures also showed that net investment, which conventional measures showed as positive at 4.6 billion pesos, was a negative 700 million pesos. Net savings, also assumed to be positives, were actually close to zero. A case study for Papua New Guinea over the same period produced similar results. There consumption exceeded output so net savings were negative (UN 1996, 63).

But there had to be a better way.

Alberta GPI

The latest work in which I have been involved as an adviser appears to have addressed both these major impediments to using the GPI in a major tool for policy planning. My challenge to the Alberta GPI Project Director, Mark Anielski at the Pembina Institute, was that the characteristics of well-being to be utilised in the Alberta GPI should reflect the values seen as indicative of well-being by Albertans themselves. The values held by Albertans should also determine how a characteristic in the GPI approach is treated. For example, in some communities, divorce is seen as a

42

negative social cost. We know it usually leads to the economic downward mobility of women. Most governments focus on single-parent-headed households as a negative phenomenon. Yet we all know cases where the separation or divorce brings about an end to prolonged violence, and the well-being of children and mothers improves substantially. Divorce can therefore, in some contexts, be seen as positive. Similarly, some communities would see the rate of oil extraction in Alberta as a positive contribution to well-being; others might see such extraction as a cost, particularly in terms of inter-generational equity.

In the time available, the Alberta GPI team was not able to conduct new research, but it was able to undertake a meta-data analysis of the Canadian and Albertan research on community values as reflected in the past five to ten years. This had the immediate effect of increasing the characteristics to be included to over 50, as opposed to the 26 in the original GPI or the 20 used in Nova Scotia.

The next challenge was to find a way of presenting all the data without ascribing notional monetary values, in such a way that all characteristics were measured in terms of their own integrity. It would obviously be useful if the system or model could also make trade-offs visible, and could be accessible for communities to understand and to participate in the analysis and planning that flows from the presentation of data. It would also be a vast improvement if the system could have 'open architecture' – that is, when a community or nation state demonstrated that a particular characteristic was no longer important to them, it could drop out of the system. Similarly, whenever a new measurement deemed important presented itself, it too could be introduced, without the tedium of 'not disturbing the comparability of the model over time', which is the outdated approach of the UNSNA and its policy of satellites.

I believe there is now this model. It is based on the healing circle used by the First Nations People of North America. It requires no expensive software: it is a simple radar diagram in an Excel Programme. The work can be downloaded from www.pembina.org.

I believe this approach offers enormous possibilities, but it must not be abused. (I dread to think of it as a tool in the hands of unethical postgraduate students who need a thesis.) In the first place, users should know the origins of opposition to the UNSNA approach, and how and why this alternative approach evolved. It must come as a whole piece of work, which is initiated by the communities whose well-being (or level of poverty, or development indicators) is or are being determined. These people themselves should determine the indicators to be included, and this list should be revisited with them every five to ten years. You can see immediately that the open architecture could deal with all the following: inflation rate, daily caloric intake, maternal mortality, the cost of a litre of water, last year's rainfall, notifiable and contagious disease levels, levels of education or literacy or school attendance, access to and use of family planning, agricultural extension programmes, micro credit schemes, the retention of indigenous languages, natural disasters, pollution of air and water, deforestation – the list can be as long as a community determines. They should also be party to the interpretation of the radar diagram, which would determine the policy inputs required for desired outcomes, with trade-offs being very explicit.

I believe this model can be rigorous, ethical and accessible in our hands as a real breakthrough for policy work, with and for women and their communities.

Conclusion

The UNSNA is still the most influential model being used universally, but it is failing women miserably as a policy instrument, regardless of all its other problems. The feminist agenda in reinventing globalisation sees the removal of this pathological arbiter of 'well-being' as a critical focus. The satellite alternative is a co-option. The Alberta model is the most exciting alternative development in my lifetime – and one we can begin to use in our own nations and communities.

Dr Marilyn Waring is Professor of Public Policy on the Albany Campus of Massey University in New Zealand. Correspondence through the editor, please.

Notes

1 This article includes material from the introduction of the second edition of my book, *Counting for Nothing – What Men Value and What Women are Worth* (1999), University of Toronto Press, Toronto.
2 The United Nations Decade for Women ran from 1975 to 1985.
3 The organisation Redefining Progress carries on Cobb and Daly's work. www.rprogress.org

References

Daly, H. and John B. Cobb Jr., (1994) *For the Common Good: Redirecting the Economy Towards Community, the Environment and a Sustainable Future*, Boston: Beacon Press

Eisner, R. (1989) *The Total Incomes System of Accounts*, Chicago: University of Chicago Press

International Labour Organisation (1982) 'Fifteenth International Conference of Labour Statisticians: Report II, Labour Force, Employment, Unemployment and Underemployment, Geneva: ILO

International Labour Organisation (1993) 'Fifteenth International Conference of Labour Statisticians: Report IV, Revision of the International Classification of Status in Employment, Geneva: ILO

Ralston Saul, R. (1997) *The Unconscious Civilization*, Ringwood, Vic.: Penguin Books

United Nations (1993) *A System of National Accounts*, New York: United Nations

United Nations (1996) *Human Development Report*, New York: United Nations

UNICEF (1997) *The State of the World's Children*, New York, UNICEF

Waring, M. (1999) *Counting for Nothing – What Men Value and What Women are Worth*, Toronto: University of Toronto Press

African women challenging neo-liberal economic orthodoxy:
the conception and mission of the GERA programme

Zo Randriamaro

Despite the many international commitments to gender equality, much remains to be done in terms of mainstreaming commitment to gender equality into development. It seems that the major global development institutions appear currently to be more concerned with mainstreaming trade into development. For example, the outcomes of the major international conferences, from the International Conference on Financing for Development to the World Summit on Sustainable Development, show a great deal of progress made in mainstreaming trade into development. Women's rights and gender activists have voiced their concern that this progress is paralleled by lip service to gender equality and women's rights. This article focuses on the activities of the GERA (Gender and Economic Reforms in Africa) programme. GERA is a pan-African research and advocacy programme which aims to increase the participation of African women in the formulation of economic policy. The article highlights some critical strategic issues that need to be addressed: the depoliticisation of economic policy, the governance of multilateral trade, and the way in which human security is conceptualised.

GERA is a pan-African research and advocacy programme, which aims to increase understanding of the different impact of economic reforms on men and women in the African setting, and ensure greater participation of African research organisations and women's groups in research, analysis and advocacy. It is the common dream of a group of African women, who created it to order to deconstruct and transform economic policies from a gender perspective. The economy is a central site of struggle for African women's empowerment in the era of globalisation. Nowadays, daring to dream and to write about a dream is not an innocent exercise, or a simple exercise of style: it is a political statement. This article discusses the concept behind GERA and some of its achievements so far, and considers its position in relation to key questions about the gender dimensions of economic policy, trade and human security in the context of globalisation. Responding to these questions is a critical element of the African women's movement's contribution to re-inventing globalisation so that it works for women and for people in poverty, rather than against them.

The conception and mission of GERA

GERA was set up in 1996. Since then, a growing number of African women researchers and activists have joined the initial group, to help make the dream come true. To date, GERA has provided support for 16 research and advocacy projects on the gender dimensions of economic reforms in 12 African countries, and for 11 projects focusing on the gender dimensions of trade and investment policy.[1] Ultimately, the GERA programme intends to create a pan-African movement of gender researchers, economists, trainers, advocates, and policy-makers, who are committed to transforming economic policy-making processes.

GERA's overall goal is to enable women better to articulate their concerns and needs, and transform economic policies from a gender perspective. Through its research activities, GERA has contributed to the body of knowledge about the gendered impacts of structural adjustment programmes (SAPs) and other policies which aim to stabilise African economies (Kerr et al. 2000). The programme research has increased awareness about macro-economic policy issues that shape the daily lives of poor women and men in the continent. The research conducted by African researchers under the GERA programme has provided evidence that macro-economic, trade and investment policies are not gender-neutral. GERA provides critical analyses of economic reform processes in Africa from a gender perspective, and works to develop alternative approaches that ensure gender equity and economic justice. Our analyses examine the intersecting causes of women's subordination and marginalisation in the economy at the micro, meso and macro level. Since 2000, GERA's focus has been on gender, trade and investment.

GERA's research extends beyond analysis which focuses on micro-level issues and interventions such as income-generating activities, micro-credit and the like. It also goes beyond the widespread view – especially among African women's organisations – that all issues related to women's empowerment and gender inequality can be resolved at the national level. We recognise that, in addition to a focus on the micro and meso level, African women's economic empowerment requires transforming policies and institutions in global economic governance.

GERA also aims to make African women's voices heard in the debate that has emerged about trade and investment policies, their impact on women, and their implications for gender relations. Undertaking research is an important means of empowering women and marginalised groups. Empowerment occurs through the participation of these groups in the different stages of the research itself, and the articulation of their own perspectives and needs. GERA's research has given a growing number of African women the opportunity to exercise their right as citizens to have a voice in decisions that shape their lives, together with the means to enter the male-dominated domain of economics and to express their concerns and needs.

At the global level, GERA participates in the global women's movement's activities to promote progressive change. GERA undertakes advocacy work to influence global economic decision-making and processes, and counter the neo-liberal economic paradigm underlying the so-called Washington Consensus.[2] We believe that advocacy is not merely a tool for achieving immediate objectives. Rather, it is a political tool to transform policies and institutions. It is an important means to address issues of power and power relations in the arena of economic policy-making, and wider society.

GERA's current concerns

The depoliticisation of economic policy

GERA is currently concerned about current attempts by the major global institutions to depoliticise economic policy. This is at the heart of the mainstream discourse on globalisation and development. But economic policy is not apolitical, and should not be seen as such. The promoters of the new economic orthodoxy are trying to promote the idea that economic policy is a technical system that should be protected from political interference. This can be clearly seen in the current liberalisation and privatisation drive in African countries. It has led to a debate among African intellectuals and activists over the role of the state in African countries.[3] While this issue has become part of the advocacy agenda of civil society groups in Africa, there is a need for wider awareness of the huge political implications. Attempts to remove economic policy from political control, by reducing economic policy to a set of technical prescriptions, imply that economic policy is the territory of experts and should not be subject to democratic debate and participation. Yet, the ever-increasing power of international financial and trade institutions shows that economic policy has actually become the major form of political action at the global level. This is a major threat to democracy in general, and women's rights in particular.

GERA advocates for a political economy approach to gender, trade and investment as the most appropriate way to uncover issues that have been hitherto considered as unintended effects of, rather than inherent to, these policies themselves. GERA counters the depoliticisation of economic policy in all its research: the starting point for its analysis of the gender dimensions of trade liberalisation and the multilateral trading system is a thorough understanding of the way in which inequalities are created and maintained by the global economic system. Production, consumption and savings may appear to be purely economic issues, but they are sustained by the ways in which society is organised. Therefore, attention needs to be given to the social dimensions of macro-economic policies (Elson and Cağatay 2000).

The role of civil society in economic policy-making

A critical question that we at GERA believe should be raised whenever possible concerns the vision of society that is promoted through the monopolisation of economic policy making by experts, which implies the exclusion of ordinary citizens from the major form of political action and subsequently, further marginalisation of women.

In the past few years, African civil society and women's organisations have been increasingly involved in consultations about some processes led by the World Bank and donors, such as the PRSP (Poverty Reduction Strategy Plan) processes. However, members of the GERA network have voiced their concerns about the way in which women's voices have been turned into instruments to legitimise economic processes imposed by the World Bank and donors (Mbilinyi 2001). In our view, in many cases, this willingness to give a voice to African women seems to be mainly motivated by the need to legitimise those processes. It comes as no surprise that the formulation of the macro-economic framework of the PRSPs, like other macro-economic policies, remains the preserve of experts – most of whom are male – and closed to public debate and participation.

What are real policy alternatives from a gender perspective?

While most women's rights and gender equality advocates agree on the need to oppose neo-liberal economic policies, there is still little consensus on what a feminist position should be on a number of issues. At GERA, we believe that the debate among women's organisations and activists has been obscured by the overwhelming focus on the impact of neo-liberal policies on women and gender relations, at the expense of a systematic analysis of the structural and inter-related causes of this impact.

An example is the issue of social protection under globalisation (that is, the extent to which the state should be able to protect and fulfil the social rights of its citizens, including the rights to employment and social security, in a globalised economy). In some cases, discussions within the women's movement focus on social protection and policies to ensure this, without relating these issues to gender biases and structural inequalities between women and men in the economy. But these discussions on women and social protection do not deal with the key factors which lead to women's requirement for social protection. Looking at social protection in this isolated way legitimises the idea that women are a category of people who only require measures to address their welfare needs, but not actions or policies for addressing the root causes of their marginalisation in the globalised economy. This gives rise to a 'politics of compassion', deployed by the promoters of neo-liberalism, in order to counter the mounting protest against the negative effects of their policies.

'Engendering' economic policies is different from institutionalising compassion towards women. Promoting gender-sensitive economic policies is not only about establishing safety nets. It is primarily about ensuring that there will be no need for safety nets. In this regard, a feminist approach would posit that sound and equitable economic policies require men and women to have equal access to, and control over, productive resources, equal participation in decision making, and equal distribution of the benefits of their work. Gender-sensitive economic policies would not be obsessed with budget deficits, inflation and macro-economic stability. They would take the care economy fully into account. They would give each country enough flexibility to meet the needs of their peoples, giving primacy to human rights and developmental needs.

Multilateral trade and the WTO: the ghost of tyranny

GERA' s work on the gender dimensions of trade seeks to inject African women's perspectives in trade policy-making and processes. In this section, I will examine some different approaches to the gender dimensions of trade liberalisation, to show the compartmentalised nature of current debates. These debates miss the inter-linkages between macro, meso and micro issues, as well as the connections between different types of economic reforms and policies. From the point of view of African women, this suggests that there is an urgent need to transform the economic model underlying the international trade regime, because of the structural and political biases that undermine gender equality and disempower women in the economy.

Gender issues forgotten: mainstreaming trade into development

The depoliticisation of economic policy discussed above can be seen in current WTO processes, and the governance of the multilateral trading system. On one level, the undemocratic and manipulative practices that characterise the WTO processes are major issues, because gender issues and women's empowerment cannot be on the agenda when people are ignored. At another level, the governance of the multilateral trading system has been – and remains – a key issue for the advocacy work of women's organisations and activists. This is not only because gender as a category of analysis, and gender relations as a key set of social dynamics, are not recognised in trade policy decision-making (Williams 2002). Most importantly, it is because trade policy formulation and decision-making needs to be challenged, if trade liberalisation is to be re-configured to ensure gender equality (Williams 2002).

The convergence between the policies of the IMF, the World Bank and the WTO has not only created a dominant discourse which promotes the trade liberalisation agenda. It has also given rise to mechanisms such as the IMF Poverty Reduction and Growth Facility (PRGF) and the World Bank-led Poverty Reduction Strategy Plan (PRSP), which are particularly powerful since they are backed by all three institutions. These mechanisms impose conditions on countries in a similar way to Structural Adjustment Policies (SAPs). The Integrated Framework for Technical Assistance, which is meant to ensure the integration of trade and development, involves the combined efforts of the IMF, World Bank and WTO, along with other UN agencies. One cannot but ask why similar but separate mechanisms have not been put in place and used to further gender equality and women's empowerment.

Gender and trade: towards an African perspective [4]

African analyses of trade liberalisation need to be heard. African countries have been integrated into the multilateral trading system, through the General Agreement on Tariffs and Trade (GATT) and the establishment of the World Trade Organisation (WTO), without any kind of meaningful participation. Their integration has also taken place under peculiar conditions that define their weak position in the global trading arrangements. In addition, there is an unresolved controversy around the issue of gender mainstreaming into the WTO. In particular, the lack of attention to African women's perspectives on this issue is important, since it has critical implications for them. The first step to ensure these perspectives are heard is to ask African women the right questions, and develop a coherent analysis which articulates their interests. The second step is to define a policy framework which will ensure not only that women gain from trade liberalisation, but also that the structural causes of their economic subordination are addressed.

GERA research aims to support the development of such a policy framework. In our view, the framework needs to take account of the following:

- the distributive effects of trade policies on African economies;
- the interaction between trade liberalisation and other types of economic reforms and policies;
- the extent to which this general context empowers or disempowers women – their empowerment in trade also depends on the general economic and political conditions into which they integrate the trading systems.

The framework needs to be based on an acknowledgment of the multiple ways in which African women are disempowered by international trading arrangements. This is not only to do with WTO agreements and rules, but also to do with the role of international financial institutions and transnational corporations, as well as the state, and institutions at national level.

Most importantly, GERA advocates for African gender researchers and activists to re-claim the concept of gender mainstreaming, so that it plays the role of a political tool for women's empowerment, instead of a technical device for legitimising inequitable trade and economic policies. The prevailing approaches to addressing the gender implications and impact of trade policies should be critically evaluated and challenged. The findings of GERA researchers[5] demonstrate that, as a first step in this direction, the ways in which different forms of inequality intersect each other to create different forms of disempowerment for particular individuals and groups should be incorporated in the analysis of trade and economic policies. Forms of inequality would include those created by gender, class, race, ethnicity and other forms of identity.

Human security from a gender perspective

In its ongoing advocacy work on the gender dimensions of investment and 'new issues' in the WTO, GERA has recently been emphasising the need for women in Africa and beyond to speak out against the way in which prevailing understandings of human security are overemphasising the security of states and corporations, at the expense of the security of individuals. Concerns for the security of investment and the protection of the rights of investors increasingly take precedence over people's security in the international agenda. Most of the time, this is presented in the name of economic efficiency – as in the case of water privatisation – and for the sake of economic growth. Women's rights activists and gender equality advocates, including the GERA programme, are focusing on the integration of the notion of freedom from want[6] and its gender dimensions, including economic security, into the international agenda.

GERA also shares the current concerns of the global women's movement about issues of human security, in the context of the establishment of the international coalition against terrorism. Civil society and women's struggles for progressive social transformation are threatened by the conflation of protest with terrorist actions, and the subsequent intensification of repression by military means (Randriamaro 2002).

It is well known that women and children are the most affected by conflicts, and the last decade has seen an increasing number of African women's organisations involved in initiatives to promote women's participation in conflict prevention and resolution. The progress that has been made as a result of these efforts is being undermined by the developments around the international coalition against terrorism, which is being established without consideration for implications in terms of internal politics in the different countries involved in the coalition.

The conceptual shift in the discussions on human security has also meant an exclusive focus on human security in times of conflict. As a result, the specific threat posed by gender inequality to women's security in times of peace is further neglected. This leads to abuse in both private and public spheres, which includes violence against women and girls, gender inequalities in control over resources as well as in power and decision-making. In addition, the current focus on military action promotes the very stereotypes of masculinity and femininity against which women's rights activists have been struggling for so long. At the Ninth International Association for Women in Development (AWID) Forum in 2002, sisters from Afghanistan amongst others provided striking testimonies of how 'the mainstream discussion of human security emphasises military might, and even occasionally justifies military action and an anti-terrorist ideology with securing women's welfare'.

GERA has highlighted that fact that the strengthening of the coalition between the international financial and trade institutions and rich countries in support of the Washington Consensus is paralleled, and potentially further reinforced, by the establishment of the international coalition against terrorism (Randriamaro 2002). Discussions on human security, and policies arising from these discussions, are resulting in the progressive elimination of gender considerations from the international agenda. The media in many different countries are reporting widespread human rights violations, along with the manifestations of a lasting economic crisis that will disproportionately affect women and marginalised groups. GERA has also pointed out that the increase in military spending is likely to lead to the diversion of scarce resources from sectors that are crucial for women and the poor, to defence budgets.

GERA has pointed to the risk that initiatives such as the New Partnership for Africa's Development (NEPAD) pose to the rights of women in poverty in Africa. They could just be the new policy platform to fight international terrorism from Africa, as opposed to tackling the other issues that are critical for women and the poor (Randriamaro 2002). Solidarity is urgently needed among the peoples affected by current developments within national boundaries by which democracy and human rights – including women's and children's rights – are traded away in exchange for their countries' support for the international war against terrorism. It is a strategic requirement, as well as an ethical imperative for the global women's movement.

Conclusion

The AWID Forum raised awareness among participants about a number of critical questions that require strategic responses from women's rights and gender activists. This article argues that the depoliticisation of economic policy, the governance of multilateral trade, and the re-conceptual-isation of human security are some of the issues that require responses from the national to the global level. These are also pointers to common front lines for solidarity within the global women's movement, which include the right to sit at the table (but also to determine what is on the table and the structure of the table itself, as well as the right to dream as a prerequisite for developing alternatives) in economic and trade policy decision-making; the primacy of people's security and the integration of gender differences and inequalities in the international human security agenda.

A major challenge for the African women's movement will be to inject its perspectives and concerns into the agenda of the global women's movement while integrating into its own thinking those elements of universality that give a sense to women's common struggles in the context of globalisation as well as to our solidarity with other marginalised groups. To that end, GERA will continue to bridge the gap between researchers and advocates in order to give a stronger voice to African women from the national to the global level.

Zo Randriamaro is a gender and human rights activist from Madagascar. She is working with Third World Network-Africa as Manager of the GERA programme. Address: PO Box AN 19452, Accra, Ghana. gera@twnafrica.org

Notes

1 The GERA programme's achievements have been described in more detail in Kerr et al. (2000).

2 The Washington Consensus refers to the shared neo-liberal vision of development on the part of the international development financing institutions, including the World Bank and IMF. The Washington Consensus inspired the set of prescriptions imposed on developing countries under the structural adjust-ment programmes (SAPs) and economic reforms, from the early 1980s. These prescriptions included fiscal discipline, deregulation, privatisation of state enterprises and trade liberalisation.

3 See, for example, Taylor 2000, for the debate within the African women's movement.

4 This subsection draws from a lecture given by the author at the 2002 Session of the CODESRIA Gender Institute, Dakar, 1–6 July 2002, on 'Gender, Trade Liberalisation and the Multilateral Trading System: Towards an African Perspective'.

5 Namely, the GERA Phase II research findings on the impact of trade and investment liberalisation on women working in the leather and footwear industry in South Africa. These findings are due for publication by TWN-Africa as part of a book compiling the findings of the eight GERA Phase II research projects.

6 UNDP 1994: freedom from want and freedom for fear are the two major components of human security.

References

Elson, D. and N. Cağatay (2000) 'The social content of macro-economic policy', *World Development*, Vol. 28(7)

Kerr, J. et. al. (eds.) (2000) *Demanding Dignity: Women Confronting Economic Reforms in Africa*, Ottawa: The North-South Institute and Third World Network-Africa

Mbilinyi, M. (2001) 'Budgets, Debt Relief and Globalisation', GERA Discussion Paper 1, Accra: GERA Programme/ TWN-Africa

Randriamaro, Z. (2002) 'The NEPAD, Gender and the Poverty Trap: the NEPAD and the Challenges of Financing for Development in Africa from a Gender Perspective', unpublished paper presented at the joint TWN-Africa/ CODESRIA International Conference on Africa and the Development Challenges of the New Millennium, Accra, 23–26 April 2002 (available from Third World Network-Africa, see postal address in biographical details above, or visit www.twnafrica.org)

Taylor, V. (2000) *Marketisation of Governance: Critical Feminist Perspectives from the South*, SADEP/DAWN: University of Cape Town, Cape Town

UNDP (1994) *Human Development Report*, New York

Williams, M. (2002) 'Gender and Governance in the Multilateral Trading System: Critical Areas of Decision-Making and Global Responses', paper presented at the GERA Mid-term Review Workshop, Accra, 25–29 November 2002 (forthcoming from the GERA programme /TWN-Africa)

In search of an alternative development paradigm:
feminist proposals from Latin America

Members of the Feminist Initiative of Cartagena[1]

This article is taken from five presentations given at AWID by members of the Feminist Initiative of Cartagena. Its main goal was to suggest that there is a Southern – more specifically, Latin American – vision of globalisation, and to identify what is needed to develop a new model of development.

1 Why did the Feminist Initiative of Cartagena start?

Alejandra Scampini, Co-ordinator, IFC, Uruguay

In July 2001, a seminar took place in Cartagena, Colombia, in preparation for the UN Conference on Financing for Development (held in Monterrey, Mexico, 18–22 March 2002). The seminar was organised by DAWN (Development Alternatives with Women for a New era), REPEM (Red de Educacion Popular Entre Mujeres) and the UNIFEM Socio-Economic and Cultural Rights Programme in the Andean region.

The Feminist Initiative of Cartagena (IFC) was founded as a result of the seminar. It was set up because Latin American feminists wished to influence the UN conference, which brought together governments, private sector (business and NGOs) and international funding organisations. The IFC is an association of active

networks in the region, which provides all its members with an opportunity to react to changing economic issues. Networking of organisations from different sectors of civil society, including women's organisations, can strengthen their ability to discuss and influence the design, execution, follow-up and evaluation of public policy, with governments and international organisations.

After Monterrey, the IFC continued producing research and developing advocacy activities. The organisations involved in the IFC take a collective position on regional macro-economic issues. Monitoring public policy and undertaking advocacy is 'a prepositional and pragmatic answer to global and local political contexts that today are more receptive to requests for gender equity' (Alvarez 1997). We propose to advance the analysis of macro-economic issues faced by our region, building on the work of other groups and existing initiatives. We want to share our experience and proposals with women from Latin

America and other regions of the world. In common with other feminist organisations, we are developing ways of linking work at grassroots level with activities at the 'macro level' of public governmental and international politics.

We aim to combine rigorous analysis with good political practice from a feminist perspective. The IFC is intended to provide an open space to strengthen the different knowledge and abilities of its members, who have different experience and expertise. It is flexible about how it does this. In terms of our ways of working, we aim to:

- meet common objectives, without becoming too formal or institutionalised

- create a common position and discourse which is built on a genuine recognition of all the personal and organisational contributions of everyone in the IFC

- maintain active and participatory communication, and a dynamic of permanent consultation, among members

- sustain exchanges with other networks and organisations.

So far, we have faced some challenges. It is challenging and complex work to generate critical debate about the impact of neo-liberal globalisation, and suggest alternatives into which gender issues have been integrated. It is particularly hard to keep up with the rhythm of regional and global events while relying mostly on short-term voluntary work, and little funding. Furthermore, there are challenges in developing new and timely responses while simultaneously maintaining our commitment to a collective process in reaching policy positions.

2 Putting the IFC proposal into practice
Alma Espino, Uruguay

As outlined above, the IFC is the result of the wish of Latin American feminists to influence the UN Conference on Financing for Development, which brought together governments, private sector (business and NGOs) and international funding bodies. We have centred our analysis on a number of key issues.

Financial resources and development
The basis for our analysis is to ask: 'What type of development are we thinking of, as groups of feminist women?' That is, in what way can our vision of the economy and economic development incorporating a commitment to gender equality, contribute to critical analysis of the current economic model? And how can our vision contribute to the development of alternative economic models? The dominant economic policies have not guaranteed equality or brought about an end to poverty, and have not tended to achieve expected rates of economic growth. And all of those are essential elements in sustainable development.

Expectations of the Financing for Development (FFD) process
Quite reasonably, the debate around the FFD process at Monterrey created expectations among those who took part. First, there is a need to mount a concrete challenge to the existing development model. Second, all those involved in development need to reach some essential agreements in order to overcome the failures of the current development process and guarantee a level of sustainability in development. This is critical not only for poor countries, but also to ensure the future of life on our planet.

By the end of the 1990s, we could already see that 'free trade' was only really free for some. Free flows of capital, in the form of speculative flows of currency in and out of government control, were destabilising different economies. As the decade came to an end, private capital flow surpassed development support as the main foreign source of capital available for developing countries. Direct investment operating in a borderless market without effective regulations conditioned the availability of funds for development, and thus conditioned state policies in our countries.

The Monterrey Consensus[2] threw all our expectations overboard. The consensus reflects the complete failure of the conference to address the poverty and hardship faced by women and men in poor countries which are integrating their economies into a 'globalised' world. The consensus did nothing to increase the availability of resources for developing countries, or improve their access to markets. Nor did Monterrey support developing countries through the development of a control mechanism, or capital regulation, which would reduce the risks of financial crisis associated with the international free market, and increase the options in terms of which economic policies countries are able to adopt.

Regional crisis

During the 1990s, the Latin American region experienced a production crisis and a large increase in unemployment, even though measures had been taken to make the labour market 'flexible' – that is, to deregulate it. These problems occurred at a time of financial and banking crisis. State sovereignty was decreased because of a number of related factors, including the fact that national debt levels were high and increasing, the institutions intended to regulate national economies were weak, and the necessary regulations were lacking.

Regional initiatives like MERCOSUR were virtually paralysed. MERCOSUR (the Common Market of the Southern Cone) is a customs union between four member states (Brazil, Argentina, Paraguay and Uruguay) and two other associate members (Bolivia and Chile). MERCOSUR was established in 1995. It is the third largest trading bloc in the world. The East Asian crisis had a strong impact on MERCOSUR, and the regional economies were not able to revitalise it. The forecast in terms of growth continues to be bleak. Conditions set by the international financial bodies not only affect the sovereignty of states from the point of view of the economy, but also threaten democracy in states where this is weak.

The challenges

Today, we in the Latin America region face the familiar challenges of development in conditions of growing economic decay and fragile democratic governance. The lessons we have learnt through our experience make us more entitled each day to insist that power relations among countries and regions cannot depend on economic theory alone. Policy making cannot neglect the realities of the relationship between economics and politics. Social and political exclusion and economic poverty should be addressed in economic proposals. Aside from being socially unjust, the exclusion and economic want experienced by particular groups of people according to their sex, race and religion, and so on, can influence the success of economic policy. So the equality issue cannot be left until poverty has been addressed: there is either growth with equity, or there is no growth.

As feminists, we need to perfect our analysis and proposals, but gender analysis, together with feminist practice, can contribute to the necessary changes in terms of access to welfare, social justice, and the strengthening of democracy and peace.

3 Placing equity at the heart of the agenda on external debt and trade

Norma Sanchís, Argentina

Latin America continues to be the most unequal region in the world. As feminists who recognise the importance of noting economic and political trends, we have consistently emphasised the importance of equality as a human value which transcends gender, social, economic, ethnic and national differences. Over the past few decades, wealth has been increasingly concentrated in a few hands, and social injustice has increased.

In the 1990s, structural adjustment policies (SAPs) led to the opening up of markets and financial deregulation in Latin American countries. At the beginning of the 1990s, the open market seemed to be leading towards a promising rise in exports and growth from the countries in the region. At the same time, some analysts flagged up the fact that countries in the region needed to transform their production processes in order to improve their reach into the world market, and that this change must be linked to proposals to improve social and economic equality (ECLAC 1991). To be competitive, we needed to upgrade our technology and the skills and qualifications of the work force. These analysts warned us of the fact that improvement in the ability to compete could not be achieved on the basis of tightening labour costs, or overexploiting the natural resources in the region.

Throughout the 1990s, the inequalities in wealth distribution that characterise the region remained strong. While economies were growing, it was not possible to counteract the patterns of unequal distribution which were observed in the 1980s. In 2001, the ECLAC *Social Panorama of Latin America* (ECLAC 2001) showed that in all Latin American countries except for Costa Rica and Uruguay, the richest 10 per cent owns 30 per cent or more of the wealth. In Brazil, the country with the highest indexes of wealth concentration in the whole region, the proportion owned by the richest 10 per cent is as high as 45 per cent, while the share of the poorest 40 per cent is around 10 per cent in all countries except Uruguay, where it is 22 per cent. In all the countries in the region as a whole, the inequality in distribution became sharper during the period 1997 to 1999.

Aside from these differences in wealth within countries, there are obvious inequalities between countries which increase vulnerability in the global free-market economy. The large foreign debts of developing countries are a key issue which has been taken up by sectors of civil society and social movements in the Latin America region in recent years. The current debt of Latin America is several times larger than it was 20 years ago, even though over the past few years debt repayments have been made which are higher than the value of the loans. According to data from the World Bank and ECLAC, Latin America has repaid US$1.4 billion over the past 20 years. This means that there was a resource transfer five times larger than the original debt, even though today the debt is three times larger.

International trade is another way in which asymmetrical power relations between countries, which shape international relations, is manifested. International trade is usually seen as a technical field, in which the negotiation mechanisms of exchange are analysed according to the specific interests of each country or region. However, this perspective ignores the fact that power defines the primary interests of the stronger economies. In the case of the FTAA (Free Trade Area of the Americas) negotiations, the supremacy of the northern economies is evident – in particular that of the US, which represents about three-quarters of the region's GDP. The remaining quarter is produced by the other 33 countries that are part of the agreement. This level of asymmetry, which became evident in the political and military spheres as well, after September 11, allows for the FTAA to serve, not only as a trade agreement, but also as a tool for the political, economic and cultural dominance of the US. Civil society movements in Latin America are mobilising to address this.

It is necessary to encourage an agenda that places social and gender equity at the centre of economics and politics. Growth in

56

itself is not enough. We need institutions that promote equality, and gender equality as a part of this; we need political systems and politicians who will fight against the inequalities that remain in our societies. They need to promote discussion on issues such as intra-state and international asymmetries in power, strategies to build alliances and negotiate, to challenge the focus on wealth creation in favour of more equal distribution, and to promote the universality of human rights (including economic, social, political and cultural rights), as a guarantee of global citizenship.

4 Forming institutions in response to the new labour relations
By Rosalba Todaro, Chile

We are facing a crisis of what has been termed 'normal labour relations'. By this phrase I mean the type of labour relations and protection of workers that characterised the capitalist industrial era in Western economies.

The fundamental characteristics of 'normal labour relations' are the following:

- full-time work, mostly performed by men, in jobs of indefinite duration, designed as a long-term relationship between worker and employer
- job provides family income, sufficient for family sustenance
- women perform essential work at home with dependents, which subsidises men's paid work
- the relationship between worker and employer is part of a set of legal norms, negotiated by different social actors
- job is of standard duration, and regulated by the working day
- workers' rights to social protection depend on their presence within the paid labour market

- sectors that are not part of the paid labour market are excluded from social protection
- hence, the economic security of women is dependent on their spouse or father.

There have always been forms of employment that are outside of this 'norm', such as contracts for specific services. But since the 1970s, the gap has widened between the norm and reality. The laws governing this kind of relationship between employers and workers are not only used less because of direct law evasion, but because their application is restricted to an ever smaller population of workers. The system loses its protective strength if it only applies to certain groups of workers. Yet, while most employment now does not conform to the norm, the regulations and forms of protection are still thought of as standards by which labour relations are defined.

Although the changes in the way labour is regulated have happened in the context of neo-liberal politics, it would be too simplistic to say that this is the sole reason they have occurred. This would bypass other important factors that influence labour structures, including new technologies, especially information and communications technologies. These make it possible for employers to co-ordinate labour processes that may be taking place simultaneously in geographically distant locations. This makes for greater financial flexibility, and a more elastic relationship between workers and working tools. The fact that productive processes can be 'farmed out' to distant regions, facilitated by technological advances, dilutes the nature of the relationship between the company and the worker and creates a grey area between employment and self-employment.

On the other hand, important changes have taken place in the relationships between women and men, linked to changes in the economic needs of families. In the description of 'normal labour relations' given above, a strict gender division of labour was a key feature. Current changes in family needs are linked to economic crisis, to commercialisation of public services, and to the growing instability and insecurity of employment. At the same time, there are also changes in women's expectations and hopes for autonomy, as they question the traditional division of labour. Family units are changing and new forms are emerging, and marriage is becoming unstable in many contexts. All this leads to the disappearance of the 'family wage' paid to a male breadwinner, and to challenges to strict divisions of labour by sex, and hence to the organisation of paid work. A paid worker used to be male, with a wife who took care of his daily needs and those of his family. This can no longer be assumed.

Overcoming poverty now requires flexibility. Currently, the new jobs are characterised by uncertainty: low incomes, instability in contractual arrangements, lack of social protection leading to greater vulnerability in times of illness, and less scope for workers to resist exploitation and negotiate terms, because of conditions of instability and high unemployment. Flexibility is not only an economic requirement for labour forces as a whole, but also a prerequisite of daily life for individuals in paid employment.

Labour relations and social protection need to be re-regulated, according to the new terms in which people are involved in paid work, and the new gender relations. Work itself needs to be understood and conceptualised correctly – not just as paid work, or work for the market, but as the totality of activities that people and society need. Feminist economics provide new models to help us understand reality, and enlarge the boundaries of the economy in theory and in practice.

Given the context of economic crisis and minimum growth among the majority of Latin American economies, high unemployment leads to companies being able to insist that their labour forces are flexible. There are currently serious difficulties in achieving a form of 'virtuous flexibility'. Institutions and regulations are required to meet the needs of women and men involved in the new forms of labour and new gendered relationships. These will come out of a new social agreement between all those involved in global trade and employment. But the problem we are facing today is the inequality among the players in the globalised employment market. Overcoming this problem is a key objective.

5 Macro economics and macro politics
Cecilia López Montaño, Colombia

Latin America in the context of the 1990s
During the so-called 'lost decade' of the 1980s, it became evident that the import substitution and popular politics model of development in Latin America was at an end. In many countries, a welfare state had been attempted at the expense of fiscal deficit and debt. Since the beginning of the 1990s, the Washington Consensus began to insist on SAPs being applied indiscriminately in most of Latin America. The same recipe was used from country to country, without any consideration of local conditions, or social safety nets. This occurred in pursuit of the goal of thrusting these countries into the globalised economy. This was an unrealistic aim, which soon became apparent. In reality, in many cases the pre-modern structures of production were not modified, nor the patriarchal relationships, nor work in precarious or exploitative conditions.

The axis of the current debate
Finding real alternatives to current economic policies requires recognition that

we are now facing new realities in which the old analysis is no longer functional. Today, it is clear that the problems of the 1990s have been replaced by new problems. The issue of inflation has been replaced by that of recession. Unemployment has become a key issue worldwide, and seriously affects our region. The old monetary and fiscal policies have shown obvious signs of weakness.

We also need to recognise the neo-colonialism that now dominates the management of world economics. With the Washington Consensus, developing countries lost autonomy in political and economic decision-making. At the same time, the power of the Western countries has been consolidated because it is they who supply financing to developing countries in debt. Only the rich countries which do not need resources are free to decide on their economic policies. Since this model benefits the rich countries, its forced implementation on the poor countries creates a neocolonial relationship.

The third thing we need to recognise is that we are facing a partial and incomplete process of globalisation. Many of the elements of a genuine globalisation process are not taking place: there is no such thing as free trade since protectionism is still the order of the day, and not everything has been globalised – in particular, the free movement of the workforce. For global-isation to work, it must go deep and integrate all factors and levels.

Finally, we need to recognise what other writers in this article have high-lighted already: macro economics is tied to, and conditioned by, international politics.

It is necessary to strengthen political parties and reclaim public space for citizens to assert their full rights.

Notes

1 The following networks are part of the Feminist Initiative of Cartagena: REPEM (Popular Education Among Women Network), DAWN, IGTN-LA (International Gender and Trade Network-Latin America), CLADEM, Women and Habitat Network, Feminists Economists Group, Women Transforming, Feminist Marcosur Coalition.
2 The Monterrey Consensus can be found at http://ods-dds-ny.un.org/doc/UNDOC/GEN/N02/392/67/PDF/N0239267.pdf

References

Alvarez, S. (1997) *The relationship between the feminist movement, democracy and State*, Flora Tristan: Peru

ECLAC (1991) *Transformación productiva con equidad*, Santiago: ECLAC

ECLAC (2001) *Social Panorama of Latin America*, Santiago: ECLAC

United Nations (2002) *Financing for Development: Building on Monterrey*, UN, New York

If I were Minister of Finance ... :
gaining understanding of financial crisis through a simulation workshop

Mehrene Larudee and Caren Grown

Financial crises (also known as debt crises, currency crises or balance of payments crises) have become endemic in the modern world. The countries at greatest risk have been developing countries. This article discusses a workshop,'If I were Minister of Finance...', which we ran at the Association for Women in Development (AWID) conference in Guadalajara in October 2002. In the workshop, participants took part in a simulation of the Argentine currency crisis. The simulation sought to give participants a better understanding of the causes of a currency crisis, and the tough, limited choices a government faces in trying to prevent it. Simulations like the one described in this article can be helpful to activists and women's organisations in moving a gender-sensitive economic policy agenda forward.

Developing countries which have faced financial crises in the past two decades include Mexico (1982 and 1994–5), Chile (1982), Brazil (1982, much of 1986–1993 and 1999), Thailand (1997), and Russia (1998), to name only a few. But even Finland (1992) and Sweden (1990) have faced similar crises, and even so-called 'fortress' Britain was compelled to devalue the pound in 1992, when it came under speculative attack. (Speculative attacks are explained below in Round 3.)

Why do financial crises arise at all? The first step is to understand that most countries' currencies – Thai baht, Indian rupees, or Argentinian pesos – are not accepted as payment when goods are sold across borders. To carry out international transactions, one has to have so-called 'hard currency': dollars, euros, or one of a very few other currencies such as the yen, the Swiss franc or the British pound sterling. (In the simulation, all kinds of hard currency are referred to as 'dollars'.) For example, suppose one wants to import goods into Argentina from another country. One must pay in dollars. Of course, if credit is available one does not have to pay those dollars immediately. But, sooner or later, one has to come up with enough dollars to pay – and if it is later, of course one has to pay back not only the principal (that is, the original money borrowed), but interest as well.

The second step in understanding financial crises and why they arise is to recognise that anyone who wants to obtain dollars normally gets them by selling the local currency and buying dollars. (For convenience, local currencies were represented by the peso in the simulation.) In most countries, only the Central Bank, or a financial institution authorised by the Central Bank, is allowed to sell dollars and buy pesos. (At least, this is the theory.) In practice, there may be a black market, but the simulation ignores that complication in the first round.

The third fact to bear in mind is that although the words 'crisis' and 'devaluation' suggest pain and suffering, there are both losers and winners in a currency devaluation. The losers are those who are holding pesos when the devaluation happens, because after the devaluation, the pesos can buy fewer dollars than before. For instance, after the Mexican peso devaluation of 1994–5, there was a steep drop in cross-border shopping by Mexicans from Ciudad Juárez, who normally spend considerable money in El Paso in the USA, buying clothes, toys, appliances and other goods. Women who are responsible for reproductive work can also lose out from devaluation, as the prices of necessities and basic goods rise; women then have to make do with less.

In contrast, the winners from devaluation are those who successfully anticipate it and buy dollars just in advance of it. After the devaluation, they can buy back twice as many pesos, and may well end up better off. In fact, all those who are holding dollars after devaluation have an advantage. For example, after the Asian financial crisis, the Wall Street investment firm Goldman Sachs was able to buy up hotels and real estate in a number of Asian countries.

The workshop process

The AWID workshop simulation was designed for participants with no previous knowledge of economics. The workshop was run twice and, all together, a total of about 30 women were taught the basic principles of balance of payments, as this affects the lives of people in developing countries. The same simulation has also been used in a class at the University of Kansas, and a simpler version was run during the 2002 UN Committee on the Status of Women meetings in New York at a teach-in hosted by UNIFEM.

Each participant took one of nine roles, and followed a script spelling out her actions during four rounds of play, during which balance of payments problems became progressively more serious, and

unfolded into a crisis. At times, the workshop seemed near chaos, as workers feverishly manufactured 'soccer balls' while toy manufacturers struggled to sell them and remain profitable in the face of imports, which were suddenly cheaper than local products. Meanwhile, Argentina's Central Bank tried to hang on to its dollar reserves, as the rich put their money into dollar savings outside the country, and currency speculators waited to pounce.

In our simulation, the nine players sit around a table, and each is given a quantity of pesos (white beans), dollars (black beans), and debt (red cards) that are appropriate to her role. There are three foreign and six domestic players. The foreigners are a Foreign Lender, a Foreign Investor who also runs an export-import business, and a Currency Speculator. The domestic players are a Central Banker, a Local Banker, the Argentine Government, a Rich Argentine, a Toy Manufacturer and a Worker in the Toy Manufacturing Business. The central banker and the toy manufacturer are the busiest and have the most complex tasks; at the other extreme, the currency speculator does nothing except watch for the first couple of rounds, and springs into action late in the game.

The worker and the manufacturer start out with nothing. The manufacturer borrows pesos from the local bank at 20 per cent interest to pay local wages, and also borrows dollars from the foreign lender at 10 per cent interest to import inputs (sheets of purple paper) with which to produce soccer balls. The workers then manufacture soccer balls (by crumpling the paper into balls), and the soccer balls are sold, some abroad (to the foreign investor with the export-import business) and some at home (to the rich Argentine). With the sales revenue, the manufacturer pays the worker, and then repays the loans with interest, making a small profit. The worker spends some of her money on imported goods, as does the rich Argentine.

The Argentine government already has $200 debt at the beginning of the simulation, and in each round has to pay 10 per cent interest on that debt. To do so, it has to use its tax revenues and exchange them for dollars with the Central Bank, since the interest must be paid in dollars. (We hand four rounds of tax revenues to the government at the beginning of the game, in order to keep matters simple.) However, the government does not have any net principal repayments on the $200 debt, since it rolls over the loan each round; that is, it pays back exactly as much principal as it borrows anew.

In addition, though, the government happens to have a persistent budget deficit – a common, though not universal, feature of economies headed for crisis – and the deficit is financed by borrowing from abroad. For this purpose, the government also borrows an additional amount in each round, so that in each subsequent round it has to pay additional interest at the world interest rate, which stays at 10 per cent throughout.

Similarly, each player buys, sells, borrows, lends, invests, or disinvests, as specified in the script. Each time such a transaction involves changing pesos into dollars or dollars into pesos, the players see the Central Bank's stack of dollars fall or rise. The main point for participants to take away is this: a financial crisis simply means that the Central Bank is running out of dollars. That stack of dollars in Argentina's Central Bank – which in real life is actually kept in a bank somewhere in New York – is called the Bank's 'foreign exchange reserves' or 'foreign currency reserves'. Some transactions cause dollars to be taken from the stack. Others cause dollars to be added to the stack.

As a rule of thumb, a central banker is happiest when the stack contains enough dollars to pay for at least three and preferably six normal months' worth of imports, and when, year after year, the stack remains around that size. The dollar reserves act as a kind of guarantee to international investors and lenders that,

even if for some temporary reason the inflow of dollars slows or the outflow increases, the country will still have enough dollars to continue making its debt payments as well as buying imports to keep its economy going. In a very real sense, the central banker is happiest if nothing happens to her dollar reserves at all. But once the dollar reserves fall close to zero, pandemonium breaks out. The approaching crisis sets off behaviour by certain economic actors which make that crisis far harder to avoid.

But this is getting ahead of our story. Our workshop unfolds over four rounds of the simulation.

How the simulation works

Round 1: A stable peso, no balance of payments problem; learning basic principles

In the simulation, the action focuses on the Central Bank: the central banker sells dollars to some players, receiving pesos in exchange, and buys dollars from other players, giving pesos in exchange. In Round 1, the exchange rate is set at 1 peso = $1. In this round, the players just get accustomed to their roles in a situation in which there is no crisis, and the balance of payments is balanced. Dollars flow in and out of the Central Bank, but at the end of the round (which represents a time period of a year or so) the Central Bank holds the same $100 with which it started.

In this round, players see that it is the flows of dollars into and out of the country that matter, and they see the various reasons why foreigners, local manufacturers, the government and various private producers and consumers might want to buy dollars and sell pesos, or sell dollars and buy pesos.

The simplest example of this is imports: if an Argentine has pesos and wants to import a car, he needs to go to the Central Bank, sell his pesos and buy dollars. He will be able to pay for the imported goods with his dollars. (Equivalently, the car dealer or importer may actually obtain the dollars; the point is that someone has to give up pesos for dollars in order for the car to be imported.) Likewise, if an Argentine bicycle manufacturer exports bicycles, then she receives dollars in payment, and goes to the Central Bank and exchanges these for pesos, which she uses to pay her employees and local suppliers. For simplicity, in the simulation we slightly altered the details of this scenario, but the basic idea is sound. If Argentina has $40 billion in imports and $40 billion in exports, then the overall effect on the dollar reserves in the Central Bank is to leave them unchanged. But if Argentina imports $5 billion more in goods than it exports, and nothing else changes, then the Central Bank's dollar reserves will fall by $5 billion as long as the exchange rate is still 1 peso = $1.

Of course, there are many kinds of transactions besides trade that bring dollars into the Central Bank: foreign lending to Argentine private firms or to the government, for instance. There are also many kinds of transactions that vacuum dollars out of the Central Bank, such as payments of interest on foreign loans (which have to be paid in dollars). A variety of these sorts of transactions are illustrated in subsequent rounds of the simulation.

Round 2: Brazilian currency is devalued; Argentina's dollar reserves shrink

In Round 2, Brazil, a major trading partner of Argentina, undergoes a large devaluation, just as it did in January 1999. Suddenly, Brazil's goods are much cheaper. Argentina now has a harder time exporting to Brazil and, within Argentina, consumers buy more Brazilian goods. A decline in exports and an increase in imports throw the balance of payments out of balance. In this round, about twice as many pesos are offered for sale as dollars. So if the exchange rate is to remain at 1 peso = $1, either some peso sellers will not find

buyers, or else the Central Bank will have to use some of its dollar reserves to buy up the extra pesos.

Once dollars seem to be flowing out faster than they are flowing in at the prevailing exchange rate, players begin to see the dilemma facing the Central Banker. She has three options, none of them appealing. The first option, the one which the script dictates in Round 2, is to go ahead and use her dollar reserves to buy all the extra pesos offered for sale, and so maintain 'parity' at one peso per one dollar. This has the advantage that it offers potential foreign investors a stable, predictable exchange rate. It prevents devaluation for the moment, but unfortunately it also reduces the Central Bank's stack of dollars. Next year, if there are more pesos for sale than offers to buy them, the Central Bank will face the same choices. But if the Central Bank sops up the extra pesos each time this occurs, it will very soon run out of dollars, and a financial crisis will ensue. At that point the government will have to appeal to the International Monetary Fund (IMF) for an emergency loan, and knuckle under to the IMF's demands for austerity measures.

A second option is to let the value of the currency be determined by letting all parties freely trade it. In other words, the Central Bank may drop its insistence on carrying out all peso–dollar trades and may let the currency float down to a new, lower value which the Bank believes will eliminate the outflow of dollars. The bank can then announce its intention to defend the new, lower value of the peso. This is what is meant by a *devaluation*. It is often unpopular – especially just before an election – because it typically causes inflation. In the simulation, the devaluation happens only in Round 4 after all other options have been exhausted.

The third option is the one used in Round 3, and is explained below.

Round 3: Central Bank raises interest rates; a crisis approaches

The third tool in the Central Bank's toolbox – to raise interest rates – is no more politically attractive than a devaluation. Round 3 illuminates why increasing interest rates can be temporarily effective.

By the beginning of the round, the level of dollar reserves has fallen so low that, at most, one or two months of imports can be purchased. This triggers responses by certain players which set in motion a destabilising process that is hard to stop. One response is capital flight: the rich Argentine sells pesos and buys dollars, in anticipation of the devaluation. Similarly, the foreign investor sells the shares in the toy manufacturing firm which she bought in Round 2, and takes her dollars out of Argentina. Alarmed by these developments, and seeing that its ability to sop up the additional pesos sold is limited by its dwindling dollar reserves, the Central Bank imposes higher interest rates. Raising interest rates persuades the foreign investor not to take her money out of the country just yet. It also slows down the currency speculator, who senses an approaching devaluation and seeks to borrow pesos in order to sell them later for dollars. However, in light of higher interest rates, she waits to be sure she has her timing right, because the higher the interest rate, the more costly any mistake will be.

The other factor that precipitates the crisis is that in Round 3 the currency speculator goes into action. She borrows huge quantities of pesos, and then exchanges the pesos for dollars at the one-for-one exchange rate. Because she is adding to the number of pesos being offered for sale, she essentially forces the Central Bank to buy those pesos, and so speeds up the exhaustion of its dollar reserves. If she gets the timing right, she forces a devaluation of the peso. Once this happens – in Round 4 – she will be able to use only about half her dollars to buy back all the pesos she needs to repay the loan with interest – and to keep the remaining dollars as profit. In 1992, when George Soros used $10 billion of his money to force devaluation of the British pound, he ultimately made $2 billion on the deal (www.soros.org).

Although the high interest rate can slow down the exit of capital, it can unfortunately also have negative effects on the economy. The toy manufacturer finds that all her profits are eaten up by interest on the loan. If high interest rates persist, she will go out of business, and her employees will lose their jobs. And if this happens to many firms, the local banks may also become insolvent. Foreign lenders may then stop lending altogether, and this will trigger a crisis.

Round 4: Capital flees, currency speculator attacks, Central Bank devalues the peso

In Round 4, the situation deteriorates even further. Both the rich Argentine and the foreign investor sell their pesos and buy dollars, and – even if nothing else changes – this capital flight uses up the Central Bank's last dollar reserves, forcing it to declare a currency devaluation.

The impact of financial crises

When crises hit, countries often turn to the International Monetary Fund for help. The Fund usually imposes a structural adjustment programme as a condition of its lending, which is not included in our simulation. Many readers will be familiar with the features of structural adjustment but, in brief, the IMF forces the government to balance its budget so that it will not keep adding to its debt, and usually also forces a devaluation of the currency, which restores near equality between exports and imports and halts that source of drain on the dollar reserves. Countries often balance their budgets by cutting public expenditure, often for education, health, and other services essential to the poor and working class, and by imposing fees for service. Public sector workers may suffer wage cuts or retrenchment, as government is down-sized. Public utilities like water and electrical power are often privatised, and fees are raised, hurting the poor.

Some financial crises have not been preceded by significant government budget deficits. For instance, in Chile in 1982, and several Asian countries in 1997–8, there was little or no government budget deficit, and the crisis was rooted in private sector debt. Nevertheless, a budget deficit might appear after the crisis breaks and austerity measures may be imposed to minimise that deficit, as was the case in East Asia.

The impact of financial crises is, by now, quite well known. Analyses of the 1998 Asian financial crises have shown that women bore a disproportionate share of the costs – see Lim (2000) and Frankenberg, Thomas, and Beegle (1999). Poor and working-class women, especially, provided the unpaid work that was critical to family and community survival. Low-income women – and their daughters – spent more time and effort to produce non-market substitutes for goods and services that became too expensive or were no longer available. In addition, women sought more paid work, often in informal employment, where returns were low, to make up for reduced family income. Girls were pulled out of school before boys, in order to help their families. In South Korea and Indonesia, job losses were higher for women than for men as the public and private sectors contracted. Studies on financial crises in other regions of the world find similar impacts.

Conclusion

Simulations like the one described here are an effective tool for teaching a complex and technical subject. At AWID, the response was overwhelmingly positive; several participants said they had had no idea how extraordinarily important it was to understand these basic principles. Perhaps most startling was the realisation of how very narrow the scope is for central banks to manoeuvre, once a crisis is well underway.

Teaching about financial crises through role-play works surprisingly well, even when the simulation is complicated. In order to play their roles, participants have to ask questions. Through the game, they gain clarity about various currency trans-actions, the reasons why one buys or sells dollars, and the effect of these transactions on different sectors of the economy. All the players see the Central Bank's dollar reserves declining, and they see that the one recourse – to raise interest rates – makes matters worse in many ways. They see, too, that once the crisis approaches, the efforts of the Central Bank to avert it can be thwarted by capital flight and speculative attacks on the currency. Like it or not, the country ends up in the stifling embrace of the IMF.

So what is the solution to financial crises? The proposal by late Nobel prize-winner James Tobin is still on the table, for a tax on international financial transactions which would limit the lurching of capital into, and then out of, developing countries. Billionaire and wizard investor George Soros has advocated the same thing, and has some ideas of his own, spelled out in his recent book, *George Soros on Globalisation* (2002). Several feminist economists – including Diane Elson, Nilüfer Cağatay, Irene Van Staveren, Stephanie Seguino and others – have also made the case for Tobin-type taxes on speculative financial capital, as well as for national-level actions that include controls on both inflows and outflows of capital, as well as changes in fiscal and monetary policy. Each of these proposals should be put on the agenda of the international women's movement.

Mehrene Larudee is Assistant Professor of Economics at the University of Kansas. Her research is on the effect of trade and investment liberalisation on employment, wages and growth, especially in Latin America. Address: Economics Department, University of Kansas, 1300 Sunnyside Ave., Room 213, Lawrence, KS 66045-7585.
mehrene@ku.edu

Caren Grown is Director of the Poverty Reduction and Economic Growth Team at the International Center for Research on Women. Her recent research has focused on the effect of gender inequality on macroeconomic and other development outcomes. Address: 1717 Massachusetts Avenue, N.W., Suite 302, Washington, D.C. 20036.
cgrown@icrw.org

References

Baden, S. (1996) 'Gender issues in financial liberalization and financial sector reform', Brighton, UK: BRIDGE Publications, Institute for Development Studies

Elson, D. (2002) 'International financial architecture: a view from the kitchen', *Femina Politica*, Spring

Frankenberg, E., D. Thomas, and K. Beegle (1999) 'The real costs of Indonesia's economic crisis: preliminary findings from the Indonesia family life surveys', *Labor and Population Program Working Paper Series*: 99–04, RAND, www.rand.org/labor

Ghosh, J. (2002) *Argentina: a cautionary tale from South America*, International Development Economics Associates Network (IDEAS), http://networkideas.org

Lim, J. (2000) 'The effects of the East Asian crisis on the employment of men and women: the Philippine case', *World Development* 28 (7): 1285–1306

Rodrik, D. (2002) 'Reform in Argentina, take two trade rout', *The New Republic*, 14 January 2002, http://tnr.com/

Singh, A. and A. Zammit (2000) 'International capital flows: identifying the gender dimension', *World Development* 22 (10): 1249–68. Oxford: Elsevier Science Ltd

Soros, G. (2002) *George Soros on Globalisation*, New York: Public Affairs

Stiglitz, J. (1999) 'Responding to economic crises: policy alternatives for equitable recovery and development', *The Manchester School* Vol. 57 (5): 409–27

Part II
Globalisation as politics

Fundamentalisms, globalisation and women's human rights in Senegal

Fatou Sow

One response to the phenomenon of globalisation in politics, economics and culture has been a resurgence of fundamentalist movements. To fundamentalists, women symbolise ethnic and cultural purity, and their rights and status have become an enormous issue. But the links between fundamentalisms, tradition and modernity are very complex. In this article I look at the example of Senegal, where traditional spiritual beliefs are mingled with the newer world religions, in very complex ways. Consequently, it is difficult to understand the connections between fundamentalism, globalisation and women's human rights. But this understanding is critical if women are to obtain and retain equal rights with men. This article is taken from a presentation given at a workshop entitled 'Fundamentalisms, globalisation and women's human rights', at the AWID Forum.

The issues of human rights, democracy and citizens' participation have never been debated as much as they are today – both internationally, and in Africa. The world is now dominated by the ideas and rules of the free market, which are forcing political changes, obliging states to open up to the world market. These changes are altering the relationship between states and citizen. The state is reshaping itself, in line with the prescriptions of the international financial institutions (IFIs) and the World Trade Organisation (WTO) that there should be a lesser state presence or even a total absence of the state, in contexts where the role of the state was previously very prominent. States currently seem more concerned about their sheer survival in the world market than in satisfying the interests of their citizens.

The talk of human rights heard in international fora masks the violation of citizen's rights in general – and women's rights in particular – which accompanies globalisation. In particular, it is increasingly difficult to address women's rights when policies reduce social budgets, and privatise resources and basic services to the poorest populations. How can we sustain the few gains made for equality between women and men, when states are unable to guarantee that these are reflected in women's lives? Women experience globalisation daily when they go in search of water at the hydrants in poor neighborhoods, or when they busy themselves in thousands of other ways to fulfill the needs of their families. These are needs that men are no longer able to meet, or needs arising from the cutting of state provision for education or health services, under the constraints of structural adjustment policies. It is primarily women who pay the actual costs of the privatisation of the economy.

All these factors have favoured the emergence of fundamentalist movements, in environments where religion is an integral part of culture. This article focuses on the example of Senegal. The resurgence of Muslim discourse, and its impact on women, is what interests us most here, because of its impact on national life.

Religion and culture in Senegal

Senegal is a country located on the west coast of Africa, which had a long spiritual tradition even before Judeo-Christianity and Islam set roots. Pre-Islamic and pre-Christian religious underpinnings are deeply embedded in daily social attitudes and practices. These form the basis for numerous informal social norms, and formal laws. For example, it is customary in many Senegalese communities to sacrifice an animal when a newborn child is given a name, or during funerals. There are other similar examples. People still spill animal blood before undertaking an important event, to call upon the spirits (*rab*) and enlist their support, or in order to mollify their wrath. People bury cola nuts and charms, or pour sour milk or animal blood on the foundations when starting to build a house. Others drink and smear their bodies with all kinds of mixtures for luck, before taking an exam, applying for a job, or to ensure that their professional or political job remains secure.

Islamic and Christian practices have flourished and mingled with traditional practices. In the first example given above, a Muslim rite may be used for the animal sacrifice, with people facing Mecca, and reciting Koranic prayers. Good luck charms are made from soaked paper inscribed with Koranic chapters. A Sereer Christian from Sine would use the Bible for this purpose. All these types of behaviour are looked upon as familiar and sensible. Whether they are popular or not, they are never considered fetishist or pagan. It does not matter to the people who practise this behaviour what traditional healers or priests think of it. To the majority of believers, whether they are Muslims, Christians, or follow indigenous beliefs,

these practices represent a call to the spirit world, to enlist the ancestors' protection. Senegalese of all religious denominations, and of all ranks and social standing, depend on religious laws and rites to define their collective identity.

Many of these rites lie within women's realm. They participate in them either as actors or leaders of worship. Female divinities govern the areas bordering the sea and rivers, between Dakar, Cape Verde and Saint-Louis on the north coast of the country. Fishermen's wives make offerings to Mame Jaare and Mame Coumba Bang as boats prepare to leave the shore at the beginning of the fishing season. This is an important activity in a country with over 600 kilometres of coastline. Women healers (*facckat*) preside over fertility rites (to cure infertility, or protect a pregnancy), and possession rites (including ceremonies of exorcism), and administer drug-yielding plants for therapeutic purposes, in cases of physical or mental illness or emotional crisis brought on by different types of problems, including difficult marital relationships.

In the newer world religions there is much less of a leading role for women. In Islam in particular, leadership of religious rites is mostly taken by men. This has had an impact on the traditional rites. By adding a few verses from the Koran to their incantations, male healers have taken over from female healers, giving the rites a new 'holy' dimension. Women have given up their roles as high-priestesses. The masters of worship and healers (who were referred to as 'shamans' in colonial ethnological terminology), have attained an even higher status than they had before the coming of the new religious beliefs. Thus, we are now witnessing subtle changes to cultural practices, in line with the gradual Islamisation of the country. A spiritual patriarchy is now established. The important titles of *Serigne, Thierno* or *Marabat* are given to men, but never to women, no matter what the degree of their acquired wisdom. The male title *Serigne* (nowadays used for 'Mr') designates a religious man; the female title, *Sokhna* (now used for 'Mrs' either designates the female relative of a Muslim holy man, or a woman who has religious knowledge and learning.

Senegal, the land of Islam

Senegal has slowly become Islamised since the ninth century.[1] Today, almost 90 per cent of its population (close to 10,000) are members of four religious brotherhoods. Each is led by a marabout or spiritual leader. These are the *Tijaania*, of Algerian origin, the *Xaadria* of Mauritanian origin (Boutlimit), the *Mourides* (Touba) and the *Layeen*. These last two brotherhoods are of local origin and can be seen as nationalist responses to colonialism, when people strengthened their sense of collective identity in the face of Westernisation and Judeo-Christian beliefs imported through formal education and changes in social and political models. While France, the colonial power, spent a century crushing monarchies from Senegambian soil, the traditional authorities gathered strength and dynamism around Islam.

Even though Senegal is a Muslim country, its culture is not an Arab culture. There are certainly Arabic terms in local languages, especially from the Koranic legal code, but Arabic is only spoken in the country sparingly, in order to read and recite the Koran. The Arabic alphabet was used to transcribe national languages,[2] even before Latin characters were adopted. Many rules of civil and social conduct such as the proper way to say 'hello', 'thank you', or conduct marital and social customs, testify to a deep Islamic imprint. This imprint has mingled with other influences, in harmony with some and in opposition or contradiction with others. For example, it needs to be emphasised that women wearing a veil, or female seclusion within domestic space, are not practices from Wolof, Sereer, Pël, Mandeng or Koniagi

traditions, which make up the cultural base of Senegal. And matriarchal lineage still defines the fundamental foundations of Senegalese kinship systems, in the face of a patriarchal Islam.

In pre-colonial Senegal, a strong religious sensibility was governed by tolerance. Into this context, French colonialism imposed the separation of religion and state. The Napoleonic code was imposed in governing family relationships. This was a partial success, with Christian families undergoing a civil ceremony before a church wedding. All civil marriages forced the spouses to abide by rules of French law, especially mandatory monogamy, legal divorce, and so on. But the Muslim communities – even including individuals within them who had been most influenced by the French – categorically opposed the use of the civil code. Koranic law, adapted in line with local traditions, continued to be administered. Muslim jurisdictions managed by a *Cadi* (Islamic judge) were reinforced as well. Their legal decisions covered various areas of expertise, especially family law (divorce, child custody, family conflicts or inheritance, for example). They were, until independence, recognised by the colonial state. The colonial state was unable to ban polygamy, or to make civil marriages mandatory. The legislation which it tried to introduce was not respected in cities or villages. People continued to abide by laws enacted by traditional custom, and then by religious law (if not at the same time).

Senegalese Islam, while giving shape to moral and social life, has been relatively gentle towards women. It recognises the importance of each family system, whether this is patrilineal or matrilineal. Beneath the general principle that women should be obedient to men, women have a degree of choice in negotiating their status and their authority within the family and society.

Secularisation, women's rights and religious laws: managing identities

In Senegal, secular forces have promoted a state based on ideas of 'modernity'. The eight constitutions that Senegal has drafted since its independence in 1960 have all been based on the principle of the secular state. This includes the current Constitution, voted upon in 2001. In its efforts at social 'modernisation', the new state, presided over by Léopold Sedar Senghor, who is a member of the Sereer ethnic group and Christian, underwent significant legal reforms. Enacted into law in 1973, the Family Law Act of Senegal was an important and original reform in the West African region.[3] The Family Law Act, which aimed to be secular and applicable to all Senegalese, no matter what their religious denomination, met strong opposition from the outset. All Muslim tribunals were abolished. Muslim authorities proclaimed their commitment to the principles of the Shari'a (fiqh) and a large majority of men believed the code to favour women too much. Indeed, the code provided impetus for women's rights insofar as it represented a series of rules set by the legislator and not by the interpretation of customs, or even by customs that were re-invented to suit various needs and contexts.

However, the code still contained an important number of Koranic dispositions, and it was left to citizens to decide whether to adopt these or not. For example, in the case of inheritance law, there are two options: either the inheritance is equally divided among children regardless of sex, or an unequal share is awarded to the two sexes (the daughter inherits half of the son's share, and only children born into wedlock have to right to inherit).

Similarly, in the case of marriage, dowry is possible, but not mandatory. But despite all the sex discrimination which appears in the Family Code, the Senegalese state was attempting to secularise the institution of marriage. Consent, celebration, and registry of marriage at City Hall were demanded of the spouses. Most importantly, divorce had to be decreed in a civil court of law. Spousal support was set by the judge. While the code does not eliminate polygamy, it requires men to choose between monogamy, polygamy with two, or polygamy with more than two. Once a man has chosen monogamy, this cannot be reversed. While Christians could marry through a civil ceremony, without going through the church, Muslim couples must celebrate their union at the mosque as dictated by their Muslim identity. A civil marriage is mainly an administrative formality.

Despite the fact that Senegal is a country in which culture, religion and secularism intermingle and contradict one another, its citizens reaffirmed their commitment to the principles of secularism in the constitution voted in 2001, and confirmed equality between men and women in so doing.

Yet, secularism seems to infringe upon people's deepest sense of identity. Modernisation, which is rapidly changing the landscape in Senegal, does not allow for disagreement with the socio-economic, political and material changes associated with it. The time for questioning the extent to which Africans remain African if they adopt aspects of Western culture seems to have gone.[4] Topical concerns now seem to consist in youngsters starting to challenge the authority of elders, especially where new ideas about female identity are challenging ideas about male identity (which have also changed).

The status of women is an issue which is at the heart of people's ideas about society and culture, and it is hence at the heart of the confrontations between Islam and modernity, between ideas about a Muslim 'Africanness' and Westernisation. Fundamentalist forces criticise the concept of modernity, which they say is imposed 'from the outside'. For them, the important thing is to reconquer and reclaim a traditional identity. In the eyes of fundamentalists, nothing should be changed (even though change is an inevitable process) and a woman is a symbol of ethnic 'purity'. Challenges to these religious and patriarchal power structures are presented through Senegalese women's new access to education (a symbol of modernisation), and the intellectual and professional freedom they can potentially gain. It should be noted, however, that while religion – which freezes ideas of women and their status in time – does not bring women freedom, modernisation and Westernisation do not necessarily guarantee that freedom either.

The globalisation of women's human rights

The globalisation of the issue of human rights should open infinite possibilities to promote the rights of women. We cannot talk about African women's rights without taking into account the globalisation of this issue. Women's claims to equality have been strengthened by the international recognition of universal human rights, and by scrutiny of the extent to which these rights are upheld in particular contexts. Two decades of world conferences on women, from 1975 to 1995, have allowed debates about women's struggles for their rights to be heard at national and international levels. Women's claims have been legitimised by various conventions signed by states.

For example, international campaigns to outlaw the different forms of female genital mutilation (FGM) have pushed some African states to legislate to abolish these practices. In Senegal, this occurred in 1999. Forms of FGM were found in the regions of Hal Pulaar and Soninké, in the north and north-east, and in the south, in Mandeng and Pulaar. While FGM is actually a pre-Islamic practice, it has been embraced in

Muslim communities as a guarantee and symbol of female purity – a concept which is so important in Islam. It is sometimes proclaimed that women who are not genitally mutilated cannot say prayers or serve meals. This is a context in which ideas of cleanliness are closely linked to ideas of religious purity: where to perform one's ablutions before prayers, and to abstain from praying and from fasting during menstruation, are religious obligations. This affects gender relations: sexual activity during menstruation is prohibited for reasons of impurity. At the end of a menstrual period, women must undergo a ritual cleansing before being allowed to pray again. Islam is invoked by those who wish to continue with the practice of FGM and to legitimise its continuation.

A similar analysis can be produced regarding violence against women. Since the reform of the penal code in 1999, this type of violence is punished more severely than before. In the old French and Senegalese penal codes, domestic violence to women was permitted if there were extenuating circumstances. In Shari'a law, beating one's wife is allowed in specific circumstances. Male public opinion was strongly opposed to the first public campaigns against domestic violence led by women's organisations, which were sparked off by the death of Dokki Niasse. Dokki Niasse was a young woman who, in 1993, was beaten by her husband while she was in the early stages of pregnancy. Taken to hospital, she died a few hours later. Her husband was arrested by the police, and jailed only after women from her neighbourhood marched, and petitions were signed nationwide. The case against him was dismissed three years later because the doctor was unable to establish that her death was a result of the beating.

Finally, international debates about the need to ensure women's equal access to politics and decision-making has contributed to a larger contingent of women entering the public sphere of political and economic power, sometimes through positive discrimination.

Fundamentalism as a response to globalisation

During important international gatherings in the recent past, the church and the mosque have forged an alliance in order to limit women's rights. It is widely acknowledged that the Christian discourse of Pope Jean Paul II plays a role in constraining women's freedoms, especially in terms of their sexuality and reproductive rights. The condemnation by the Vatican of contraception, including condoms, and abortion, weighs heavily on the sexual and reproductive rights of Christians. Muslim women are relatively free: they may use contraception, and therapeutic abortion, if life is threatened. However, Muslim women cannot refuse to see pregnancy to term for any personal reasons, or undergo an abortion if they have been raped. Hundreds of women have died from secret pregnancies and abortions as a result of the imposition of these religious dictates.

During the 1970s, the Koranic discourse was brought together with the power of money. Islamic power emerged as a major force with the Iranian revolution, and with the wave of activism generated from the escalating price of oil from countries in the Maghreb and the Middle-East. The influence of this new religious movement has been significant in the sub-Saharan Muslim world, and gave a boost to already existing movements within the region. As Islamic power became evident in the Senegalese political landscape, Senghor, the Christian President of Senegal for over 30 years, made efforts to strengthen secularism, and maintained a certain balance between communities of different religious denominations.

In 1981, his successor was immediately seen by a part of public opinion as a Muslim President. Certainly, he allied himself spiritually to the very powerful brotherhood of *Mourides*, mentioned earlier, which controls the production of peanuts,[5] other tradeable products, and craft industries. Migrations of people from the *Mourides* brotherhood to other parts of Africa, and to North America, have resulted in significant sums of money being sent back for re-investment in the country. During his 20-year presidency, between 1981 and 2000, manipulation and mutual influence became established between the Senegalese state (initially ruled by a single party system, then a multi-party system), and the religious leaders, for the control of the mainly rural electorate. The *Mourides* spiritual leader would encourage the believers to vote for a particular candidate.

The March 2000 elections overthrew the socialist party in power for the previous 40 years. The new President proclaimed himself a Muslim, a *talibé*[6] of *Mourides*, to the surprise of the political establishment. A lawyer and professor of economics – an exemplification of modernity – he has encouraged the progression of a fundamentalist discourse. This has caused concern to civil society and women's organisations. It is true that Senegal is certainly not a religious state such as Iran or Algeria. There is no 'Islamist' power as such; indeed, the constitution prohibits the creation of political parties based on religious, ethnic or gender affiliation. Nonetheless, during the presidential elections of March 2000, three parties claiming Islamic denomination offered their candidatures. They were effectively ignored by the electorate, but their speeches about a return to faith and to Shari'a law, and their promise to abolish the Family Law Act in the event of an electoral victory, presented a threat to women.

Dahira, and other fundamentalist religious groups have now emerged, and attempt to impose a totally retrograde and alienating rhetoric on women, which is disseminated by local radio. Their stipulations include the wearing of the veil by girls in schools, in city streets and in villages; a taboo against touching women's hands; revival of religious vigils; a return to the Islamic practice of patriarchal control over women, women's seclusion in domestic spaces, and rule of a male household head; and condemnation of social changes which are rooted in secular law. The airwaves are taken over by Islamic preaching until very late into the night. Women and children's rights are heavily contested, and are subject to fights between 'modernists' and 'Islamists'. Others even question the legitimacy of laws voted on in Parliament. Obedience to the patriarchal order is looked upon as a sign of commitment to God and religious faith. The fundamentalist discourse on culture has gone as far as to deny the civilised cultural values which Senegalese communities had preserved in the face of both Islamisation and Christianisation. Wolof Islamic customs are questioned in the name of a united, outward-looking Islam.

At the time of writing, the state is getting ready to implement changes to the Family Law Act. Resistance to this is strong. One of the changes proposes a modernisation of the concept of paternal authority, so that parental authority over the children is shared by the mother and the father. This change is in line with the principle of equal rights as stipulated in the constitution. The parliamentary debate on this has so far been unable to resolve the issue. To debate women's issues is also to debate the question of male identity.

Conclusion

Religious forces in Senegal are demanding greater power in the public sphere and in decision-making institutions which shape the lives of citizens. The intention of certain religious groups is to influence the political process through their interpretation of divine texts. Fundamentalist groups manipulate religion for ideological and political means, and women's rights issues are a particular focus. We cannot allow them to succeed, or leave it to society to introduce the necessary changes to abolish discrimination on the basis of gender, class or race. We need laws to reduce violence, to prohibit marriage and family practices which harm women, such as polygamy and divorce by repudiation, and to give states the power to renegotiate power relations between the sexes in the pursuit of greater social justice. Here lies the real challenge of democracy.

Fatou Sow is Professor of Sociology, and a member of the Groupe de Recherche sur les Femmes et les Lois au Sénégal (GREFELS), affiliated with the solidarity network Women Living Under Muslim Laws. Address: Université Cheikh Anta Diopb, P206 Dakar, Senegal.
fatousow@sentoo.sn

Notes

1 Christian communities live mainly on the coast and the south of the country.

2 *Wolofal* refers to the transcription of Wolof using the Arabic alphabet.

3 Cote d'Ivoire, Mali and Guinea formulated their Family Codes much later. Benin ratified its code as late as 2002, while Niger and Chad, which have strong Muslim communities, refuse to adhere to secular law on the family for religious reasons and questions of identity. Except for Mauritania (which by establishing itself as an Islamic republic in the 1980s has followed Shari'a law) all these countries have written secularism in golden letters in their constitution.

4 This is a reference to Cheikh Hamidou's *L'aventure ambiguë*, a Senegalese novel published in the 1960s to highly enthusiastic reviews. The author questions

the construction of the African identity in light of Western culture.

5 Peanuts are Senegal's main export crop.

6 A *Talibé* is a pupil of the Koranic school, given up by his family, who must beg to make a living for himself and his teacher.

A daring proposal:
campaigning for an Inter-American Convention on Sexual Rights and Reproductive Rights

Valéria Pandjiarjian

Can women in Latin America and the Caribbean really exercise their sexual and reproductive rights? Are economic globalisation and state policies in our region creating conditions which will help us claim the rights we have gained in international fora, or are we going in the opposite direction? And is it possible to have a society which respects human rights under a neo-liberal model of development? These questions were asked in a workshop at the Association for Women in Development (AWID) Forum, which focused on the new Campaign for an Inter-American Convention on Sexual Rights and Reproductive Rights.

Sister Juana Inés de la Cruz lived in Mexico from 1651–1695. She was a poet and nun, a woman of genius, whose intellectual prowess, ideas and accomplishments were ahead of her time. She was a precocious writer who, from an early age, was renowned not only for her beauty, but for her wisdom and poetry. When she was 16, Sister Juana joined a convent, since this was one of the few places in the seventeenth century in which a woman could gain access to education and intellectual pursuits.

At the ninth AWID Forum, an actor playing the role of Sister Juana opened a workshop which focused on women claiming their sexual and reproductive rights in the era of globalisation. There could be no better image than that of Sister Juana to open such a workshop. Her life shows how women throughout history have found ways of gaining control over their minds and desires, as well as over their sexuality and fertility, to enable them to be free to contribute to the good of the world. Being a

nun enabled her to pursue her talent, rather than taking on the conventional roles of wife and mother, with no control over her sexuality and fertility.

Sexuality and reproduction are essential dimensions of the life of each human being. Historically, women's ability to express choices in these areas of life have been conditioned and constrained under economic, political, religious and cultural patterns, responding to a model of 'normality', which disallows any kind of behaviour which deviates from this. Reproduction has been the basis for the social inequality between men and women; women's identities have been limited to motherhood. Society and the law have repressed any behaviour that could challenge the reproductive role of women in societies throughout the world.

The dramatisation of Sister Juana's life at the AWID workshop prompted the participants to learn about and discuss a bold and daring proposal, for a Campaign for an Inter-American Convention on

Sexual Rights and Reproductive Rights. The workshop participants were as diverse as they could possibly be. Around 90 people attended; among them were women and men of different ages, races and ethnicity, from different continents, regions and countries, representing many kinds of movements, networks and organisations. All were interested in gender equality and human rights, and concerned about the impact of economic globalisation and current state policies on these.

The aims of the workshop were:

- to share the idea of the proposal of a Campaign for an Inter-American Convention on Sexual Rights and Reproductive Rights
- to gain further support for this proposal
- to invite more organisations and networks to participate in the campaign
- to publicise the campaign, in order to create a favourable environment for discussions on the proposal at national level within the Latin American and Caribbean region.

About the campaign

The idea of the campaign came first from CLADEM, the Latin American and Caribbean Committee for the Defence of Woman's Rights. I have worked for CLADEM for the last ten years, in my capacity as a feminist lawyer, researcher and consultant in gender and human rights, with a specific focus on sexual rights and reproductive rights. The proposal for the campaign has been discussed and adopted by many well-known networks and organisations from the Latin American and Caribbean women's movement.[1] The workshop at the AWID Forum resulted from collaboration between representatives of some of these organisations.[2]

An inter-American Convention on Sexual Rights and Reproductive Rights would effect profound mid- to long-term changes in society's – and the law's –

understanding of sexual and reproductive rights. This is because traditional attitudes to sexuality and reproduction have been oppressive for everyone, but particularly cruel for women. Control of women's bodies by men, and the significance attached to chastity, fidelity and child-bearing within marriage, have resulted in social and legal codes which are based on the need to control female bodies. We hope that the Convention would shape political, social and economic development, by ensuring that women are able to benefit from the agreements on reproductive and sexual rights which have been reached at the international and national levels.

The main goal of the campaign is to challenge the laws and social beliefs in our countries concerning sexual practices and reproductive choices. We want to make policy makers and the public aware of the connections between reproductive choice, sexuality, and economic, social and political development. We aim to mobilise people and organisations to lobby for change. To achieve this, we have to work out strategies, organise political action, generate alliances, and accumulate and consolidate power, so that we can put our point of view to decision-makers in powerful positions. We want to create the space in public debates to express different views on sexuality and reproduction, which would promote mutual understanding.

What would the convention do?

The basic ideas presented and discussed in the workshop were those drafted in the manifesto 'Our Bodies, Our Lives' (See www.convencion.org.uy, available in Spanish). An inter-American convention on sexual rights and reproductive rights would ensure state accountability for respecting sexual rights and reproductive rights, as well as for monitoring and resolving conflicts and human rights violations and abuses at international levels related to this subject. It would ensure that international treaties of human rights on reproductive and sexual rights are created and implemented by countries, via the development of national standards and norms. It would also ensure that arguments defending women's reproductive and sexual rights are heard in political and legal fora. Women and men want their rights as citizens upheld, and an aspect of citizenship is the right to protect the exercise of our sexuality and our reproductive capacity. We want to speak, hear, and debate. Through this, we will eliminate prejudices, break myths, and open up minds, windows and hearts.

While the ideas underlying our campaign are constantly being debated, there are some principles and ideas that are non-negotiable. Participants at the workshop discussed some of them and the main issues are presented below.

The universality, interdependence and indivisibility of human rights

The workshop participants discussed the fact that human rights are held by all human beings, and all human beings must be able to exercise the whole range of rights simultaneously. There is no hierarchy among human rights; that is, there are no rights more important than other rights. In particular, civil and political rights are not more important than economic, social and cultural rights. For instance, the freedom to express oneself freely is not more important than the right to food, health or education, and vice-versa. This means that governments cannot excuse a failure to protect one right by saying they have prioritised another. For human well-being, everyone needs employment, health, and education, but also liberty, integrity, dignity and a life free from violence and discrimination.

Protection of human rights regarding 'market logic'

Currently, globalisation is causing people in particular contexts to lose the battle to guarantee a good quality of life. It is also responsible for the widening gap between rich and poor in Latin America and the Caribbean. Some people and groups are now excluded from full participation in our economies, societies and political systems. The so-called 'logic' of the market is in clear opposition to international human rights standards, which hold that the well-being of people is paramount. States have obligations to pursue progressive, not regressive, economic and social policies. Any economic development which contradicts the principles of human rights and well-being should be seen as an obstacle to be overcome by state policy.

The secular state and its role in protecting human rights

It was clear to all of us in discussions at the workshop that keeping the separation between the churches and the state in our region is the only acceptable way of governance. States must adopt a neutral position regarding the different dogma of beliefs. The churches have relevance and jurisdiction only over their members, while states act in line with public interest, upholding citizenship for all. Because they try to shape the behaviour of everyone, all forms of fundamentalism are a threat for states which have a commitment to uphold human rights.

Feminist perspectives on sexuality and reproduction

Workshop participants agreed that women have not often had freedom to decide how to exercise their sexuality. Society treats them differently according to their age and marital status, but in general all women are expected to remain sexually faithful to their husbands and to bear children. They are punished severely when they veer away from the role of a traditional, heterosexual wife and mother. The sexual freedom of lesbians is not respected, and neither are the choices of bisexual, transsexual and transgender persons. These women present a challenge to religious and moral mandates, and the traditional male-dominated family, with its objective of reproduction. They challenge ideas of what is 'normal' and 'natural', and undermine the idea that the traditional family is the only type of family possible.

Distinguishing between sexuality and reproduction

Following on from the last paragraph, the assumption that there is always a link between sexuality and reproduction – i.e. that one leads to the other – reinforces the widespread assumption that women must have children. There has not been a free choice about this in our societies. Once, there was no contraception and only hetero-sexuality was allowed in our societies, which meant that sex was usually linked to having children. But now we have sex without reproduction due to contraception, and even reproduction without sex through fertility technologies ... so how can we, and why should we, keep dealing with these issues in a traditional way?

Each one of the topics above is very complex, and cannot be discussed fully in this article. We want to be as democratic as possible in constructing our proposal for the convention, so we invite readers of this article to join us in thinking about the issues and designing the convention. The proposal is a seed to be watered by creativity, dreams, and ideas.

Designing the convention

In this first phase of the campaign, we are spreading the idea and discussing its principles. This process is strengthening the campaign at national levels. We are aware that some sectors and groups can initially feel resistant to the idea of a regional convention, because they do not want

international legislation on sexual and reproductive rights. But an inter-American convention on sexual rights and repro-ductive rights would not regulate our bodies, in order to control our sexual and reproductive lives, as many of our national laws have done in the past. On the contrary, it would be an instrument guaranteeing the full enjoyment of this important dimension of human life, establishing standards that respect and strengthen the conditions for women and men to make choices and decisions on their own reproductive and sexual lives, based on principles of gender equality and non-discrimination.

Designing a convention like this is going to be a long-term process, since it involves a set of complex issues on which consensus will be hard to reach. There are many steps to take before we can draft the text of the convention, and then work on mechanisms for its implementation.

The convention will sit beside those that already exist in the inter-American system of human rights protection. We have good models of how social movements can participate in constructing legislation in the inter-American system, for example, the 1994 Inter-American Convention on the Prevention, Punishment and Eradication of Violence Against Woman (Convention of Belém do Pará). Nowadays, the issue of domestic violence against women is understood and approached as a human rights violation. However, it was a different story until very recently. The Inter-American Convention on Violence against Women is legally binding for those countries that have adopted this convention, and it has been incorporated into their national systems. Consequently, much national legislation on domestic violence has been created and implemented in different countries of the Latin American and Caribbean region. In Brazil, for example, the state was declared responsible for negligence, omission and tolerance related to domestic violence against women. Brazil has also implemented many recommendations established by the Inter-American Commission on Human Rights, including the development of public policies to prevent and eradicate domestic violence against women in the country (see Case 12.051, Maria da Penha vs Brazil, www.cladem.org). An Inter-American Convention on Sexual Rights and Reproductive Rights could have the same kind of impact.

Conclusion

The final point we discussed at the workshop was the fact that rights are only useful when they can be exercised. Even if women know they have a right to decide whether to sex with a man, in many situations they will not be able to prevent being raped or coerced. What happens when these rights are not clearly defined to the people they could help? Or people are unaware of how to claim their rights in court? One consequence of the non-exercise of women's rights is the fact that thousands of clandestine abortions take place each year, presenting very high health risks to the women concerned.

We know that democracy is still a challenge; it is a goal which no society has yet reached. Because of this, we need to rethink the political, juridical, economic, social and cultural systems we have in each of our countries, and ensure that they assist all human beings to expand and strengthen their capacities, in conditions of substantive equality and real liberty. We want a convention because it would be a long-term means of guaranteeing and strengthening a key group of human rights for all persons. We need to incorporate a discourse of rights into our political and legal systems, enabling women to reclaim their right to control their own bodies and lives. This discourse of rights would also equip women to recognise that they are full citizens, with independent rights. Such a recognition would empower women to claim their right to choose freely how to lead their lives, according to a principle of equality and non-discrimination.

Valéria Pandjiarjian is Regional Co-ordinator of the gender violence area of the work of CLADEM, the Latin American and Caribbean Committee for the Defence of Woman's Rights. Contact her at Rua Oscar Freire, 1967, apto. 122-A, CEP: 05409-011 São Paulo, SP, Brasil. lela.alp@zaz.com.br

For more information on the campaign contact CLADEM e-mail and website: oficina@cladem.org / www.cladem.org

Notes

1 Many networks and organisations are now supporting the campaign, including: CIDEM, Cotidiano Mujer, FEDAESP, Flora Tristan, Instituto de Estudios Ecuatorianos, Movimiento El Pozo, SOS-Corpo e Gênero, Campaña 28 de Septiembre, Católicas por el Derecho a Decidir, Red de Salud de las Mujeres Latinoamericanas y del Caribe (RSMLAC), Red Feminista Latinoamericana y del Caribe contra la Violencia Doméstica y Sexual, Red Latinoamericana y Caribeña de Jóvenes por los Derechos Sexuales y los Derechos Reproductivos, Rede Nacional Feminista de Saúde, Direitos Sexuais e Direitos Reprodutivos, REPEM-DAWN, GELEDÉS, CEPIA, CFEMEA, AGENDE, AMB, IPAS, THEMIS, Comissão de Cidadania e Reprodução – Programa de Saúde Reprodutiva e Sexualidade do NEPO/UNICAMP, Rede Mulher de Educação.
2 The workshop was run by: Mayara Antunes (artistic performer), Roxana Vásquez, Ximena Machicao, Alejandra Domínguez, Lidia Alpízar, Lucy Garrido and Valéria Pandjiarjian. Supportive contributions were also made by: Celita Eccher, María Consuelo Mejía, Sandra Gonzáles, Marita Pareja and others.

Free markets and state control:
a feminist challenge to Davos Man and Big Brother

Mona Danner and Gay Young

In this article, a sociologist and a criminologist argue that recent analysis from feminist men's studies points to ways to challenge the masculine institutions involved in global economic restructuring and the global war on terrorism. The expansion of state control – in the name of security and fighting terrorism – represents a new aspect of globalisation, which, in the US, carries significant consequences in terms of less freedom, more incarceration and tremendous costs. As with economic restructuring, women will bear much of this burden. However, the forms of masculinity dominant in global social institutions are subject to challenge. This gives feminists opportunities to transform existing relations of social inequality in states and markets.

> *'The hidden hand of the market*
> *will never work without a hidden fist –*
> *McDonald's cannot flourish without*
> *McDonnell Douglas,*
> *the builder of the F-15 [military jet fighter]'*
> (Friedman 1999)

Economic globalisation, in the form of reigning neo-liberal development strategies, enshrines two key ideals: de-regulation of markets, and the notion that less government is the best government. The creed of 'Davos Man'[1] is that the key to allowing global markets to work naturally is to minimise state intervention. However, this conviction is based on a misrepresentation of the state's active role in global economic restructuring, over two decades (Beneria 1999). Often, so-called 'state de-regulation' simply amounts to different regulation; that is, protection and benefits now accrue to corporations and elites, rather than to workers or to the public.

Belief in that state power has contracted, yet a dramatic expansion of state control has been camouflaged in the current global war on terrorism. Pursuing this objective means an extension of the state's long-standing task of controlling populations, both within and outside its borders. This occurs through the criminal justice system, as well as the military. The consequences of Big Brother's[2] increased control are less freedom and more incarceration, supposedly to ensure security. The tremendous economic cost of this strategy carries liabilities for ordinary members of society – especially poor women in both the North and the South.

General familiarity with critiques of global economic restructuring exists among gender and development analysts and policy makers. We highlight certain of those themes here, as they link in key ways to our critical appraisal of the expansion of state control beyond the control of crime to homeland security and the global war on terrorism. Like the outcomes of market-led development, evidence from the United States, our home country, shows that expanding state control of populations exacerbates gender-, race-, and class-based inequalities (Wonders, Danner, Solop 2002).

How can feminists respond to these global issues? We feel they need to struggle for justice for women in the face of both aspects of globalisation: the global war on terrorism, and global economic restructuring. As we discuss here, possibilities do exist for feminist intervention in the institutions involved. The forms of masculine domination that drive and legitimate institutional practices in markets or states are not immune to challenge and transformation. Such feminist challenges potentially open the space for progressive institutional changes to dismantle relations of gender, race, and class domination (Wonders and Danner 2002).

The consequences of control-oriented state expansion

Increased surveillance

The escalation of the war on terrorism, in the context of intensified crime control, means heightened surveillance of citizens and immigrants. In the aftermath of the attacks on the World Trade Centre and the Pentagon, the US government passed the USA Patriot Act and, later, the Homeland Security Act. The US government justifies increased surveillance of citizens and immigrants because it might help detect terrorist activities before they occur.

However, the surveillance methods employed and proposed represent a significant incursion into civil rights. Hundreds of Arabs and Muslims have been arrested and detained, held, tried, imprisoned, and deported, in secrecy. The FBI's terrorist watch list was released to government agencies and private corporations; its numerous errors resulted in the harassment of people with absolutely no involvement in terrorist activities (Davis 2002). The Pentagon's Total Information Awareness Programme – an electronic surveillance programme – will eventually enable the government to track people's daily activities, including their use of libraries, email, the Internet, telephones, and credit cards, and the contents of their medical records.

As a result of the attacks, the legal standard required to initiate intelligence surveillance of US citizens has been lowered, and information learned can be turned over for unrelated criminal prosecution. Previously forbidden 'sneak and peek' searches, in which government agents search homes without notice, are now allowed. Government officials may now listen in on previously confidential attorney-client conversations without notice. In contrast to the increased surveillance and decreased civil rights of citizens, the new laws protect private industries from scrutiny if they are part of the 'critical infrastructure' of national security, even if their actions endanger public safety.

Decreased space for civil dissent

The expansion of the state in controlling populations has also led to attacks on the acceptability of civil dissent. US colleges and universities have, in the past, been considered relatively safe spaces for civil dissent, in large part because of their commitment to academic freedom. However, the new state emphasis on homeland security and the war on terror has made college campuses an important focus for government surveillance. A university police officer on the University of Massachusetts-Amherst campus was recruited to work with the FBI's Anti-Terrorism Task Force as part of his campus job. This affiliation led to the questioning of a faculty member about his political views and organisational affiliations, even though no specific suspicious activity was reported (Smallwood 2002). Universities are also more sensitive to public opinion, and academics can no longer assume university

support for free speech, including participation in anti-war teach-ins. Even tenured
professors are in danger of losing their jobs
for their political opinions and affiliations.

Increased incarceration

State actions taken as part of homeland
security and the war on terrorism are
following the punitive pattern demonstrated by the US war on crime and drugs,
which is now in its fourth decade. While
there has been little decrease in drug use or
the problems associated with drug use, this
policy resulted in the incarceration of
nearly 2 million people in prisons and jails
in 2001 alone. This amounts to more than a
fourfold increase in just 20 years. Another
4.6 million adults were under some other
form of correctional supervision, such as
probation or parole (US Department of
Justice 2002). Over 167,000 of those
imprisoned were women, and another
960,000 women were on probation or
parole (Beck, Karberg and Harrison 2002;
Glaze 2002).

The rate of women's imprisonment has
increased nearly twice as much as the rate
for men, and 34 new women's prison units
have opened across the US, beginning in
the 1980s (Immarigeon and Chesney-Lind
1992). The number of black women
imprisoned for drugs has increased to more
than three times that of white women
(Bush-Baskette 1998). Black men and
women are seven times more likely to be
imprisoned than are white men and women
(Beck and Karberg 2001); the expansion of
mandatory and increased sentences for
drug law violations accounts for much of
this difference (Mauer 1990). African-
Americans, who represent 13 per cent of
the population, make up 45 per cent of
those incarcerated (Beck and Karberg 2001);
25 years ago they were 35 per cent of those
locked up (Maguire, Pastore, and Flanagan
1993, 618). Nearly all of those behind bars
are poor.

The war on crime and drugs has
included a practice known as racial

profiling – for example, traffic stops of
African Americans or Latinos solely
because of their race/ethnicity. Racial
profiling is now evident in the war on
terrorism as well, as officials selectively
enforce immigration law on the basis of
nationality, race and ethnicity. Men and
women of Middle Eastern appearance can
expect to be stopped on the street or called
in for questioning by local and federal law
enforcement and immigration authorities.
The slightest visa violations can lead to
imprisonment and deportation, and even
legal immigrants are being detained for
minor offences and technical violations
(American Civil Liberties Union 2002,
Human Rights Watch 2002). As state
authority expands and civil rights shrink,
practices associated with crime control and
now homeland security and the war on
terrorism will likely add immigrants and
citizens of Arab descent to the racial and
ethnic minorities with incarceration rates
far higher than their proportions in the US
population.

Counting the cost

The final consequence of the expansion of
the state in this context is the costliness of
the control policies associated with the war
on terrorism. The White House has
estimated that the US will spend $100
billion per year on homeland security, not
including costs associated with the military
(Office of Homeland Security 2002, 63).
Establishing the new Department of
Homeland Security is expected to cost $3
billion (Congressional Budget Office 2002).
The US Conference of Mayors estimated
that cities would spend more than $2.6
billion on additional security costs by the
end of 2002 (Hasson 2002). The latest
estimates put the cost of a war in Iraq
between $60 billion and $95 billion; and
higher outlays are expected to pay for
occupation, reconstruction and humanitarian relief (*The Washington Post* 2003).

The effects of such high levels of
control-oriented spending are significant.

Note that the cost to imprison one person in the US stands at $20,000 per year. As a result of increased incarceration, state spending on corrections has grown at six times the rate of spending on higher education, and states now spend more money building prisons than colleges (Ziedenberg and Schiraldi 2002). The enormous and expensive prison construction programme undertaken during the 1990s meant that prisons represented 'the only expanding public housing' in the US (*The Nation* 1995, 223). And now the costs associated with maintaining these facilities and incarcerating citizens are dwarfing the costs of construction. In addition, the current economic downturn has resulted in significant shrinking of governmental budgets. Social service programmes aiming to benefit people living in poverty, most of whom are women, are those frequently targeted; education and health care also face cuts. Budgeting for prisons and criminal justice agencies, however, remains relatively safe. Thus, the expansion of state inter-vention aimed at crime control, the pursuit of homeland security and the war on terrorism parallels the contraction of state activities devoted to meeting human needs.

In addition to incarceration, women bear many of the other visible, as well as the hidden, costs of expanding a punitive and expensive criminal justice system (Danner 1998). Not only do women as beneficiaries suffer directly when the state cuts education, health care, and social services, but they also suffer indirectly due to cuts in various services, which increase women's unpaid labour. To pay for state expansion beyond crime control into homeland security and the war on terrorism, deeper cuts will be made to these services. In addition, the jobs cut in education, health care, and social services are primarily jobs done by women. In contrast, the jobs created in the crime control/ homeland security/war on terror apparatus are, overwhelmingly, jobs in sectors

dominated by men. Finally, in the context of more limited social services and fewer jobs, female relatives must shoulder the emotional care and economic support of the children of mothers and fathers in custody, whose numbers will certainly increase with control-oriented state expansion aimed at homeland security and fighting the war on terrorism.

This analysis depicts patterns in the US. UN documents on crime and justice parallel the US emphasis on drug trafficking, counterfeiting, and copyright piracy – in sharp contrast, we note, to their limited attention to crimes of corporate theft and violence or to crimes of concern to feminists, such as human trafficking and the violation of women's human rights. Through multilateral agencies as well as direct bilateral linkages, the US 'exports' experts to the so-called developing world to support the creation of systems of criminal law and crime control. In an ironic way, this importing of US models for state control of populations fits the preference for 'trade not aid' incorporated in neo-liberal development strategies. However, we assert another connection between control-oriented state expansion and global economic restructuring. That is, raising challenges to the 'predestined' march of market-led development across the globe likewise affirms the possibility of resisting the prescribed strategies for the global war on terrorism.

Alternatives to market-led development

For the past two decades, neo-liberal economic policy – the so-called 'Washington Consensus'– has demanded dedication to principles of market-led development (Williamson 2000). The worldwide spread of this ruling policy framework of market fundamentalism has propelled global economic change (Baker et al.1998). This approach has intensified a longer-term trend, in which over-reliance on market systems has led to the organisation of social life in a way which serves a global economy based on values of profit and gain. Society runs as an accessory, or an adjunct, to the capitalist economic system (Polanyi 1957). Because the primary concerns of 'free-marketeers' are growth and efficiency and not human or social goals, more and more people – especially women and their dependents – are losing the struggle 'to live in a society, rather than [exist] in an economy' (Bayes et al. 2001, 4).

However, 'the market' is a social construction not a 'natural' phenomenon, and the growth of global markets in the past two decades has been achieved largely by macro-economic policy makers' interventions. Recognising the socially constructed nature of markets reveals the possibility of creating alternative economic systems, which operate in the service of social life, rather than the reverse, and in which growth and efficiency are promoted as means to increase collective well-being, not valued as ends in themselves (Beneria 1999). Until recently, economic global-isation has succeeded as a 'totalising story' – a grand vision of inevitable and irresistible global market integration – stifling discussions of economic diversity, and making alternative economic practices invisible (Gibsen-Graham 1996). As in the short poem with which we introduced this article, many commentators assert the necessary connection between militari-sation and McDonaldisation. But we can envision alternatives to the governing agenda of 'making the world safe for markets' (MacEwan 1998, 65). In particular, analysis from feminist men's studies suggests potentially powerful ways to challenge the dominant institutions involved in global economic restructuring and in the global war on terrorism.

Challenging Big Brother and Davos Man

Feminist scholars in the fields of macro-economics and international relations first undertook analysis of the gendered nature of large-scale institutions, such as states and global markets (Elson 1995, 1999 and Tickner 1992 being but two examples). Important new directions in feminist men's studies are advancing the understanding of masculinity as an attribute of global social institutions (Connell 2000). This work builds on several key points about masculinity (the social status and personal identity of being a man). First, societies and social institutions contain many forms of masculinity, but a dominant, or *hegemonic*, form of masculinity usually exists, which is most desirable in a given social context. Second, men actively construct masculinities, and because they contain contradictory elements, masculinities are subject to reconstruction, including the unseating of one ruling form by another (Connell 2000). The dominant form of masculinity is an idealised model rather than a description of the actual traits of the majority of men in a society, but it influences and is a key aspect of virtually all institutional practices (Connell 1987).

The institutions of the globalised world number not only corporations and markets for capital and labour, but also armies, bureaucracies and criminal legal systems. These institutions, involved in global economic restructuring and the global war on terror, are masculine in two senses: on the one hand, men (or, more precisely, a small number of elite, white, Western men) dominate these institutions, and their views and interests prevail; on the other hand, such institutions serve as sites where particular notions of masculinity are created, maintained and legitimated in the context of ongoing global processes (Hooper 2001). Global social institutions, then, are places in which a particular form of globally dominant masculinity is forged and exercised. Key analysts have dubbed the ascendant form of dominant masculinity, typified by the men who control the institutions central to economic liberalisation, 'transnational business masculinity' (Connell 2000). A leading publication of mainstream economics, *The Economist* (1997), created the character 'Davos Man' to represent the new style of elite masculinity which fits a globalised world of accelerated capitalist accumulation.

However, any form of masculinity is subject to challenge. Just as processes of globalisation have disrupted and displaced earlier forms of dominant masculinity, current responses to ongoing international events may undermine the dominance of Davos Man. The escalation of the global war on terrorism has reinvigorated the 'control-oriented military-style' masculinity of Big Brother – who, before the attacks on the World Trade Centre and the Pentagon, was a 'fading threat' to the dominance of transnational business masculinity (Connell 2000, 59). The competition between different potentially dominant forms of masculinity in global institutions offers feminists opportunities to take action. Because this competition shows that masculinity is not fixed or monolithic, institutions – even those of international finance and security apparatus – become vulnerable to feminist intervention (Hooper 2001).

At the AWID conference, we introduced 'Guadalajara Woman' as a character epitomising feminist action. She can be a potentially 'disruptive' presence in settings where the masculinity of military control now vies for dominance with the masculinity of fast capitalism. While enterprising alliances between these two groups of elite men are certainly possible, the tensions and contradictions between them can be manipulated by feminists to undermine their power to maintain gender inequality. And even in global social institutions, elite men – despite their power and advantage –

do not simply impose forms of masculinity from above; rather, they construct and reconstruct them in their ongoing social practices (Hooper 2001).

Who, then, is Guadalajara Woman? She is not some essentialist vision of universal womanhood or the version of ever-compliant femininity emphasised by dominant masculinity. She has a complex identity and an activist agenda. She takes her name from the location of the AWID conference. She knows another world is possible, and knows that the cumulative effect of scores of local small-scale feminist interventions can round out large-scale global campaigns multiplying their potential for institutional change (Hooper 2001).

Thus, she participates in women's NGOs and progressive community action to resist control-oriented state expansion. An example is Families Against Mandatory Minimums (FAMM), a woman-founded and -led organisation that challenges US mandatory drug law imprisonment policies. FAMM has had significant impact because of the sophisticated use of new technologies, including the World Wide Web, to organise against excessive prison sentences to tell the stories of individual women and men sentenced to long prison terms, and to reveal the plight of families, poor communities, and communities of colour, in the wake of high rates of imprisonment. Guadalajara Woman also works with organisations such as Human Rights Watch, challenging not only the conditions in prisons, including the sexual abuse of women in custody, but also the provisions of government legislation that endanger human rights. In addition, she supports civil liberties organisations to confront governments by filing freedom of information requests and lawsuits, and generating publicity. Through these and other progressive actions, Guadalajara Woman struggles for institutional accountability, and demands gender, racial and class justice from the state.

Likewise, Guadalajara Woman has been building alliances with a broad cross-section of social justice advocates who are engaged in highly visible protests against international financial institutions. Women have lifted their voices and decried corporate-led globalisation, beginning in Seattle in 1999, through the 'A16' action against the meetings of the World Bank and IMF in Washington DC in the spring of 2000, and on to Prague and other sites where the international financial elite have gathered (Staudt et al. 2001). Guadalajara Woman knows economic activity can be motivated by values such as reciprocity and redistribution, solidarity and altruism.

Her goal is to see that institutions which give macro-economic prescriptions to governments in the North and South will be held accountable to women, and work in service to people-centred development. The workings of neither free markets nor state control extend beyond the reach of collective action to globalise feminist visions of economic justice and just peace.

Gay Young is associate professor of sociology at American University (on leave) and resident scholar at the Institute of Women's Studies, Bir Zeit University (2002–2004). P.O. Box 20175, Jerusalem-East 91200, Israel. gyoung@american.edu

Mona Danner is associate professor of sociology and criminal justice at Old Dominion University. Old Dominion University, Department of Sociology and Criminal Justice, Norfolk VA 23529. mdanner@odu.edu.

Notes

1 Introduced by *The Economist*, 'Davos Man' refers to the international business and political executives who meet annually in Davos, Switzerland for the World Economic Forum.
2 'Big Brother', introduced in George Orwell's *1984*, was always watching you via telescreens mounted everywhere, including people's homes, such that everyone was always under surveillance by the state.

References

American Civil Liberties Union (2002) *Caught in the Backlash: Stories from Northern California*, San Francisco, CA: American Civil Liberties Union Foundation of Northern California

Baker, D., G. Epstein, and R. Pollen (eds.) (1998) *Globalization and Progressive Economic Policy*, Cambridge: Cambridge University Press

Bayes, J.H., M.E. Hawkesworth, and R.M. Kelly (2001) 'Globalization, democratization and gender regimes,' in R.M. Kelly et al. (eds.) *Gender, Globalization and Democratization*, Lanham, MD: Rowman and Littlefield

Beck, A.J. and J.C. Karberg (2001) *Prison and Jail Inmates at Midyear 2000*, Washington, DC: U.S. Department of Justice, Bureau of Justice Statistics

Beck, A.J., J.C. Karberg, and P.M. Harrison (2002) *Prison and Jail Inmates at Midyear 2001*, Washington, DC: U.S. Department of Justice, Bureau of Justice Statistics

Beneria, L. (1999) 'Davos man,' *Feminist Economics* 5 (3): 61–83

Bush-Baskette, S.R. (1998) 'The war on drugs as a war against black women', in S.L. Miller (ed.) *Crime Control and Women: Feminist Implications of Criminal Justice Policy*, Thousand Oaks, CA: Sage

Congressional Budget Office (2002) *Cost Estimate: H.R. 5005 Homeland Security Act of 2002*, as introduced on 24 June 2002

Connell, R.W. (1987) *Gender and Power*, Stanford, CA: Stanford University Press

Connell, R.W. (2000) 'Masculinities and globalization', in M. Baca Zinn et al. (eds.), *Gender Through the Prism of Difference*, Boston, MA: Allyn and Bacon

Danner, M.J.E. (1998) 'Three strikes and it's women who are out: the hidden consequences for women of criminal justice reform', in S.L. Miller (ed.) *Crime Control and Women: Feminist Implications of Criminal Justice Policy*, Thousand Oaks, CA: Sage

Davis, A. (2002) 'FBI's post-Sept. 11 "watch list" mutates, acquires life of its own', *The Wall Street Journal*, A1, A10, 19 November 2002

The Economist (1997) 'In praise of the Davos man', 1 February 1997

Elson, D. (1999) 'Labor markets as gendered institutions: equality, efficiency and empowerment issues,' *World Development* 27(3): 611–27

Elson, D. (1995) *Male Bias in the Development Process*, New York, NY: Manchester University Press

Friedman, T.L. (1999) 'A manifesto for the fast world', *New York Times Magazine*, 28 March 1999

Gibson-Graham, J.K. (1996) *The End of Capitalism (As We Knew It)*, Malden, MA: Blackwell Publishers, Inc.

Glaze, L.E. (2002) *Probation and Parole in the United States*, 2001, Washington, DC: U.S. Department of Justice, Bureau of Justice Statistics

Hasson, J. (2002) 'Funding holdup irks mayors', *Federal Computer Week*, 9 December 2002

Hooper, C. (2001) *Manly States: Masculinities, International Relations, and Gender Politics*, New York, NY: Columbia University Press

Human Rights Watch (2002) *Presumption of Guilt: Human Rights Abuses of Post-September 11 Detainees*, Washington, DC: Human Rights Watch

Immarigeon, R. and M. Chesney-Lind (1992) *Women's Prisons: Overcrowded and Overused*, San Francisco, CA: National Council on Crime and Delinquency

MacEwan, P. (1998) 'Comment' in D. Baker et al (eds.) *Globalization and Progressive Economic Policy*, Cambridge: Cambridge University Press

Maguire, K., A.L. Pastore, and T.J. Flanagan (eds.) (1993) *Sourcebook of Criminal Justice Statistics 1992*, Washington, DC: U.S. Department of Justice, Bureau of Justice Statistics

Mauer, M. (1990) *Young Black Men and the Criminal Justice System: A Growing National Problem*, Washington, DC: The Sentencing Project

The Nation (1995) 'The prison boom', 20 February 1995

Office of Homeland Security (2002) *National Strategy for Homeland Security*, Washington DC: U.S. Government

Polanyi, K. (1957 [1944]) *The Great Transformation*, Boston, MA: Beacon Press

Smallwood, S. (2002) 'University of Massachusetts faculty members protest FBI meeting with scholar', *The Chronicle of Higher Education*, 13 December 2002

Staudt, K.A., S.M. Rai and J.L. Parpart (2001) 'Protesting world trade rules: can we talk about empowerment?' *Signs* 26 (4): 1251–7

Tickner, J.A. (1992) *Gender in International Relations*, New York, NY: Columbia University Press

U.S. Department of Justice (2002) *U.S. Correctional Population Reaches 6.6 Million*, Press release, 25 August 2002

United Faculty of Florida (2003) *The United Faculty of Florida Defends the Due Process Rights, and Academic Freedom and Tenure Rights of USF Professor Sami Al-Arian*. http://w3.usf.edu/~uff/AlArian/Overview.html

The Washington Post (2003) 'Tax cuts plus war equals a record deficit', 2 March 2003, H2

Williamson, J. (2000) 'What should the World Bank think about the Washington Consensus?' *World Bank Research Observer* 15 (2): 251–64

Wonders, N.A. and M.J.E. Danner (2002) 'Globalization, state-corporate crime, and women: the strategic role of women's NGOs in the new world order', in G.W. Potter (ed.) *Controversies in White Collar Crime*, Cincinnati, OH: Anderson

Wonders, N. M.J.E. Danner, and F.I. Solop (2002) 'Gender, race and class divides in the U.S. under globalization: new injustices, new opportunities', paper presented at the Society for the Study of Social Problems, Chicago, IL, August 2000

Ziedenberg, J. and V. Schiraldi (2002) *Cellblocks or Classrooms?: The Funding of Higher Education and Corrections and its Impact on African American Men*, Washington, DC: Justice Policy Institute

Using the master's tools:
feminism, media and ending violence against women

Sanya Sarnavka

Worldwide, women are harnessing the power of mainstream media to change minds and hearts about women's human rights. In particular, they are focusing on ending violence against women as depicted in the media. Violence against women is here understood in two ways – not only as violence against women in society, but as violence committed in the media. By this we mean all misrepresentations, distorted reflections, sexism and silencing of women's voices, which violate women's right to equal access to public discourse. In a workshop at the AWID Forum, three leading feminist media analysts – from Croatia, India, and Uruguay – presented short video clips from their work, and discussed the successes and failures of women's human rights activists who use mainstream media as a vehicle for change. Their presentations were followed by a discussion about the successes and failures of women's human rights activists to engage with mainstream media as a vehicle for change.

There have been many statements by governments that equality between women and men is an integral part of democratisation. The need to reform the way in which women are represented in the media, especially in the mainstream media, has been recognised as part of the process of achieving equality. For example, the Fourth Ministerial Conference on Equality between Women and Men, was held in Istanbul in 1997. This affirmed, in its final declaration, 'Democracy must become gender-aware and gender-sensitive; this includes gender-balanced represent-ation as a demand for justice and a necessity for attaining genuine democracy, which can no longer afford to ignore the competence, skills and creativity of women...' (www.humanrights.coe.int/equality/Eng/WordDocs/Document/20list.htm).

The media, taken together, are a very important societal institution, which shapes public discourse and gives legitimacy to the existing social structure, describing, defining and creating a power basis within a culture. The media serve not only as carriers of information and messages, but also as interpreters, supporters and advocates of certain social, political and cultural values. Today especially, the media play a significant role in determining people's perception of their view of the world and their place in it, regardless of whether they are based in First-, Second-, or Third-World countries, as 'almost 80 per cent of the total news flow emanates from Western-based major transnational agencies; one-fifth of the total number of foreign correspondents of the Western agencies are based in the developing nations where four-fifths of the world's population lives; no wonder that Western agencies devote only 20 to 30 per cent to developing countries' (Pattanayak, 1985).

The international media are dominated by several (at the moment, eight) trans-national corporations, and are predominantly profit-driven. The conquest of markets for the benefit of economic gain also means control over people, if the mass media are used as transmitters of dominant ideology, and audiences lack media literacy in order to engage in independent analysis and arrive at a diversity of readings. Because of all these facts, it is of utmost importance to initiate a debate to try to work out how feminist activists can use the master's tools in order to advocate for a more just presentation in the mainstream media. Little progress has been made in implementing strategies in line with statements like the one above. The representation of women in mainstream media remains mostly stereotypical and discriminatory. This reinforces the unequal terms on which women participate in public life, and prevents them from taking a more active role in shaping the political, cultural and economic environment in society. This remains a huge and seemingly very difficult problem to solve

The workshop

If anyone needed proof of how important the issue of the representation of women in the public media remains, this was provided at the AWID Forum in the shape of the number of women who joined our session, their interest in the presentations, and their participation in the discussion that followed. The panel at the workshop were: Loreto Bravo, of CORSAPS (Area de Salud y Género de la Corporación de Salud y Políticas Sociales), Chile; Mallika Dutt of Breakthrough, India/USA; Lucy Garrido of Cotidiano Mujer, Uruguay; Joanne Sandler of UNIFEM, USA; and Sanja Sarnavka of Be active, Be emancipated (B.a.B.e.), Croatia.

The first part of the session presented facts from different surveys of media content, together with texts that illustrated persistent stereotypes of 'maleness' and 'femaleness'. It was important to show participants how media literacy should become one of the priorities of the women's movement if we want to empower women and enable them to become less vulnerable to the messages that are disseminated daily

through different media: the beauty myth, with anorexic models who are paid to expose their bodies, but are never allowed to speak; stories about women's lack of interest in politics and economic issues; fairy tales about women who are joyful in serving others, but who have no interest in gaining power and attaining decision-making positions.

The most powerful and exciting part of the workshop came when women activists presented video materials they had produced, to challenge such stereotypes and promote equality between women and men. These were a cartoon commercial used in the '16 Days of Activism Against Violence Against Women Campaign' in Croatia, musical videos produced in India, one of which had been nominated for an MTV award, and a video clip against fundamentalisms produced in Uruguay. It proved that it is possible to promote gender equality through lively, interesting, commercially competitive media products that can draw a wide audience.

However, the production of attractive media artefacts – created according to the highest professional standards, as well as being empowering and not sexist or discriminatory – has not been among the priorities of women's movement so far. From time to time, women's NGOs have been supported, usually with small grants, to research the media or produce materials independently. These materials have usually had connections to campaigns on violence against women. No ongoing education of women activists on media production and media literacy has been conducted. Nor has the education of journalists on gender issues been a priority. While many donors and agencies have given support of various kinds to journalists and the media in developing countries, and this support has been declared to promote professionalism, openness, and a non-partisan approach, somehow gender discrimination was always left out and 'forgotten'.

Conclusion

At the end of the session, we concluded without any hesitation that if gender mainstreaming is our true goal, more elaborate projects addressing critical issues related to the media should be carried out. We need to work in collaboration with each other – across countries and across professions – and to take a long-term perspective.

And the message should be sent to all who want to re-think globalisation and women's position in the world that, without women's voices in the mainstream media, all our struggles and networking will remain marginalised and invisible.

Sanya Sarnavka works for B.a.B.e., Vlaska 79, Zagreb 10000, Croatia.
babe@zamir.net

Reference

Pattanayak D. (1985) 'Diversity in communication and languages. Predicament of a multi-lingual nation state: India, a case study', in N. Wolfson and J. Manes, *Language of Inequality*, Berlin: Mouton

Part III
Specific issues of
global concern

Strategic advocacy and maternal mortality:

moving targets and the millennium development goals

Lynn Freedman

The UN Millennium Development Goals (MDGs) are the latest international development strategy.[1] The debates around the choice of MDGs, and the first steps of implementation, have threatened to push many women's health concerns off the policy map. But I argue in this article that there is space for feminist action around the remaining MDG on reducing maternal mortality. I discuss strategies to address maternal mortality and emphasise the importance of all women having access to EmOC (emergency obstetric care) in the event of birth complications. Using this MDG, we have an important opening for strategic advocacy focused on accountable health systems that can deliver the care necessary to save women's lives and improve their health. That focus will enable us to demand that attention be given to the globalisation policies that have contributed to the devastation of health systems in many parts of the world.

'Health care systems that do not offer care – that take a narrow or an abusive view of their duties... contribute profoundly to people's experience of what it is to be poor' Mackintosh, 2001

There are moments for 'strategic advocacy', when certain issues and approaches should be raised and fought for because of the considerable possibility they offer for advancing women's health and rights, and because of the danger that looms if we fail to seize our opportunity and instead allow other interests to take control. I believe we are in one such moment in the fight to secure good health and human rights for women worldwide.

In September 2000, the United Nations General Assembly issued the Millennium Declaration, designed to focus and intensify development efforts. Drawing on the UN conferences of the 1990s, the declaration sets out eight broadly stated goals of social and economic development: the Millennium Development Goals or MDGs, and specific, time-bound targets for each goal. A year later, in September 2001, the Secretary General issued a *Road Map to Implementation of the UN Millennium Declaration*, that structured and formalised the goals and targets, and put forth a set of indicators to monitor progress. The goals and targets that make up the MDGs are shown in Table 1.

That the Millennium Declaration is a negotiated political document becomes apparent when we see the fate of reproductive health, the central concept elaborated in the Programme of Action issued at the International Conference on Population and Development (ICPD) in Cairo in 1994. The concept of reproductive health incorporated many of the most significant developments in the analysis and practice of women's health and women's human

Table 1: Summary of the Millennium Development Goals and Targets

Goal 1	Eradicate extreme poverty and hunger	• Reduce by half the proportion of people living on less than one dollar a day • Reduce by half the proportion of people who suffer from hunger
Goal 2	Achieve universal primary education	• Ensure that all boys and girls complete a full course of primary schooling
Goal 3	Promote gender equality and empower women	• Eliminate gender disparity in primary and secondary education preferably by 2005, and at all levels by 2015
Goal 4	Reduce child mortality	• Reduce by two-thirds the mortality rate among children under five
Goal 5	Improve maternal health	• Reduce by three-quarters the maternal mortality ratio
Goal 6	Combat HIV/AIDS, malaria and other diseases	• Halt and begin to reverse the spread of HIV/AIDS • Halt and begin to reverse the incidence of malaria and other major diseases
Goal 7	Ensure environmental sustainability	• Integrate the principles of sustainable development into country policies and programmes; reverse loss of environmental resources • Reduce by half the proportion of people without sustainable access to safe drinking water • Achieve significant improvement in the lives of at least 100 million slum dwellers, by 2020
Goal 8	Develop a global partnership for development	• Develop further an open trading and financial system that is rule-based, predictable and non-discriminatory. This includes a commitment to good governance, development and poverty reduction – nationally and internationally • Address the least-developed countries' special needs. This includes tariff- and quota-free access for their exports; enhanced debt relief for heavily indebted poor countries; cancellation of official bilateral debt; and more generous official development assistance for countries committed to poverty reduction • Address the special needs of landlocked and small island developing states • Deal comprehensively with developing countries' debt problems through national and international measures to make debt sustainable in the long term • In co-operation with the developing countries, develop decent and productive work for youth • In co-operation with pharmaceutical companies, provide access to affordable essential drugs in developing countries • In co-operation with the private sector, make available the benefits of new technologies – especially information and communications technologies

rights made during the decade that preceded ICPD – and has grown to capture many of the developments in those fields made since. Reproductive health had therefore been one of the international development targets advanced during the five-year process leading up to the Millennium Declaration (Devarajan, Miller et al. 2002). But, at the last moment, under apparent pressure from the United States and its conservative allies on this issue, reproductive health was expunged from the Millennium Declaration document (Berer 2001; Girard 2001).

Although achievement of many of the other MDGs will certainly have positive effects on women's health, only one goal having any explicit connection to women's health remained. Goal 5, to 'improve maternal health' is put into action with a target on maternal mortality – that is, women's death in pregnancy and childbirth. The target is to 'reduce by three-quarters between 1990 and 2015, the maternal mortality ratio'. The road map suggests two indicators for tracking progress toward the target: first, the maternal mortality ratio, and second, the proportion of births attended by skilled health personnel.

Of course, reproductive health is inextricably connected to the goal of improving maternal health. As countries and the international community develop strategies for achieving the MDGs, reproductive health services will need to play a central role – both as a matter of good evidence-based public health policy, and as a matter of human rights (Freedman, Wirth et al. 2003). Women's health and rights advocates will need to work hard to ensure their appropriate inclusion.

At the same time, it matters very much what targets and indicators are chosen for the maternal health goal. In public health practice, what you *count* is what you *do* and where your resources go. Many international

health policy actors, including the World Bank, UN agencies and bilateral donors, are taking these specific targets and indicators seriously, investing enormous amounts of time, energy, and political capital on developing strategies for their achievement. There will be a push to use the MDGs at the country level as well.

It is now critical, therefore, that the women's health and human rights communities turn their attention to maternal mortality in a new and more intensive way. As the target and indicators for maternal mortality reduction are translated into new policies, programmes, and spending priorities, we will need to have a clear vision about their implications for women's health and human rights. We will also need a clear strategy to ensure that the MDG targets are used to confront – rather than to avoid – the globalisation policies that have had such a profound influence on health and rights.

Maternal mortality: basic facts

Maternal mortality accounts for approximately 515,000 deaths of women each year. For each death, an estimated 30 to 50 women suffer short- or long-term disability due to complications of pregnancy and childbirth (Fortney and Smith 1996). The distribution of maternal deaths across the world is telling. As shown in Table 2, almost 99 per cent occur in poor countries, with Africa and South Asia overwhelmingly bearing the brunt. By contrast, in the global North, maternal mortality has virtually ceased to exist as a public health problem.

Why? Why has the level of maternal mortality registered barely any change globally, despite nearly 15 years since the Safe Motherhood Initiative[2] was launched? Why have child mortality rates steadily declined, while maternal mortality rates have stayed unchanged? Why is there such

Table 2: Maternal mortality worldwide

UN region	Maternal mortality ratio (maternal deaths per 100,000 live births)	Number of maternal deaths	Lifetime risk of maternal death 1 in:
World total	400	515,000	75
Africa	1,000	273,000	16
Asia*	280	217,000	110
Europe	28	2,200	2,000
Eastern	50	1,600	1,100
Northern	12	140	3,900
Southern	12	170	5,000
Western	14	280	4,000
Latin America and the Caribbean	190	22,000	160
Northern America	11	490	3,500
Oceania*	260	560	260

*Japan and Australia/New Zealand have been excluded from the regional averages and totals

Source: WHO, UNICEF, and UNFPA, 'Maternal mortality in 1995: Estimates developed by WHO, UNICEF, UNFPA', 2001, Geneva: World Health Organization

a dramatic difference in death rates between rich and poor countries when it comes to death in pregnancy and childbirth (where child mortality shows a twenty-fold difference, maternal mortality ratios show nearly a hundred-fold difference)? Why does one in every 16 women in sub-Saharan Africa die in pregnancy and childbirth, compared to one in every 5,000 women in southern Europe?

Something is deeply wrong. While this scenario can be taken apart and analysed in many ways, and through different lenses, I believe that the medical and historical evidence, and analysis of contemporary health policies, point to one critical fact: without exception, high-mortality countries have failing, grossly deficient, often inequitable health care systems that have been unable to provide the interventions necessary to save women's lives.

Of course, there are many other differences between high and low mortality countries that one could point to; differences in income and poverty, gender equity, and education would also map in roughly the same way as maternal mortality, with sub-Saharan Africa doing dramatically worse on most social and economic development indicators than other parts of the world. But for women's health and rights advocates, it is absolutely essential to push past these broad associations between development and maternal mortality, to ask: *what is the mechanism of action?* What is the route through which gender inequity or income poverty influences maternal mortality? Until we can answer that question, we will fail to develop effective strategies that focus on the critical things that can make a difference.

To understand the importance of a functioning health care system to reduction of maternal mortality, it is crucial to recognise several basic facts about how maternal mortality happens. Eighty per cent of maternal deaths are caused by five direct obstetric complications: haemorrhage, infection, hypertensive disorders (pre-eclampsia and eclampsia), obstructed labour, and unsafe abortion.[3] The vast majority of these obstetric complications cannot be predicted or prevented (the exception is deaths due to complications of abortion, which could be almost totally eliminated by access to safe abortion services). Most non-abortion-related obstetric complications happen suddenly and unexpectedly, in women with no known risk factors, and even in women who are otherwise in good health. Yet virtually every one of these complications can be treated by well-known, relatively simple techniques: blood transfusion for haemorrhage, antibiotics for infection, anti-convulsant drugs for eclampsia, Caesarian section for obstructed labour. Together, these health interventions to treat complications are called emergency obstetric care (EmOC).

The fact that most life-threatening complications cannot be predicted or prevented means that many of the actions and interventions that we commonly associate with women's health care that is effective – for example, antenatal care programmes and nutrition programmes – *will not substantially reduce maternal death.* To make a dramatic change in maternal mortality – certainly to meet the MDG target of 75 per cent reduction – all women must have access to EmOC, in case they experience complications.

Emergency obstetric care should therefore be seen as a core element of essential health care services for women. This does not mean that all women must give birth in a health facility, nor does it imply a focus on urban, high-tech hospitals. But it does mean that every woman must have access to a facility that can provide EmOC, so that if she experiences a life-threatening complication, she can get there and be treated in time. EmOC will only be accessible to all women, rich and poor alike, when countries have functioning, equitable health care systems. Until then, whatever else is done to improve their overall health, women will continue to die in pregnancy and childbirth in unacceptably high numbers.

Strategies for addressing maternal mortality

In 1985, a groundbreaking article, 'Where is the "M" in MCH?' (Rosenfield and Maine 1985) first focused attention on the neglected issue of maternal mortality. Through 15 years of the international Safe Motherhood Initiative led by UN agencies, and a decade-long campaign to reduce maternal mortality spearheaded by women's health activist movements, strategies to reduce maternal mortality have evolved significantly. In addition to the provision of safe abortion services, which has been and remains an essential part of maternal mortality reduction efforts, early recommendations centred on the training of traditional birth attendants (TBAs) and improved antenatal care. Yet, as discussed above, neither antenatal care nor trained TBAs can prevent the vast majority of obstetric complications from happening; and once a complication occurs, there is almost nothing that TBAs, by themselves, can do to alter the chance that death will ensue. Thus, neither of these interventions has had a substantial impact on maternal mortality levels (Goodburn, Chowdhury et al. 2000; Greenwood, Bradley et al. 1990; Smith, Coleman et al. 2000).

Risk-screening programmes – another early recommendation in this field – have also proven ineffective. Because most life-threatening complications occur in women with no known risk factors, a screening program that identifies high-risk women for special monitoring and treatment can catch only a small fraction of those who will die in childbirth (Maine 1991; Maine and Paxton 2003).

Today, there is a clear international consensus that scarce resources should not be spent on trying to predict which women will have life-threatening complications. Instead, maternal mortality reduction programmes should be based on the principle that every pregnant woman is at risk for life-threatening complications. Thus, all women must have access to high-quality delivery care. That care has three key elements:

- a skilled attendant at delivery
- access to emergency obstetric care (EmOC) in case of a complication
- a referral system to ensure that those women who experience complications can reach life-saving EmOC in time.

It is important to note that 'skilled attendant' refers 'exclusively to people with midwifery skills (for example, doctors, midwives, nurses) who have been trained to proficiency in the skills necessary to manage normal deliveries and diagnose, manage or refer complications' (WHO, UNFPA et al. 1999, 31). This is a level of skill and training substantially higher than that of most trained TBAs or community health workers. Although TBAs have a role to play during childbirth, they are not substitutes for skilled attendants (Safe Motherhood Inter-Agency Group 2002).

What priorities should be set?

There is currently much discussion about how best to frame and promote this constellation of services. Some have framed this whole package as 'skilled care', meaning the person of the skilled attendant and the conditions, including EmOC and a referral system, that enable the attendant to manage complications, as well as a range of other maternal and newborn health measures. Others feel that 'skilled care' may be too broad a concept to be strategically effective: their view is that EmOC must be explicitly identified as high priority in a maternal mortality reduction strategy in order to ensure that attention to health systems and emergency care does not slip off the agenda as has happened so often in the past.

These two approaches can certainly complement each other. But the difference between them is not just a question of semantics. It is a question of strategy: of setting priorities, and of linking activism on maternal mortality reduction to other important aspects of women's health and human rights.

'Skilled care'
The skilled care strategy (or skilled attendant strategy, as it is sometimes called) in theory includes a broad set of maternal and newborn health interventions during pregnancy, delivery and the post-partum period (WHO 2003). It is often interpreted to mean that top priority should be given to training, equipping, supporting, and supervising enough new health workers (with midwifery skills) to reach every woman of reproductive age, whether she gives birth at home or in a facility. This interpretation is reinforced by the MDG indicator, 'proportion of births attended by skilled health personnel'. This interpretation exposes a serious drawback to the 'skilled attendant' indicator for the MDGs: it focuses on the *person* who attends a birth, but not on the *system* into which the attendant must be integrated in order to save women's lives.

Prioritising EmOC
In contrast, those who emphasise EmOC first advocate a strategy that aims to ensure that all women who experience life-threatening complications have access to the care necessary to save their lives. In this view, 'access' means physical and financial access to non-discriminatory, culturally sensitive, high-quality, facility-based services. This strategy begins with a focus on the health system, ensuring first that EmOC is in place – a process that includes community involvement in the development of accountable health services – and second, that women with complications can and do use it (Maine and Rosenfield

2001; Freedman 2001). The UN recommendation for minimum levels of coverage is one comprehensive EmOC facility and four basic EmOC facilities per 500,000 people.[4] Progress in improving availability and utilisation of EmOC can be monitored with a set of health system indicators which were issued in 1997, by WHO, UNICEF and UNFPA (Maine, Wardlaw et al. 1997; Paxton, Maine et al. 2003)

In an ideal world, both strategies would quickly arrive at the same end result of every birth being attended by a person with midwifery skills. That person would be able to do some procedures that can prevent certain complications in women (for example, active management of third stage labour to help prevent post-partum haemorrhage) and in newborns as well (for example, resuscitation for birth asphyxia). In the event of a complication, there would be an accessible facility able to deliver the appropriate level of emergency care needed to save a woman's life; and the skilled attendant could stabilise and quickly refer the woman to that facility.

Reaching this goal through strategic advocacy and health systems

But how should most countries get to this goal? And what should the international community do to facilitate the process? What should the health, human rights, and development advocacy communities do to ensure the most appropriate and effective steps are taken – and how does this relate to other advocacy agendas?

Activists in the public health field often find themselves in an ambivalent relationship with formal health systems. For many of us, the touchstone of our work has been Primary Health Care (PHC) and the principles of PHC articulated in 1978 in the Alma Ata Declaration.[5] Recognising that poor health is not just a biological phenomenon, PHC brought into focus the social and economic determinants of poor health and the need to link health to other sectors of social development. It thereby made health work an affirmative, socially-engaged, politically-aware process of action. Among PHC's most important contributions was to move the focus of health work away from building high-tech urban hospitals – 'disease palaces', as some called them – into communities, engaging with and empowering the people whose health was at stake (Morley, Rohde et al. 1983).

As originally articulated at Alma Ata, PHC was a broad and comprehensive vision that contemplated an integrated system of basic and referral health services, delivered in as close proximity as possible to where people lived. PHC was intended to respond to their most pressing needs in a respectful and empowering way. But the idealism of PHC quickly hit the stone wall of international economics and a new development orthodoxy which was ushered in with the debt crisis of the 1980s. The broad programme of PHC which had been set in 1978 at Alma Ata rapidly became an agenda of 'selective primary health care' focused on households and communities with simple interventions (such as oral rehydration therapy, immunisation and family planning) often delivered vertically, and often side-stepping the health system altogether (Claeson and Waldman 2000).

Such interventions have been vitally important for people's health and the attention to household and community-based health care was long overdue. But the scaling back of PHC into almost *only* these interventions has left the formal public health system unattended and unprotected. The decades of structural adjustment and health sector reform programs that followed have taken their toll, not only on the health of people, but on the infrastructure and functioning of health systems (Simms, Rowson et al. 2001).

Today, health systems are in profound crisis.

In vast parts of the world, health centres stand empty and deteriorating. In others, they are overwhelmed and unable to cope. User fees and exemption schemes have routinely failed to protect the poor, with 'informal' or illicit payments sometimes being the only way health providers can earn a living wage, while drug shortages force patients into the streets to find life-saving supplies or to forgo needed care altogether. In many countries, the public health system is plagued by personnel posting and transfer policies that put patients' interests last, and by absenteeism as public employees (sometimes driven by necessity) engage in private practice and steer patients accordingly. At the same time, massive 'brain drain' draws trained professionals out of countries while IFI (international financial institutions) policies pressure for bans on government hiring. Those who remain are often poorly trained and supervised, leaving even the best-intentioned providers without confidence or skills. Over-worked and demoralised, they can barely cope with their workloads much less follow protocols for improved inter-personal relationships with clients. And, all the while, patterns of social and gender discrimination that shape society as a whole often end up reflected in health systems where shocking maltreatment of patients and their families is almost routine.

But for many health activists and public health professionals, attention has been focused elsewhere. This has had profound effects for women – not least because of the futile search for maternal mortality reduction strategies that could be implemented regardless of the current state of national health systems. Despite the fact that almost every single maternal death is avoidable with access to appropriate treatment delivered through a health system, maternal mortality – the leading killer of women of reproductive age in developing countries – has been allowed to continue virtually unchecked, as health systems crumble under economic reform policies and a host of other domestic and international pressures.

Reconnecting households and communities to health care systems

If, 25 years ago, the politically and medically appropriate move was to take health care out of the urban hospitals and into households and communities, today the politically strategic – and medically vital – move is to reconnect those households and communities to local health care systems, but in a new way – a way based on fundamental principles of human rights. That will require a different vision of health care systems – what they do, how they work, and who should guide them (see WHO 2000). It will also require new, multi-disciplinary, flexible approaches to human rights (Freedman 2000).

A new vision should be premised on the recognition that, by its operation, a health system forms part of the very fabric of social and civic life. This fact often goes unnoticed in societies where health systems basically work. But where health systems have failed – and even more, where they have failed for poor and marginalised populations – that failure is experienced, to quote Maureen Mackintosh, 'as a core element of social exclusion . . . Health care systems that do not offer care – that take a narrow or an abusive view of their duties – thereby contribute profoundly to people's experience of what it is to be poor' (Mackintosh 2001; Tibandebage and Mackintosh 1999). Equally important is Mackintosh's insight that 'the culture and operation of the health care system (as a whole, public and private) is the way in which claims are established, legitimated and denied or fulfilled by "society"' (Mackintosh 2001, 185).

This has significant implications for the development of rights-based approaches to health, including mechanisms that will ensure constructive accountability. I use the phrase '*constructive* accountability' to make clear that accountability is not primarily about blame and punishment when things go wrong. Rather, it is about developing an effective dynamic of obligation and entitlement between people and their government, and within the complex system of relationships that form the wider health system, both public and private. It is, first and foremost, about building health systems that function for the benefit of people (see Freedman 2000; Freedman 2001).

A strategy built on ideas drawn from human rights transforms the health system from a static agglomeration of buildings, equipment, drugs and staff, into a dynamic entity through which citizens interact with their government and the wider civil society. Mechanisms of constructive accountability give people the potential to effect change – from the micro level of interactions with local health workers, to the macro level of health sector reform in the context of international development policies.

In the context of the MDGs, the target on maternal mortality, and a strategy based first on EmOC, gives us an opportunity to realise a new kind of analysis and activism, grounded in the basic needs and perspectives of women, but linked to the wider set of social and economic forces that shape their experience. For just as people's health status cannot be detached from the social and economic conditions in which they live, so the health policies that structure health systems are not set in isolation from the forces of globalisation and the specific agendas of IFIs and other actors (private and governmental) that drive globalisation and the social and economic changes it entails (Kim, Millen et al. 2000; Lee, Buse et al. 2002).

Because EmOC cannot be delivered outside of a functioning health system, its inclusion and emphasis forces a confrontation with the social and economic policies that, at the global and national levels, have decimated health systems and dramatically increased health inequity. In short, a maternal mortality strategy that focuses on EmOC gives health and human rights advocacy a *structural* perspective and concrete, do-able agenda that simultaneously addresses some of the most important challenges in the health and human rights fields in an era of globalisation.

This strategy for women's health advocates can link synergistically to emerging trends in the child health field and in the HIV and tuberculosis fields as well. For example, although household and community-based PHC interventions have certainly had a positive impact on child mortality, coverage is beginning to plateau or decline, as gaps between rich and poor grow ever wider (see Leon and Walt 2001; Evans, Whitehead et al. 2000). Vertical programs such as EPI (Expanded Programme on Immunisation), once championed and supported by international donors, but often delivered outside the broader health system, are now experiencing stagnation or even reversal, as donors begin to withdraw and the health system is unable to sustain immunisation coverage levels (Starling, Brugha et al. 2003). There is growing evidence that the weakness of health systems, particularly in low-income, highly-indebted countries, now presents a serious constraint to the scaling-up of appropriate child health interventions, such as IMCI (Integrated Management of Childhood Illnesses), and to efforts to address inequity (Black and Troedsson 2002; Gwatkin 2001).

A similar concern is growing in the community of health workers and activists focusing on HIV/AIDS. Even if access to essential medicines is ultimately secured, the need for a health system strong enough to deliver treatment adequately will still present an enormous obstacle in many countries struggling to cope with the epidemic. The same is true for effective interventions to cope with the resurgence of tuberculosis, such as DOTS (Directly Observed Therapy Short-Course). Without a health system that is strong enough to support the therapy properly, the poorest and most marginalised remain out of reach.

Conclusion

The strength of the Millennium Development initiative is that it brings these different aspects of health together, and it puts them at the table not only with other social sectors critical to health (e.g. water and sanitation, education), but also with representatives in ministries of finance and planning, and with the parts of World Bank and other international actors, who truly hold the power and resources necessary to make real change. It is a moment for strategic advocacy focused on accountable health systems that can deliver the care necessary to save women's lives and improve their health. We dare not miss it.

Lynn Freedman is Associate Professor of Population and Family Health, and Director of the Law and Policy Project at Mailman School of Public Health, Columbia University, 722 West 168th Street, Suite 1030, New York NY10032, USA.
Lpf1@columbia.edu.

Notes

1 At the Millennium Summit in September 2000, the Millennium Declaration, signed by all UN member countries, set out a number of Millennium Development Goals.
2 The Safe Motherhood Initiative is a worldwide effort that aims to reduce the number of deaths and illnesses associated with pregnancy and childbirth. The Initiative was launched at a conference held in Nairobi, Kenya in 1987.

3 The remaining 20 per cent are indirect complications, i.e. pre-existing conditions such as HIV and malaria that are aggravated by pregnancy and delivery. In areas where HIV and malaria prevalence is high and growing, these indirect deaths may account for an increasing proportion of maternal mortality.
4 Each country organises its health system differently. Basic EmOC can be delivered in a health centre that is more sophisticated than a health post, but not a full-service hospital. Comprehensive EmOC, which includes the capacity to do blood transfusions and surgery (e.g. Caesarian sections), is generally delivered at the level of a district or sub-district hospital (see Maine, Wardlaw et al. 1997).
5 The Alma Ata Declaration was defined following the UN Conference on Primary Health Care (PHC) in Alma Ata in the former USSR in 1978 (www.who.int/hpr/archive/docs/almaata.html). Alma Ata recommended that development plans concentrate on establishing community health centres and training community health workers, to benefit predominantly rural communities, rather than funding expensive urban hospitals, advanced technologies and specialist medical staff.

References

Berer, M. (2001) 'Images, reproductive health and the collateral damage to women of fundamentalism and war', *Reproductive Health Matters* 9: 6–11

Black, R. and H. Troedsson (2002) 'The Future Agenda for Child Health', Powerpoint presentation, 16 December 2002 (on file with author)

Claeson, M. and R. Waldman (2000) 'The evolution of child health programmes in developing countries: from targeting diseases to targeting people', *Bulletin of the World Health Organization* 78(10): 1234–45

Devarajan, S., M.J. Miller and E.V. Swanson (2002) 'Goals for Development: History, Prospects and Costs', Washington, DC: The World Bank

Evans, T., M. Whitehead, M. Wirth et al. (eds.) (2000) *Challenging Inequities in Health: From Ethics to Action*, New York: Oxford University Press

Fortney, J. and J. Smith (1996) 'The Base of the Iceberg: Prevalence and Perceptions of Maternal Morbidity in Four Developing Countries', Research Triangle Park, North Carolina: Family Health International

Freedman, L.P. (2000) 'Human rights and women's health' in M. Goldman and M. Hatch (eds.), *Women and Health*, New York: Academic Press

Freedman, L.P. (2001) 'Using human rights in maternal mortality programs: from analysis to strategy', *International Journal of Gynecology and Obstetrics* 75: 51–60

Freedman, L.P., M. Wirth, R. Waldman, M. Chowdhury, A. Rosenfield (2003) 'Millennium Development Project Task Force 4 Background Paper on Child Health and Maternal Health' (on file with author)

Girard, F. (2001) 'Reproductive health under attack at the United Nations (letter)', *Reproductive Health Matters* 9(68)

Goodburn, E., M. Chowdhury, R. Gazi et al. (2000) 'Training traditional birth attendants in clean delivery does not prevent postpartum infection', *Health Policy and Planning* 15: 394–9.

Greenwood, A., A. Bradley, P. Byass et al. (1990) 'Evaluation of a primary care programme in the Gambia: the impact of traditional birth attendants on the outcome of pregnancy', *Journal of Tropical Medicine & Hygiene* 93: 58–66

Gwatkin, D.R. (2001) 'The need for equity-oriented health sector reforms', *International Journal of Epidemiology* 30: 720–3

Kim, J., J. Millen, A. Irwin, J. Gershman (eds.) (2000) *Dying for Growth: Global Inequality and the Health of the Poor*, Monroe, Maine: Common Courage Press

Lee, K., K. Buse, S. Fustukian (eds.) (2002) *Health Policy in a Globalising World*, Cambridge: Cambridge University Press

Leon, D.A. and G. Walt (eds.) (2001) *Poverty, Inequality and Health: an International Perspective*, Oxford: Oxford University Press

Mackintosh, M. (2001) 'Do health care systems contribute to inequalities?', in Leon and Walt (eds.) (2001)

Maine, D. (1991) *Safe Motherhood Programs: Options and Issues*, New York: Center for Population and Family Health

Maine, D. and A. Paxton (forthcoming 2003) 'Evidence based strategies for prevention of maternal mortality', in R. Johanson and S. Daya (eds.) *Evidence-based obstetrics*, Oxford: Blackwell Publishing

Maine, D. and A. Rosenfield (2001) 'The AMDD program: history, focus and structure', *International Journal of Gynecology and Obstetrics* 74: 99–103.

Maine, D., T. Wardlaw, V. Ward et al. (1997) *Guidelines for Monitoring the Availability and Use of Obstetric Services*, New York: UNICEF

Morley, D., J. Rohde and G. Williams (1983) *Practising Health for All*, Oxford: Oxford University Press

Paxton, A., D. Maine, N. Hijab (2003) 'Using the UN Process Indicators of Emergency Obstetric Care: Questions and Answers', New York: AMDD Program, Heilbrunn Department for Population and Family Health

Rosenfield, A. and D. Maine (1985) 'Maternal mortality – a neglected tragedy: Where's the M in MCH?' *The Lancet* ii: 83–5

Safe Motherhood Inter-Agency Group (2002) 'Skilled Care During Childbirth: Policy Brief', New York: Family Care International

Simms, C., M. Rowson, S. Peattie (2001) 'The Bitterest Pill of All: The Collapse of Africa's Health Systems', London: Save the Children Fund UK

Smith, J., N. Coleman, J. Fortney et al. (2000) 'The impact of traditional birth attendant training on delivery complications in Ghana', *Health Policy and Planning* 15: 326–31.

Starling, M., R. Brugha, G. Walt (2003) 'New Products into Old Systems: The Initial Impact of GAVI from the Country Level', London: Save the Children

Tibandebage, P. and M. Mackintosh (1999) 'Institutional Cultures and Regulatory Relationships in a Liberalising Health Care System: A Tanzanian Case Study', ESRF Discussion Paper for WIDER workshop on 'Group Behaviour and Development', September 1999

WHO (2000) *World Health Report 2000*, Geneva: World Health Organization

WHO (2003) 'Maternal and Newborn Health: Making Pregnancy Safer', http://www.who.int/reproductive-health/mpr/index.htm

WHO, UNFPA, UNICEF, World Bank (1999) 'Reduction of Maternal Mortality: A Joint WHO/UNFPA/UNICEF/World Bank Statement', Geneva: World Health Organization

HIV/AIDS, globalisation and the international women's movement

Sisonke Msimang

The spread of the HIV/AIDS pandemic is closely connected to processes of globalisation in the South and, in particular, in Africa. It is clear that, for the most part, these processes are bad for poor people, women, and a range of marginalised groups, both within the global South and in some communities within the North. While globalisation certainly has a strong relationship to AIDS, groups such as the Treatment Action Campaign[1] are fighting back and demonstrating that in the new world order the need for a vigilant civil society is all the more important. At the global level, feminists from the North have not as yet engaged with HIV/AIDS as a critical issue. Given that in my country (South Africa), HIV prevalence hovers at about 22 per cent, and not a weekend goes by without a funeral of someone my age whose death no one can explain, it feels like there is an almost deafening silence on AIDS in the global women's movement. In this article, I propose that by analysing the complex intersections between different forms of inequality,[2] feminists from the South can move such critical issues further up the global agenda.

HIV/AIDS and globalisation

Globalisation has been described as 'the drive towards an economic system dominated by supranational trade and banking institutions that are not accountable to democratic processes or national governments' (Globalisation Guide, www.global isationguide.org /01.html). It is characterised by an increase in cross-border economic, social, and technological exchange under conditions of (extreme) capitalism. As human bodies move across borders in search of new economic and educational opportunities, or in search of lives free from political conflict and violence, they bring with them dreams and aspirations. Sometimes, they carry the virus that causes AIDS, and often, they meet the virus at their destinations.

As corporations increasingly patrol the planet, looking for new markets, and natural and human resources to exploit, they set up and abandon economic infra-structure – opening and closing factories, establishing hostels. In so doing, they create peripheral communities hoping to benefit from employment and the presence of new populations where previously there were none. And when they move on, once they have found a cheaper place to go, they leave in their wake communities that are extremely susceptible to HIV/AIDS.

This is because the virus follows vulnerability, crosses borders with ease, and finds itself at home where there is conflict, hunger, and poverty. The virus is particularly comfortable where wealth and poverty co-exist – it thrives on inequality. It is not surprising, then, that Southern Africa provides an excellent case study of the collusion between globalising processes and HIV/AIDS.

The economy of the region has been defined in the last two centuries by mining:

gold and diamonds. In an era of plummeting gold prices, and an increasing shift towards the service industry, Southern Africa is shedding thousands of jobs. Yet the last century of globalisation has provided a solid platform for the current AIDS crisis.

If there was a recipe for creating an AIDS epidemic in Southern Africa, it would read as follows: 'Steal some land and subjugate its people. Take some men from rural areas and put them in hostels far away from home, in different countries if need be. Build excellent roads. Ensure that the communities surrounding the men are impoverished so that a ring of sex workers develops around each mining town. Add HIV. Now take some miners and send them home for holidays to their rural, uninfected wives. Add a few girlfriends in communities along the road home.

Add liberal amounts of patriarchy, both home-grown and of the colonial variety. Ensure that women have no right to determine the conditions under which sex will take place. Make sure that they have no access to credit, education, or any of the measures that would give them options to leave unhappy unions, or dream of lives in which men are not the centre of their activities. Shake well and watch an epidemic explode.'

There's an optional part of the recipe, which adds an extra spice to the pot: African countries on average spend four times more on debt servicing than they do on health. Throw in a bit of World Bank propaganda, some loans from the IMF and beat well. Voilà. We have icing on the cake.

As the gap between the rich countries of the North and the poor countries of the South grows, we are beginning to see serious differences in the ways that states can afford to take care of their citizens. Access to technology, drugs, and strong social safety nets in the North, mean that HIV/AIDS is a manageable chronic illness in most developed countries. Yet there are pockets of poor, immigrant, gay, and otherwise marginalised communities within these countries, where HIV prevalence is on the rise. An analysis of the complex intersections between inequalities tells us that it is not enough to belong to a rich country – that alone does not protect you from vulnerability to HIV infection, nor does it guarantee treatment. Where you sit in relation to the state is equally important – whether you are a woman, a poor woman, a black woman, an educated woman, a lesbian, a woman with a disability who is assumed not to be having sex, an immigrant who is not entitled to many of the social security benefits of citizens. All these factors determine your vulnerability to HIV/AIDS.

Now what does this mean for a 25-year-old woman living in Soweto? Jabu works as a security guard at a shopping centre in Johannesburg. Every day she spends two hours travelling to work because of the distances the architects of apartheid set up between city centres and the townships that serviced them. Jabu is grateful to have a job. Her two little ones are in KwaZulu Natal with their grandmother until Jabu can get a stable job. She is on a month-to-month contract with the security company. She watches expensive cars all day, protecting their owners' investments while they work. The company doesn't want to take her on as staff so each month she faces the uncertainty of not having a job the next month. Joining a union is not an option – she's not technically a staff member and she can't afford to make trouble. Jabu's boyfriend Thabo drives a taxi. Their relationship saves her cash because he drives her to and from work every day – a saving of almost one third of her salary each month. She has another boyfriend at work, who often buys her lunch. She has to be careful that Thabo doesn't find out.

In addition to race, class, and gender, Jabu's life is fundamentally shaped by the forces of globalisation – where she works and how secure that work is, where her children live, even how she arrives at work.

These factors all influence her vulnerability to HIV infection.

HIV/AIDS and feminism

During the last eight years of my work on sexual and reproductive rights, my focus has been primarily on HIV and AIDS. For me, the pandemic brings into stark relief the fact that states have failed to provide their citizens with the basic rights enshrined in the declaration of human rights.

Twenty years ago, AIDS was known as Gay Related Immune Disease – so associated was it with gay men. Today, the face of AIDS has changed. It looks like mine. It is now black, female, and extremely young. In some parts of sub-Saharan Africa, girls aged 15–19 are six times more likely than their male counterparts to be HIV positive. Something is very wrong.

In the next ten years, the epidemic will explode in Asia and in Central and Eastern Europe as well as in Latin America. The pandemic will have profound effects on the burden of reproductive work that women do, and this in turn will have far-reaching consequences for the participation of women in politics, the economic sector, and other sectors of society. The very maintenance of the household, the work that feminist economists like Marilyn Waring, Diane Elson and others tell us keeps the world running, may no longer be possible.

As older women are increasingly called upon to care for children, and as life expectancy shrinks to the forties and fifties, in Africa we face the prospect of a generation without grandparents, and an imminent orphan and vulnerable children crisis that will effectively leave kids to take care of kids. As the orphan crisis deepens, child abuse is on the rise. Girls without families to protect them are engaging in survival sex to feed themselves and their siblings, and we are told that communities will 'cope.' There is a myth of coping that pervades the development discourse on

AIDS. What it really means is that women will do it. What it translates into is that families split up, girls hook for money and food,[3] and a vicious cycle is born.

While there is some feminist analysis of the AIDS epidemic, we have not yet heard a rallying cry from the women's movement. A recent article by Noeleen Heyzer, UNIFEM's Executive Director begins to formulate some arguments about why in the context of AIDS, women can no longer wait for equality with men (www.csmonitor. com/2002/0718/p13s02-coop.html). Dr. Heyzer points out that it takes 24 buckets of water a day to care for a person living with AIDS – to clean sheets fouled by diarrhoea and vomit, to prepare water for bathing (sometimes several times a day), to wash dishes and prepare food. For women who must walk miles, and still do all the other chores that always need doing, the burden becomes unbearable.

This past spring in New York, I was asked to speak to a group at a high school in Brooklyn about HIV/AIDS and violence against women in the South African context. They were an intelligent group, well versed in feminism. I was not the only presenter. A young American woman who had worked with *Ms. Magazine* talked about pop culture, and the politics of wearing jeans and letting your G-string[4] show. I left the meeting feeling disconcerted. I had made my presentation and received a few awkward questions about men in Africa. I cringed on behalf of my brothers because I certainly was not trying to demonise them, but the students were feeding into a larger narrative of the familiar discourse of black male laziness, deviancy and sexual aggression that I was careful to point out to them. Aside from that, they found little else to talk about.

On the other hand, the woman from the US struck a chord with them. They talked about eating disorders and the media, about Britney Spears and Janet Jackson. It was fascinating. Having lived in the US, I was able to follow and engage, but my interests as an African feminist do not lie in this subject matter. It was a clear example of how far apart we, as feminists, sometimes are from one another.

Contexts vary, and of course the issues that are central in the global North will be different from those of Southern feminists. And amongst us there will be differences. I understood where the high school students were coming from. Indigenous feminism must be rooted in what matters most to women at a local level. At a global level within feminism, however, I fear that we may be in danger of replicating the G-strings versus AIDS conversation. I am worried by the relative silence from our Northern sisters about a pandemic that is claiming so many lives.

A way forward

In the context of HIV/AIDS, it is no longer enough to frame our conversations solely in terms of race, class, and gender. These are primary markers of identity, but increasingly, we need more. We need to look at where women are located spatially in relation to centres of political, social, and economic power. We need also to examine how where we live – rural, urban, North or South – intersects with poverty and gender. We also need to think about how the experience of poverty interacts with, and not just intersects with, gender. Culture is another factor that deserves attention.

We are beginning to see dangerous patriarchal responses to the epidemic – from virginity tests to decrees about female chastity from leaders. In part this is simply an extension of deeply rooted myths about female sexuality. However, with HIV/AIDS, it can also be attributed to the fact that in many cases women are the first to receive news of their sero-positive status. This is often during pre-natal screening, or when babies are born sick. Bringing home the 'news' that there is HIV in the family often means being identified as the person who caused the infection in the first place.

We know that, in the vast majority of cases, this is simply not true.

The Treatment Action Campaign (TAC), a movement begun by and for people living with HIV/AIDS in South Africa, has managed to mobilise national and international support for the idea of universal access to drugs for people with AIDS. The group began their campaign by using pregnant women as their rallying cry. The right to nevirapine for pregnant women opened the door for TAC's broader claims about the rights of all people with HIV/AIDS to HIV medication. The campaign has been hugely successful. TAC encouraged the South African government to take the pharmaceutical industry to court and the government won, paving the way for a win at the World Trade Organization. Companies' patent rights can no longer supersede the rights of human beings to access life-saving medicines.

TAC's strategy needs to be vigorously debated and analysed by feminists. TAC did not use arguments about reproductive and sexual rights. They simply said, 'It is unfair for the government not to give drugs to pregnant women so they can save their babies' lives.' It was a classic 'woman as the vessel' argument. TAC's interest was not in women's rights – but in the rights of people living with HIV/AIDS, some of whom happen to be women. The campaign's success was largely based on the notion that the average South African found it difficult to accept that 'innocent' babies would die because of government policy. This requires some serious feminist interrogation. TAC has since been pushed by gender activists within the movement to ensure that the drugs do not stop when the baby is born.

Gender activists to date have struggled to get their voices heard in the doctor-dominated AIDS world. The mainstream women's movement needs to get on board and face up to the challenge of HIV/AIDS. AWID's 'Globalise This' campaign provides an opportunity to highlight the HIV/AIDS epidemic and the threat it poses to women.

At precisely the moment when we need international solidarity to focus on the impact of AIDS on poor women's lives, and their need to be able to control their lives and their bodies, we have to oppose the US administration's cutbacks on funding for essential reproductive health services. We are also still waiting for the G8 to enact their long-standing commitment to spend 0.7 per cent of GDP on overseas development assistance each year. How likely is it that they will ever reach this target if they focus instead on supporting the war against Iraq?

Our sisters in the North need to develop a consciousness about the fight against AIDS as a feminist fight. We need civil society and feminist voices in developing countries to challenge their governments to tackle HIV/AIDS as a health issue, as a human rights issue, and as a sexual and reproductive rights issue. If we lose this fight, it will have profound effects on the lives of girls and women into the next century.

Sisonke Msimang lives in South Africa and works on gender and sexual and reproductive health and rights issues including HIV/AIDS. She has worked with a number of NGOs and international agencies based in sub-Saharan Africa. Postal address: Youth Against AIDS Network, PO Box 56950, Arcadia 0007, South Africa. Tel. +27 12 392 0500; Fax. +27 12 320 2414

sisonkem@iafrica.com

Notes

1 Treatment Action Campaign, a movement begun by and for people living with HIV/AIDS in South Africa, which began in the late 1990s.
2 I have based my idea of 'intersectionality' on Kimberle Crenshaw's definition: for her, intersectionality is about 'challenging those groups that are home to us, in the name of those parts of ourselves that don't feel so at home' (Crenshaw Williams 1994).
3 Girls engage in survival sex/sexual relationships for financial gains.
4 Fashionable underwear.

Reference

Crenshaw Williams, Kimberle (1994) 'Mapping the margins: intersectionality, identity politics, and violence against women of color', in Martha Albertson Fineman and Rixanne Mykitiuk (eds.) *The Public Nature of Private Violence*, New York: Routledge

New genetic technologies and their impact on women:
a feminist perspective[1]

Lisa Handwerker

In wealthy countries such as the United States, new genetic and reproductive technologies, including human reproductive cloning, are being developed. To date, the short- and long- term consequences for women of human reproductive cloning have remained largely unexamined. This article analyses ten common misconceptions about new genetic technologies, especially human reproductive cloning, and shows that women will bear the major physical, psychological, social, moral, legal, political and economic burdens of these genetic manipulations. Despite the great diversity of women and differing feminist perspectives towards new reproductive technologies, I argue that we need a united position which opposes human reproductive cloning. This article is based on a presentation that formed part of a panel at the Association for Women's Rights and Development (AWID) 9th International Forum entitled 'The Genetic Revolution, Biotechnology and Women's Rights'.

In late January 2001, a breaking news story announced that a well-known Italian infertility specialist, Dr Severino Antinori, and his colleague, Panayiotis M. Zavos, Professor of Reproductive Physiology at the University of Kentucky, USA, had plans to clone human beings within the next 12 to 24 months (*Los Angeles Times*, 28 January 2001). This announcement by medical professionals who supported new genetic technologies was a culmination of efforts to overcome public repulsion of and resistance to human reproductive cloning. On the one hand, scientists, researchers, and bio-ethicists who favour human genetic manipulation had been insisting that these techniques are low-risk, helpful to women and children by reducing disease and producing a physically and mentally 'superior' baby by design, and inevitable. On the other hand, there was concern from other members of the scientific community and broader public which led President Clinton's National Bioethics Advisory Committee to declare human reproductive cloning unsafe and to recommend a ban. The result was a five-year moratorium (June 1997–June 2002) on federal, not private, funds for human cloning in the United States. Since there was no moratorium on private funds, scientists backed by private funding sources raced to be the first to clone a human being. In late 2002, Clonaid, the Raelians' for-profit company[2] claimed the birth of the first cloned baby, named Eve. While the Raelians initially promised to provide evidence that the baby was indeed a clone, to date no proof has been provided.

This paper is a critique of human reproductive cloning,[3] from a feminist perspective, focusing on the impact on women and women's health. It is based on research that I conducted both as a consultant for the Exploratory Initiative on the New Human Genetic Technologies (known today as the Centre for Genetics and Society) in 2001, and my own ongoing research. At the start, I want to acknowledge that very important differences are bound to exist among and between women and women's groups about new human genetic manipulations. Where individual women draw the line between acceptable and unacceptable practices will be influenced by our multiple identities, including ethnicity, class, wealth, sexuality, religion, age and disability. In addition, our decisions will be influenced by our political persuasions.

Among those of us who are feminists, some may be members of the Feminist International Network of Resistance to Reproductive and Genetic Engineering (FINRRAGE), a group which is opposed to all new reproductive technologies on the grounds that they are ultimately oppressive and dangerous for women. Others may be post-modern feminists, who reject grand theory to explain inequalities, but as a result, may also shy away from a political position. Or we may be cyborg feminists, who are interested in the ways we can produce forms of resistance as part-machine/part-human. We may be libertarian feminists, who are committed to individual reproductive liberty and procreative freedom. Or we may take an egalitarian feminist perspective, dedicated to social justice, and to understanding how social position influences the ways in which technologies are used and inform us.

While respecting these differences, I argue that women need to consider a united position, which opposes human reproductive cloning. These new genetic techniques are not in the best interests of all women. Women, more than men, will bear the burdens – physical, psychological, social, moral, economic, political, and legal – of these technologies, and any negative consequences.

Ten misconceptions

My purpose in outlining ten misconceptions about human reproductive cloning is to debunk some existing myths. In so doing, I am focusing on the potential technological harms, and discussing these within the broad context of US culture.

1 Diseases, abilities, and personalities are genetically determined; thus, solutions to human problems are genetically based

'Genomania', is a term coined by Ruth Hubbard, a biologist and Professor Emeritus from Harvard University, and board member of the Council for Responsible Genetics,[4] to refer to the way in which biological determinism has entered into the public's consciousness through the media (Hubbard and Wald 1997). Biological determinism refers to ways our lives are increasingly pervaded by a flow of bio-medical knowledge showing a connection between biology and identity, and biology and disease. We are witnessing the 'over-geneticisation' of people and life; genes alone do not determine a person's health, ability or personality. In fact, the majority of diseases, abilities, and personalities are influenced by multiple genetic and environmental factors. Ultimately, we are complex social and biological beings.

2 The human genome sequence and the human genome project are 'neutral'

The human genome project, an international effort to map and sequence human DNA, was officially launched in 1990. Interestingly, the questions of *whose* genome is being matched, and *whose* sequences we are being compared to, are often overlooked (Mahowald 2000) in this area of research. The generic human genome sequence, developed mainly from a composite of existing cell lines of healthy individuals of both sexes from different ethnic groups, is referred to by scientists as 'neutral'. It is this 'neutral' human genome sequence that women's genome is compared to. Based on past lessons, we know that research on male subjects cannot always be accurately applied to women. Thus, is there really such a thing as a 'neutral' human genome sequence, which disregards sex and other factors? Regardless of whether it is or not, clearly political, social, and economic decisions stemming from this project are not neutral. Women in the United States need to question the justification for spending over three billion dollars on genetic research, given the limited funding for research and inadequate coverage of basic rights of women including food, clothing and shelter.

3 Human reproductive cloning is relatively risk-free, and whatever risks exist will be worked out in a short time

In the media, pro-human reproductive cloning scientists are building their case and hoping that a single success will erase all ethical and safety concerns. It is suggested that human reproductive cloning is inevitable and just a matter of time, despite bans in most of Europe and in several US states. Dr Zavos, one of the team members who will attempt human reproductive cloning, has said, 'We have a great deal of knowledge. We can grade embryos, we can do genetic screening, and we can do quality control' (www. DailyNews.yahoo.com/h/n/m/20010126/ cloning_ dc_1.html). Seemingly as an afterthought, he is reported to have added: 'It's not the easiest thing. The stability of the genetic information is what's important. We are cloning a human being now; we are not trying to create a Dolly. You don't want to create a monster (ibid).' In a recent television interview, he added, 'We don't intend to step on dead bodies to get there. But cloning babies is only a matter of time' (World News, ABC, Channel 7, 13 February 2001).

We should be *very* concerned when potential risks of human reproductive cloning are played down or ignored. To create animal clones, scientists frequently made hundreds of failed attempts to develop viable embryos. Many, including medical professionals and ethicists, have posed the possibility of cruel failures in human cloning, where genetic abnormalities result in grotesque foetuses unable to survive outside the womb (www.DailyNews. yahoo.com/h/n/m/20010126/cloning_dc_ 1.html). According to newspaper reports, 'All sorts of things can go wrong', said George Seidel, a cloning researcher at Colorado State University. Cloned cattle and sheep are often born dangerously large. A calf might normally weigh 100 pounds, but a clone might weigh 160 pounds. This excessive size prevents the calf from having room to grow and wiggle, resulting in all sorts of limb deformities. 'Sometimes the kidneys aren't right – they're just plain put together wrong – or the heart is, or the lungs, or the immune system,' he added. 'It can be a unique abnormality in each case. They can die within a few days after birth, or sometimes they just can't make it after you cut the umbilical cord.' Nobody really knows why (*The New York Times Magazine*, 4 February 2001).

Even Dr Harry Griffith, assistant director of the Roslin Institute, Scotland, which successfully cloned Dolly, the sheep, has said on BBC News Online, 'It would be wholly irresponsible to try to clone a human being, given the present state of technology. The success rate with animal cloning is about one to two per cent in the published results, and I think lower than that on average. I don't know anyone working in this area who thinks the rates will easily be improved. There are many cases where the cloned animals die late in pregnancy or soon after birth' (BBC, http://news/bbc.co.uk/hi/English/sci/tech /newsid_11440001/114694.stm). Others have cited risks to women in carrying clones. For example, several scientists stated that the first 100 attempts to clone will result in spontaneous abortions because of genetic or physical abnormalities, putting the health and lives of the surrogate mothers at risk (*Washington Post*, 7 March, 2001).

Scientists and doctors who support human reproductive cloning argue that any woman undergoing these new techniques will be told about all the risks in order to make an informed decision. Dr Zavos has said, 'Cloning has already been developed in animals. The genie is out of the bottle. It's a matter of time when humans will apply it to themselves, and we think this is best initiated by us... with ethical guidelines and quality standards' (*The Nation*, 2 Jan, 2001).

But can these same doctors, working at such high stakes for success and fame, and Institutional Review Boards (IRBs), within private hospitals and clinics motivated by profit, be entrusted to develop informed consent protocols that are in the best interests of women? This, I argue, is a serious conflict of interest. We have examples from the past of abuses, and the need for additional mechanisms to protect women and women's health. Women who underwent in-vitro fertilisation (IVF) techniques, often to overcome male infertility problems, read and signed informed consent forms. However, some women later learned that information about possible risks had been withheld from them. Specifically, some women were not informed about a study which linked multiple failed attempts at IVF to an increased risk of ovarian cancer (Turkiel 1998). When I asked several doctors why this information was not reported to infertile couples, they said the results were not statistically significant. But why were women not allowed to read the study to determine that themselves? Last year, I was interviewed on two radio stations, including KPFA in Berkeley, California and National Public Radio (NPR) about the social and ethical issues of IVF with egg donation. Also on one of the radio programmes was a woman who had donated her eggs on three separate occasions. Her doctors, whom she trusted, repeatedly told the woman that the hormones she was given to stimulate egg production had no known health risks. Since there is evidence about potential risks, this kind of misinformation is irresponsible and unethical.

Women are rarely provided with what the US-based National Women's Health Network[5] refers to as, 'evidence-based, independent information' to empower them to make fully informed decisions. There are very few organisations which, like the network, act as an independent voice for women's health by not accepting money from companies that sell pharmaceuticals, medical devices, dietary supplements, alcohol, tobacco, or health insurance. We must ensure that women have access to evidence-based, independent information to enable them to make their decision from a fully-informed perspective.

In addition to physical risks, women will face serious social, psychological, moral, and legal risks if they are involved in reproductive human cloning. They will be burdened with complex moral decisions about their embryos and be held responsible for future generations. If human reproductive cloning is allowed, social relationships between people will become very complex and we will need additional guidelines about how to act towards one another. A cloned child may question his/her relationship with his/her adult caregivers, and will want to know, 'Are you my mother, sister, or twin?'[6] What will happen if a woman refuses to use new genetic tests and her baby is not considered 'normal' by some external standard or committee? Furthermore, who sets the standards and decides what is 'normal'? Many involved in the disability rights movement are rightfully concerned about these and other issues, including how embryo decision-making occurs at the pre-implantation stage.[7]

What will happen if and when a woman makes a different decision from that of her doctor? What will happen if a woman and her partner (male or female) cannot agree on similar qualities for their baby? Will these women face criminal charges or wrongful birth suits? In a social context where women have been criminally charged for failing to agree to a Caesarean or charged with taking drugs that endanger their newborn as has happened in some US states (Handwerker 1994), these women might well face criminal charges or wrongful birth lawsuits. Such a scenario is not paranoia, but rather raises some serious concerns about both the short- and long-term consequences of new human genetic manipulations, including human reproductive cloning.

4 The commercialisation of reproduction is not a problem, and will not adversely impact women

According to a recent newspaper report in the US, Mark Eibert, a cloning advocate and attorney, said he received requests daily from people asking whether they can participate in clinical trials of reproductive cloning. Of those, he estimates that 90 per cent are infertile, one per cent gay or lesbian, and the rest are worried about genetic diseases (*UPI Science News*, 28 January 2001). This raises the question of who the first subjects of these new experiments will be. What selection criteria will doctors use to decide? Will they be wealthy women, mainly Caucasian, who can afford to pay the estimated $50,000 fee? Or poor women, especially women of colour (this is a term used in the US to refer to any woman who is not white, or who identifies with any ethnic group other than Caucasian), who are too often subjects of human trials? Within the United States and abroad, I can imagine a scenario in which both would be possible. Despite recent evidence that in the US, black women suffer 1.5 times more from infertility problems than white women, it is disproportionately white women who use expensive technologies to bear children, while black women disproportionately undergo surgical procedures that prevent

them from being able to bear children (Roberts 2001).

5 New genetic technologies, including gene therapy and human reproductive cloning will save a dying child, replace a dead child and reduce human suffering

I think we would all agree that we would want to save a dying child, or reduce human suffering. The question is whether new genetic technologies can really save a dying child and cure diseases. In Western societies where average life expectancy is high, people are terrified of the idea that they will die eventually, and particularly by the idea that this may be before a ripe old age. Some strive to find solutions. For example, scientists and doctors held out hopes for experimental gene therapy, but overall it has been largely unsuccessful, and sometimes quite dangerous. In 1999 the untimely death of a young man, 18 years of age, who underwent gene therapy in the US raised many concerns about the process. His father, who had originally agreed to this treatment, questioned its experimental nature after his son died. In 2002 gene therapy trials in both the US and France have been halted after a child undergoing treatment developed a leukaemia-like disease (Lemonick 2003). These and other examples have forced a critical re-examination of the health risks of gene therapy.

Marcy Darnovsky, a staff member of the Center for Genetics and Society located in Oakland, California, has told the story of how a female bio-ethicist, testifying as an expert witness at a California Advisory Committee on Human Cloning, argued that one reason reproductive cloning should be allowed is to replace the loss of a child. What an insult to human dignity – as though a child who dies can so easily be replaced! Among some grieving parents there is a misperception that a cloned child will be the exact replica of a child that died. An irony of human cloning, if it happens, is that it may finally disprove biological determinist theories! It will become clear that a clone, while s/he may look alike, will never be the exact replica of the person because of environmental influences and cultural experiences (Diane Beeson, Professor of Sociology at California State University, Hayward, US, personal communication, 1999).

Since each child is unique and can never be replaced, this sets up a dangerous precedent. George Annas, a biomedical ethicist and lawyer, has said, 'perhaps [the] most compelling [reason to clone a human] is cloning a dying child if this is what grieving parents want. But this should not be permitted. Not only does this encourage the parents to produce a child in the image of another, it also encourages us all to view children as interchangeable commodities. The death of a child thus need no longer be a singular human tragedy, but rather an opportunity to try to duplicate the no longer priceless deceased child.' (Annas 1998, 12). And yet the clone claimed to have been produced by Clonaid, was said to have been cloned from a ten-month-old deceased baby girl (*The New York Times Magazine*, Feb 4 2001).

6 Human genetic manipulation will not lead to the commodification of and geneticisation of children

We have already witnessed ways in which children have become commodities in the twenty-first century. For example, in 2001, twin babies were sold on the Internet to the infertile couple who bid the highest. Genetic manipulation is likely to result in the further commodification of children because people will begin having what Marcy Darnovsky and others refer to as 'designer babies'. Advocates of human reproductive cloning tell us that parents will be able to design a 'superior' child through the selection of personality traits, physical attributes, sex, and intellectual and moral qualities.

However, the consequences of selecting specific characteristics in a child may lead to devastating consequences including psychological backlash of anger, stigma, and discrimination against any child, and especially one who cannot or does not live up to expectations. Women making the decisions will also face incredible pressures, moral decision-making, and potential backlash if babies do not work out as planned. In addition, some in the disability community argue against any form of pre-implantation diagnosis, because of the potential further stigmatisation of disabled people in our society (Wolbring 2000). The movie, *Gattaca* (1997), vividly illustrates societal impacts when one attempts to control a baby's destiny from birth. There is an incorrect assumption that diseases, personalities, and characteristics are all genetically predetermined. In 1999 a *New York Times* magazine article predicted a future scenario called 'The Genetic Report Card' in which a baby's first official check-up would be in the petri dish while s/he is an eight-cell embryo (*The New York Times Magazine*, 1999).

7 Human reproductive cloning cures the 'incurably' infertile and offers a last chance for a genetic connection

Professionals, such as lawyers and in-vitro fertilisation (IVF) doctors, make this argument professing to speak on behalf of infertile couples. Ironically, one of the rationalisations for human reproductive cloning is the low success rate of IVF. While testifying at the California Advisory Committee on Human Cloning, one well-known IVF doctor relied on the same statistics used to convince infertile couples of IVF's success, to make his argument that IVF's low success rates justified the need for human reproductive cloning. Yet, IVF is currently one of the steps in the human reproductive cloning process.

Among some women, especially infertile women and lesbians, human reproductive cloning may be a potentially divisive issue. In the case of infertile couples, even within RESOLVE, a national organisation for infertile couples, women are divided about whether or not to support human reproductive cloning. In the rare case of an infertile couple in which neither person produces gametes (or a reproductive cell that can unite with another similar one to form the cell that develops into a new individual), human reproductive cloning would allow for a genetic connection that no other reproductive technology could offer. Nevertheless, many feel this is dangerous threshold to cross to help a few (Hayes 1999).

Generally speaking, lesbians have relied on alternative technologies, and embraced many new reproductive technologies as a form of resistance to heterosexual nuclear families and as an opportunity for motherhood. Human reproductive cloning offers lesbian couples, in a society that is obsessed with biological connections and often uses this as a marker in legal custody battles, the rare opportunity to be genetically linked to both women. Egg donation cannot accomplish this. (With egg donation, a lesbian couple may choose one woman to supply the egg and the other woman to carry the pregnancy to term and/or breastfeed). To date, sperm banks, especially those serving mainly lesbians, have not taken a formal position for or against these new technologies.

Professionals who support reproductive cloning would like people to believe that if anyone is against human reproductive cloning, then we are against infertile couples. An anti-reproductive cloning position is *not* unsympathetic to the pain of infertility, or to women and men experiencing infertility in their lives. Infertility is a painful life experience, but even within the infertility community, members are divided about their support or lack of support for human reproductive cloning. In considering infertility, there are several important points to be made. Firstly, new reproductive technologies never 'cure' infertility but rather, they only offer temporary solutions to infertility or

treatment, which may or may not result in a live birth. Anyone who has faced infertility problems and later had a child, through birth or adoption, will tell you that the infertility experience is still a part of her/his identity. Secondly, there is no indication to believe that new technologies such as human reproductive cloning will have any better 'success' rates ('success' being measured by the live birth of a healthy child) than IVF, GIFT (Gamete Intra-Fallopian Transfer) or GIUT (Gamete Intrauterine Transfer). Thirdly, while I whole-heartedly support low-risk research efforts to help infertile women, men, and couples, I also endorse preventive efforts. The majority of causes of infertility are preventable including occupational health hazards, environmental toxins, drug-induced infertility like DES,[8] sexually transmitted diseases, accidents, and rare cases of complications following childbirth or abortion.

8 Human genetic technologies will lead to new ways to rid society of all unwanted and unplanned pregnancies

Martine Rothblatt has written a book proposing 'inocuseed', a technique for banking all men's semen as a way to end teenage pregnancies (Rothblatt 1997). In her vision, each male will undergo a vasectomy at puberty and their sperm will be stored in a bank and reproduction will be controlled with no unwanted pregnancies. Certainly, this idea which relies on new technologies seems an extreme measure to prevent unwanted pregnancies. What has happened to the promotion of condoms or other contraceptive methods to prevent unwanted pregnancies?

9 Women who are anti-human reproductive cloning are anti-procreative liberty and anti-science and in a democratic society, that is unacceptable

In a recent book, *Genes, Women and Equality*, Mary Briody Mahowald, a philosopher, has outlined two feminist positions (Mahowald 2000). Firstly, the feminist libertarian position, which emphasises women's right to pursue individual liberty and reproductive freedom. A majority of feminist libertarians would argue that women should have access to such genetic technologies, if and when they become available, and be free to choose between them. The problem with this approach is that it fails to consider social inequalities among and between women based on race, class, ethnicity, disability, and sexual orientation. Not every woman will have equal access to these technologies, and nor will there always be autonomy to make a decision. For example, a libertarian feminist position fails to consider what happens if a heterosexual couple disagrees on these technologies; who makes the final decision?

The second position Mahowald outlines is the feminist egalitarian position, which operates from a social justice framework (Mahowald 2000). It considers the fact that a woman's autonomy is contextually located and social location – class, disability, race, ethnicity, gender – influences our ability to make decisions and have access to technologies. Thus, feminist egalitarians are not only interested in women's access to a new technology, but also how women's social location impacts the use or misuse of that technology. If a new technology increases inequality, women need to pay attention to this. We, as a society, need to make the benefits and burdens associated with genetics more equal for both men and women. Genetics is neither gender neutral nor colour-blind. Even if all women had access to these technologies, we still might not want them. A feminist egalitarian might support some gene technologies, and still reject others, if and only if, they were both equally available and women had equality within the broader social context.

10. Women who are anti-human reproductive cloning are also anti-abortion.

This misconception has far-reaching implications for women and women's groups. The human genome project potentially makes for interesting political alliances between groups that have usually been oppositional including the religious right and the democratic progressives. For example, both the religious right led by the Vatican and the democratic progressive movement are against human reproductive cloning. But the Vatican does not distinguish between reproductive cloning and non-reproductive cloning (or stem cell research). It is opposed to stem cell research on the grounds that such research, although not necessarily, may involve embryos or aborted foetuses.

Many women and women's organisations support stem cell research, but are opposed to human reproductive cloning. Furthermore, they do not want to be aligned with the Vatican's anti-abortion position. Rather, they prefer to collaborate with like-minded people who support a women's right, if necessary, to have a safe and legal abortion. The challenge for women and women's groups is how to work with other groups, on a policy that is anti-human reproductive cloning, but which is clearly not anti-abortion rights. (I am deliberately refraining from using the word 'choice', since professionals who support human reproductive cloning use this word to mean reproductive freedom.)

There is another interesting twist. I believe that scientists and doctors in support of human reproductive cloning inadvertently feed into anti-abortion politics, by further delineating the pregnant woman and foetus as separate and opposing entities, as in cases of pregnancy and drug abuse, forced Caesareans, and with the use of ultrasound screening during pregnancy. This is ironic, because human reproductive cloning may actually further the need for safe and legal abortions at a historical juncture when this legal right is being threatened. If human reproductive cloning occurs, we may be performing more late-term abortions than we have had to do in the past. Brigitte Boisselier, a French chemist who is the 'scientific director' of Clonaid, the Raelians cloning venture, has said, 'We want a healthy baby.' All of the 50 young females eagerly volunteering to serve as egg donors and surrogate mothers were prepared to undergo abortions if defects were revealed by ultrasound or amniocentesis. If one pregnancy failed, another surrogate would automatically step into line; there would be no need to wait another month, as you would if you were dependent on the cycles of one woman (*The New York Times Magazine*, 4 February 2001). While scientists claim that pre-implantation diagnosis can detect poor quality embryos and grade embryos while still in petri dishes, we know this is not always possible. Furthermore, not all 'mutations/defects' are genetic, and thus identifiable at an early stage. In fact, evidence from research conducted on sheep suggests that high rates of foetal anomalies were discovered in late term pregnancy or soon after birth. Potentially, if human reproductive cloning is allowed this could have devastating consequences for women.

Conclusion

Both the short- and long-term consequences of these new human genetic manipulations, especially human reproductive cloning, must be seriously considered for diverse women. Some have argued that these new technologies offer potential for resistance and building new family forms. Others have argued these technologies can help infertile couples with no gametes. While this may be the case for a few, I am concerned that many more women will be harmed than helped. Overall, women – not men – will bear the major physical, psychological, social,

moral, legal, political, and economic burdens of these genetic manipulations. Finally and most importantly, human reproductive cloning and germ line alteration, whatever their risks, are unprecedented and irreversible.

The discussion in this article about what is happening to women in the US has far-reaching implications for women in a global context, where women still face all kinds of social, political, and economic injustices. I seriously doubt that human reproductive cloning would tip the scale towards balancing these inequities, including poverty, violence, stigmatisation, unemployment and unequal wages and exploitation, for women in a global context.

Lisa Handwerker, Ph.D., M.P.H., is a medical anthropologist, international health consultant and recently, a conflict mediator. For over 20 years, she has worked on women's health issues as a teacher, activist, researcher, writer, and policy maker. Postal address: UC Berkeley, Institute for the Study of Social Change, c/o 2333 Prospect Street, Berkeley, CA 94704 USA.
lisahand@juno.com

Notes

1 A version of this paper was first presented as a talk on 3 February 2001 at a meeting in San Francisco, California US, on 'human genetic manipulation and its implications for women and women's organisations' co-sponsored by The Exploratory Initiative on the New Human Genetic Technologies and the Boston Women's Health Book Collective (BWHBC). This talk was later turned into an article and posted at www.ourbodiesourselves.org. A shortened version of this paper was presented at the AWID conference on 4 October 2002. A version of this article will also appear in *Medical Anthropology Quarterly*, special edition in honour of Professor Joan Ablon, my mentor from the joint

Berkeley–UC San Francisco Medical Anthropology Program.

2   The Raelians are a religious sect based in Canada, who believe that humans are clones of extraterrestrial scientists and that human cloning is the key to eternal life.

3   Human reproductive cloning is asexual reproduction. An egg is removed from a woman's body. The nucleus is removed from that egg which, after it has been stripped of its genetic materials, is called an ovacyte. The regular body cells (skin, hair etc.) or undifferentiated stem cells of another individual (man or woman) are inserted into the ovacyte. (Stem cells are undifferentiated cells that can later develop into other body parts. Stem cell research is at its earliest stages, and stem cells of different origins, including embryos and fetuses, are being explored for research purposes.) A clone does not have a genetic mother or father, as in sexual reproduction when an embryo gets half its genes from the woman's egg and half from the man's sperm. It has a 'nuclear donor' and also gains some genetic material from the original egg.

4   Council for Responsible Genetics (CRG), located in Cambridge, Massachusetts, has been a forerunner of important policy statements on genetics and social responsibility.

5   Founded in 1975, The National Women's Health Network's mission is to advocate for national policies that protect and promote all women's health and to provide evidence-based, independent information to empower women to make fully informed decisions (www.womenshealthnetwork.org).

6   Rich Hayes first brought these concerns to my attention at a groundbreaking meeting on human cloning in early 2000. Currently, he is the director of the Center for Genetics and Society.

7   Pre-implantation diagnosis or genetic testing is an experimental method designed to identify genetic defects or chromosome abnormalities at two different stages: either in an ovum (unfertilised egg) before fertilisation or in an embryo before fertilisation. Both Marsha Saxton, a researcher at the World Institute on Disability (WID) in Oakland, California and Debra Kaplan have written extensively on this subject. Also, please see publications by Gregor Wolbring including *Science and the Disadvantaged* published by the Edmonds Institute in Canada, 2000.

8   Diethylstilbestrol, a powerful synthetic estrogen, was a drug prescribed to an estimated 4.8 million women in the US between 1938 and 1971, in the mistaken belief that it would prevent miscarriage. Instead, it was found to be linked to many reproductive health injuries, including increased rates of vaginal cancer, and infertility in the children born to those women.

References

Annas, G. (1998) *Some Choice: Law, Medicine and the Market*, New York: Oxford University Press

Handwerker (1994) 'Medical risk: implicating poor pregnant women', in *Social Science and Medicine*, 38(5): 665–75

Hayes, R. (1999) Appendix D in *Reproductive Human Cloning: Key Arguments*. For this and other published and unpublished publications, please refer to the Center for Genetics and Society, 436 14th Street, Suite 1302, Oakland, California, US, 94612. The website address is: www.genetics-and-society.org and e-mail is: info@genetics-and-society.org

Hubbard, R., and E. Wald, (1997) *Exploding the Gene Myth*, Boston: Beacon Press

Lemonick, Michael D. 'The DNA revolution: a twist of fate', in *Time: A Special Report*, 17 February 2003 49–58

Mahowald, M.B. (2000) *Genes, Women and Equality*, New York: Oxford University Press

Roberts, E. D. (2001a) 'Race and the New Reproduction' *GeneWatch* 14(1)

Roberts, E. D. (2001b) Interview conducted on 'Cloning Babies: It Is Only a Matter of Time', ABC World News, February 13

Rothblatt, M. (1997) *Unzipped Genes: Taking Charge of Baby-making in the New Millennium*, Philadelphia: Temple University Press

Turkiel, J. (1998) *Beyond Second Opinions: Making Choices about Fertility Treatment*, Berkeley: UC Press.

The Boston Women's Health Book Collective (1998) *Our Bodies, Ourselves: For the New Century*, New York: Touchstone

Wolbring, G. (2000) *Science and the Disadvantaged*, Canada: Edmonds Institute

Trafficking and women's human rights in a globalised world

An interview by Pamela Shifman

According to the United Nations, the global industry of human trafficking generates an estimated 5–7 billion dollars annually, with at least 700,000 victims every year.[1] By all accounts, trafficking in human beings is increasing at staggering rates. Increased economic inequality, with its discriminatory impact on girls and women, ensures a supply of desperately poor women and girls willing to do anything to survive. Within continents and across oceans, women and children are bought and sold to serve the demands for exploitative sex or cheap labour. In this interview, Pamela Shifman talks to four women involved in challenging the international traffic in women which is a feature of globalised poverty and unemployment.

Local sex industries have gone global: expanding rapidly, and filled with girls and women from the global South and newly independent states of eastern Europe. Traffickers and pimps no longer need rely on the traditional routes into sex work, as women and girls can now be sold on the Internet. Globalisation has, in short, encouraged new routes and new methods to exploit women and children for profit. Ethiopian women are trafficked for domestic work to Lebanon; Nepali girls are trafficked to the brothels of Mumbai; and Russian women to the red light district of Amsterdam.

But globalisation has also allowed unprecedented collaboration between feminist activists in source countries, transit countries and countries of destination. In order to explore the links between trafficking and globalisation, I facilitated a discussion following the Association for Women in Development (AWID) Forum between four leading activists involved in the struggle against trafficking in women.

Ruchira Gupta (from India), Esohe Agheteste (from Nigeria and Italy), Aida Santos (from the Philippines) and Colette DeTroy (from Belgium) came together to explore the challenges that globalisation poses to end the trafficking of women and girls and the opportunities it opens for activists to fight it. Below is an edited version of that conversation.

Pamela:
What do you think the relationship is between trafficking and globalisation?

Colette:
Globalisation is mostly concerned with the globalisation of trade, of goods and services. All over the world, women, sexuality, and sexual services are considered as good trade for people who have money. So a big trade in human beings – mostly in women – has developed.

Aida:
Globalisation has a specific impact on developing countries, like the Philippines.

One of the key features of globalisation is the use of technology. In the Philippines and other Asian countries, the use of technological advances has been an avenue for a serious rise in trafficking of women and children. For example, a lot of the negotiations for 'mail order brides', [now also called Internet brides] are happening through Internet technology. So, while there may be some good features of globalisation (a debatable point of course) in terms of our experiences it does not serve our women and children well.

Esohe:

I see globalisation in a much broader way, as including not only the economic aspects, but also the cultural and the political aspects. With regard to most African countries, it's been in terms of acquisition of cultural, economic and political models, which have not been able to be transformed into something useful for the African people. And so you find a distorted transformation of these models in these countries. And this has led to a distorted view of the Western world.

And then, on the other side, in the Western world, commodities, services and also people from other countries are seen as something that the Western world has to acquire. And so the trafficking of women and children, and young persons, is seen within this context.

Ruchira:

The tools of globalisation are beneficial to traffickers. For instance, technology is helping them use the Internet to market girls all across the world, through all kinds of Internet sites which auction girls. It has made it easier for traffickers to operate their trafficking networks, keep in touch with each other, and find out the sites where girls can be sold cheaply, and it is easy for buyers and clients to log on to Internet portals to find out where to go. At the same time, it has made it more difficult for girls in the Third World to understand that they are going to be exploited in these ways. Because they might be in Delhi, and they can't comprehend that they would end up in New York through the Internet as virtual goods. So that is one part of globalisation which has been very advantageous to traffickers.

The other is that globalisation has changed the definition of choice itself. So, for people in the First World, or from richer countries, globalisation just means checking into a hotel room anywhere. For people from the Third World, or poor countries, globalisation could very well mean that there are certain rules imposed by the World Trade Organisation (WTO), or the World Bank which say that the public sector unit has to be closed down, because it's not making a profit. Many people in a household lose their jobs, and the girl in the family has to travel further to look for work. And, because it is not efficient or productive to be in the place where she is, she becomes vulnerable to traffickers.

Colette:

In addition, globalisation has resulted in free exchanges of goods and services, but there are strong obstacles to persons and therefore no easy entry to Western countries. The borders are simply closed, particularly to Western Europe. This provides a good way for traffickers to make money. They can 'help' people to enter a country, where there is no opening for people to enter.

Aida:

One aspect that is very problematic is the discourse within globalisation about a 'level playing field'. A lot of our migrants who eventually will be trafficked think that there is a possibility of a better life in the future. And so migration has been an avenue for bettering their lives. And then there is the consumer's attitude of 'I have to have this.' I look at globalisation and trafficking in terms of the abuse of the right to mobility; of the right to travel; of the right to better one's life; of the right to development.

Ruchira:

I want to add something to what Aida is saying, on the issue of sex tourism. Because everything becomes marketable, and everything becomes a commodity in the new world of globalisation, men can travel thousands of miles just to buy girls from poorer countries. And countries are actually promoting some of their cities as sex tourism sites.

Esohe:

There is a general tendency to black-mark globalisation in itself, as something negative. I personally don't think of globalisation, itself, as something negative. It's rather an abuse of globalisation. Right now, we have huge movements of goods and services, these highly facilitated communication systems that are spreading all over the world – but there are no checks and controls. And I believe this is where the problem starts.

As Aida just said, I think it's right, and proper that people should try to develop, to try to attain to a better life for themselves. And I'm afraid that if we give this negative idea of globalisation this will block that possibility. And that is overlooking what causes the negative aspects of globalisation, and just looking at the damage that its abuse is causing.

Pamela:

One example of the women's movement using globalisation toward a good end was the passage of the Transnational Crime Protocol on Trafficking in Women. Despite the efforts of powerful governments and NGOs who advocated for a very narrow definition of trafficking, which would not protect women or facilitate traffickers being punished, the international women's rights movement was very successful in organising for a broad and protective definition. This is just one example.

Ruchira:

One of the positive aspects I have found personally as an activist is that I can sometimes bypass the pressure of my own government, and link up with an activist in Europe, or in America, and get them to put pressure on the Indian government, to do more work on trafficking, or to create better laws to improve the lives of women.

Pamela:

I want to go back to something Ruchira said earlier about how globalisation has changed the nature of choice. Do you think the idea of free choice, particularly in terms of women who are trafficked into the sex industry, has been detrimental to the anti-trafficking movement?

Aida:

I have just finished a five-country research project with the Coalition against Trafficking in Women (CATW). I asked my respondents all over the Philippines about whether they chose to migrate. Many of them did know that there was a large potential for being trafficked into prostitution. They said, 'I chose to migrate despite the risk of being trafficked.'

And then I look at their vulnerabilities – the vulnerabilities of being poor, with low education, being enticed by the possibilities of greener pastures – being enticed by the possibilities beyond their little villages. Some of them said, 'Nobody put a gun to my head', but when I examine their actual lives, I saw that there were severe vulnerabilities that they face as women – poor women – in a Third World country. What was the real choice of these women, even if they knew they could be trafficked?

I don't think that women choose to be exploited. I think that they would choose to migrate despite the potential harm, because there are no other possibilities for them. In my country particularly, the women did not have a real choice. When you speak of choice as if it were about free will, in the way we know free will, in the context of human rights, then I pose big questions about this kind of discourse in relation to women migrants who are trafficked. I think it's a dangerous discourse for women who have no choice, really, in their lives.

Esohe:

There is also the issue of cultural colonialism, when television programmes create a certain image of the Western world. And then you compare it to the kind of life women live, in which there are very few possibilities. Every day, they can choose only whether to eat once or twice a day.

When somebody comes and offers you the possibility of leaving that misery, that poverty, to go to this wonderful world, I don't think the person has all the information necessary to make a real choice. And, from this point of view, I don't think we can call it choice, really. It's more of an imposition by somebody who has experience and complete information, and uses this to convince another person who does not have information. Most of these girls know, of course, that they may end up in prostitution, in very violent situations, but they say, 'Yes, I choose.'

I put this word 'choose' in quotation marks. In reality, there is no choice. It's like a blind person who is led into some place, and told: 'Look you're going into heaven', and taken into hell.

Collette:

This word 'choice' is coming from the new liberalism. In the neo-liberal economic model, everybody has a choice and is responsible for their success. That's what is presented. That's totally false, and ignores the difficulties, and the imbalances, both among and within countries, where not everybody has the same choices and the same chances. But it is presented like it is an individual choice. But I think this word 'choice' has to be analysed in the context of the economic model we are living in, and the consequences in the lives of millions of women.

Ruchira:

Choice also has to be seen in the context of time, of space, and also of economic models of development. For instance, in America, when I was living there I noticed that a lot of feminists used the pro-choice arguments for the pro-prostitution arguments. And they would say that a woman should have the right to control her body in any way she wants to. This is true with regard to abortion, of course. But then they say that she also has the right to sell her body for sex.

This is a superficial and fallacious argument, because a woman actually loses control over her body in prostitution. In rich countries they understand and manage globalisation differently from people in poor countries. When people do choose to be trafficked or get into prostitution, they're choosing it as a survival strategy for a very limited period of time, under tremendous pressure – economic pressure, pressure from the family, from children crying for food, husbands beating up wives, and no income in the village. And once they choose, the degree of choice exercised by a person in prostitution changes according to her stage in a cycle.

When a girl is about seven or nine years old, she always talks about the fact that she wants to go back home, and she's sick of being in the brothel, and she blames her trafficker as the biggest villain, and the first client who raped her repeatedly. After five years inside a brothel, there is a period of socialisation within the brothel, and this girl is allowed to keep half of what she earns, and she also becomes dependent on drugs and alcohol. She is forced to have a couple of babies by the brothel madam. And at that point, when you talk to her, she sees no way of going back home. She begins to suffer from the Stockholm syndrome, almost beginning to love her kidnapper, which is the brothel Madame. She is desensitised, she is dependent on drugs and alcohol, and at that point if you talk to her she will say, 'Yes, I choose to remain here' because she doesn't see a way of going back home.

Another five years down the road, when her earning capacity comes down, she is disease-ridden, she has two or three children, and then you talk to her about choice, and she says, 'I want to get out of here, I want to acquire some skills so that I can earn a living some other way. I want to keep my daughter from getting into prostitution.' So again the choice changes. And of course, in the last five years should she survive, she is completely disease-ridden, she is thrown out of the brothel, she is on the sidewalk, and she is just dying. And she has no pension scheme, no home to return to, no extended family structure, nothing to protect her daughters or sons from prostitution.

At that point, of course, she regrets that she was ever sold into prostitution, or trafficked into prostitution. So in a life span of 20 years, for about five years a girl may say that she chooses to be in prostitution. And that's true, but her choice is in a very limited context, where she sees no other way out. So choice does vary, from different parts of the world, in different times of life, and also just different economic circumstances.

Aida:
In the Philippines, there is a continuing erosion of what I would call national consciousness, a sense of national identity. For example, one form of trafficking is trafficking of women to become brides. When I talked to a number of mail order brides, they said it is better to marry a foreigner. To marry a Filipino is downgrading their potential opportunities. A lot of the women, not just involved in prostitution locally, but women who have graduated from universities and colleges, have articulated this. And so there is a sense of a loss of pride in being a Filipina.

The Philippines is a centre for mail order brides. Thousands of women marry foreigners, and in the research that I did, not one of my respondents talked about love.

They talk about economic opportunities for a better life, of being able to help their families.

So, again, when I look at the data and the actual interviews with the women, I see a problem with this discourse of choice. It seems to me the choice is a false notion, when you have an environment where there is a real lack of many things.

Esohe:
I was just thinking about ways that globalisation itself could be used to change some of these aspects. For instance, with regard to trafficking, what is being done on an international level, using pressure on an international level to change internal policies on women, to give more respect to the rights of women – I think this is also an aspect of globalisation.

And there are various other aspects, especially economic aspects. You see cases where money is being given to corrupt leaders in developing countries, when they know that money is not being spent to develop the countries. And they keep doing it. This is something that, for instance, happened for more than 30 years with the European Union which gave money to develop the ACP (Africa, Caribbean and Pacific) countries. The European Union kept pouring in money, even knowing that most of this money didn't go to those projects it was supposed to go to. And so, 30 years later, you still find that the countries are even more behind than before. We need a change of attitude on a political level. Because as long as their interests are being protected, as long as profits are being obtained with the rules on the market being manipulated whenever it's convenient, then the situation is going to remain like that.

Collette:
I think Esohe's is a very good example. If the European Union had given the same money to women, there would be quite different development. Women know that

it's more important to develop basic needs and to have money for education or health than to develop monoculture and industry.

Given the way that women could work to make a globalisation which has different values and is not just about the market economy, it is important to support the women's movement. I agree with Esohe that it's a struggle between those who have power and those who don't have power. And even if all women are not poor, women still don't have power, although they are the majority. So we need to unite and to exchange and to develop capacity to limit globalisation or exert pressure for globalisation which is based on different things.

Pamela:
I want to move in a different direction and ask you all to talk about the demand for sexual services that comes from men in rich countries, or among richer men, in poor countries and the link to globalisation.

Aida:
We need to look at the issue of the middle-man. For a long time, we have always looked at the women and the children, and sometimes the men, in prostitution. We've got to turn the table around and ask the question, why is there so much demand for sexual services? I think governments must begin to look at the way that they are not only promoting patriarchal values, and patriarchal socialisation processes, but how the commodification of sex and sexuality has been part and parcel of the negative side of globalisation.

We need to go back to a universality of rights. No one should be selling her body just to be able to eat a meal a day. It's beyond human dignity. One of the issues that can be tackled internationally, in terms of reinventing globalisation from a feminist perspective, is addressing the issue of male demand and asking the hard questions. We all know that international peacekeeping forces have been involved in buying sex.

Why do we accept this? Why is this not being challenged systematically?

Esohe:
There is this myth that men will be men. And so they have their needs, which must be satisfied and so on, and so forth. This is a myth that has to be destroyed. It all comes down to what men see as culturally and socially acceptable. I don't believe that men cannot do without paid sexual services any more than I believe it's 'the women who choose'. These are ideas that have been bastardised to increase trafficking and the commercialisation of women's bodies. These aspects have to be addressed.

Collette:
Yes, I think we have to deconstruct the myth, but also this analysis. The presentation of prostitution as linked to sexuality, is so wrong. Male sexuality is also associated with power. It's the same with rape. It doesn't have anything to do with sexuality, or desire. It's just power. Prostitution and rape show that men control women. A man can pay for sex and use her as an object. I think it's really important to deconstruct this myth, in this framework of power relationships between a man, who could purchase his wife or another woman or a child. Equality between women and men cannot include the possession of a body.

Pamela:
Sweden has been groundbreaking in this regard. Colette, can you talk about the Swedish law?

Collette:
For the first time in the world, in Sweden, legislation has been enacted under which it is forbidden to buy sexual services. It is punishable. It's only the man, the buyer, who is responsible. Prostitution is seen as violence against women, violence against a human being. It is part of broad legislation on violence.

The legislation has been in effect for two years. The pro-prostitution lobby says it doesn't work. That's the main argument. They never say that the legislation against torture does not work since there is still torture in the world. They just say that the Swedish legislation doesn't work. This is actually not true, but it's also important in itself as a symbol – I believe that legislation has a very strong symbolic power. European women are trying to lobby for this kind of legislation in different countries.

It is important that we address the myth that Esohe spoke about earlier. The myth of men's sexuality – that they need to go to prostitutes – we need to challenge that in the context of the legal framework of human rights. In this sense, we are not helped by the pro-prostitution lobby, who speak about choice. Men want to hear about the choice of prostitutes. They don't want to hear that the woman doesn't have a choice, and does not want to be there, and is in a vulnerable position. They don't want to know that.

Ruchira:
Sexuality is, of course, rooted in concepts of power and violence. And men are constantly trying to reinforce their sexual beings by reinforcing their sense of power, or by being violent. And this is something that they're conditioned to believe in, from the time that they're boys, as individuals, as members of a family, as members of a community, and as part of the state. And so, they sometimes don't even know any other way of expressing their sexuality. And they connect all these three things in their head: power, violence, sex.

So, while women are taught that there is an appropriate time and place to have sex, men are not. And it's almost accepted at every level of society, that men have to have sex when and how they want to. So if they don't have a woman around, and they don't have the social skills to actually build a relationship with a woman, they go looking for prostitutes.

Again and again, when I try to do my work on trafficking and prostitution, I am confronted with the statement that prostitution is the oldest profession in the world.

Pamela:
I like to say it's the oldest oppression.

Esohe:
The myth of prostitution being the oldest profession in the world has to be deconstructed. It comes to my mind, for example, that murder has always existed and is heavily punished. I don't think there's any country in the world that accepts it as part of the social order. And it continues to happen, but nobody resigns him or herself to it and says 'you know, human beings will always be human beings, and so there is nothing we can do about that.'

Aida:
We must begin to pose the question about the harms of prostitution. For it to be seen as a choice, when there is inherent violence in it and inherent human rights violations in it, is something that we must resist.

Pamela:
Does anyone have final comments about re-inventing globalisation in the context of trafficking?

Aida:
We need to seriously address – at the practical as well as strategic level – the issue of reinventing globalisation, vis-à-vis sexual exploitation, migration, and mobility. We need to push governments to look seriously at the strategic impact of trafficking and sexual exploitation in terms of its cost: the loss of productivity of nations and individuals.

Esohe:
I very much support the last statement, and I would also like to add that there is a practical need to create strategies and programmes based on this analysis. And then there's also the issue of beginning to work on deconstructing myths that tend to create space for continued exploitation of

women, and the destruction of women's rights.

Collette:

We will continue this struggle between the more vulnerable and the more powerful. We have to unite and see the powerful complementarities between us, and the power of our being together. And we have to lobby and to exert pressure on the institutions, and the places of power.

Esohe Aghatise is the Executive Director of Associazione Iroko Onlus, based in Turin, Italy. She is a lawyer and ethno-cultural mediator by profession and has been an activist working against the international trafficking of women and children for prostitution for the past ten years. Address: Via Ceva, 40 10144 Turin, ITALY. esoheaghatise@libero.it

Colette De Troy is the co-ordinator of the European Women's Lobby (EWL) Policy Action Centre on Violence against Women. Address: 18, rue Hydraulique, B-1210 Bruxelles. centre-violence@womenlobby.org www.womenlobby.org

Ruchira Gupta is Trafficking Expert for Development Alternatives Incorporate. She is also the Executive Director of Apne Aap Women Worldwide, a not-for-profit organisation set up in Bombay and Kolkata's red-light area to end sex-trafficking. Address: c/o 364 8th Street, Brooklyn, NY 11215, USA.

Aida Santos is a board member of the coalition against trafficking in women for the Asia Pacific region and works as a gender and development officer with WEDPRO (The Women's Education, Development and Productivity and Research Advocacy Organization), and other institutions. Address: Building 15, Unit 41, BL Condominium, Road 3, Pag-Asa, Quezon City 1105, Philippines. afs@pacific.net.ph

Pamela Shifman is Project Officer at UNICEF on sexual exploitation and abuse in humanitarian crises. Address: 364 8th street, Brooklyn NY 11215, USA. pshifman@yahoo.com

Note

1 United Nations figure, quoted in Arlacchi (2000)

Reference

Arlacchi, P. (2000) 'Against all the godfathers: the revolt of the decent people' in 'The World Against Crime', Special Issue of *Giornale di Sicilia*, 7

Part IV
Building a global voice to protect women's rights

The women's movement in the era of globalisation:
does it face extinction?

Andrea Medina Rosas and Shamillah Wilson

This article is based on an inter-generational dialogue between younger and older women regarding the future direction of the women's movement. Like other social movements, the women's movement is currently experiencing tensions as feminists of different ages negotiate their place within it. In this article, we will highlight some of the issues raised in this session, and relate them to our personal experiences and points of view, as young feminists.

The contributions and gains made by the women's movement[1] over the past 20 or 30 years have assisted in creating a very different world. Currently, there are many new challenges for the movement. One is the issue of ensuring that commitments to women's rights are turned into reality for every woman, and another comes from the new global political situation, which threatens to unleash a new World War. But there is another key challenge, which comes from inside the movement itself. This challenge – which is felt in other social movements too – is how to deal with inter-generational tensions within the movement. Young women, either already in the movement or considering entering it, are asking questions about the movement, including where it is headed. We think this creates several distinct tensions and experiences that have not been sufficiently discussed and addressed.

At the AWID Forum, an attempt to develop the dialogue among young women and older women in the women's movement took the form of an inter-generational panel. The structure of the engagement was an open and honest exchange among participants about the tensions that seem to the participants to exist between the generations of women in the movement. We then moved on to discuss the challenges and strategies for inter-generational activism. When we came to distil this article from the discussions we had had, we decided to focus it around three main questions raised most often by the panel. These questions are, first, 'Is the women's movement "missing in action"?', second, 'What are some of the tensions between different generations of women in the movement?', and third, 'What strategies can we use for inter-generational organising?' The article aims to reflect on all these questions and put forward some suggestions for action.

Is the women's movement 'missing in action'?

The question 'Is the women's movement "missing in action"?', as well as the title of the panel 'Is the women's movement on the way to extinction?', are both important, and represented radical starting points for the discussion. In reflecting on these questions, some of the women at the workshop felt, that in fact, the movement is in some state of paralysis. Evidence for this includes stronger right-wing and fundamentalist groups who obstruct our actions and goals; a feeling of inability to draw more people into the movement; and a sense that the women's movement has entered a period of relative inaction in comparison to the success-ful mass mobilisations of feminists that took place around the world in the 1990s.

We feel that before anyone pronounces a final verdict on the current state of the women's movement, it is very important that we take a look at the diversity that can currently be found in the global women's movement, and consider the possibilities open to us to organise as a women's move-ment. The issue of diversity kept emerging throughout the panel at AWID. The agenda of women within the movement seems to widen every day. Women's experience of inequality does not only depend on gender, but also on other factors including their age, race, and culture, their political, economic and social situation, their health, their erotic preferences, their education and experience, and so on. The differences between life in different contexts, and the inequalities between regions and countries, affect the way in which we engage with issues. The state of the women's movement differs in every place, according to history and current conditions. Even in the same country, we can find radical differences in women's situation from one region to another, because of differences in access to information, services, the condition of civil and political rights, and the presence or absence of war.

Sometimes we hear criticism about the emphasis currently being given to diversity within the women's movement. One particular criticism is that in focusing on only one aspect of the multiple agenda (for example, the rights of young women), we risk forgetting about the global agenda, and betraying the women's movement. We think it is important to state explicitly that all the context-specific issues we bring up are informed by the same feminist vision, and contribute to the global feminist agenda. We feel that through focusing on specific issues affecting us as women in particular contexts, we strengthen our capacity and ability to challenge existing relations of power in our situations. This focus also strengthens our ability to contribute meaningfully to the global women's movement. It is important that we do not lose sight of this, given the new challenges that women are facing in a globalised world. In the end, it is most important to be explicit that all these specific issues have the same feminist vision, and contribute to the global feminist agenda.

Nowadays, there are more women who identify themselves as feminist or have a commitment to equality and women's rights than ever before, across all generations.

This presents us with a choice: we can either develop a strong global movement which supports women in their diversity, and is able to act, influence and advance even further; or we can forfeit a unique opportunity through our own short-sightedness.

As a first step, we think it is important for all women within the movement to acknowledge that the movement *is* advancing, in many very different ways because of the diversity of women within it. In the end, the critical issue is to analyse and evaluate the advances, rather than dismissing them if they are not in line with our own vision of feminism. We think that women within the movement sometimes try to find some signs of the movement advancing, but only look for signs that it is advancing in the way that we want it to. If they are not there, we conclude that the movement is not advancing at all. We have not necessarily looked more widely and asked others how they see the progress of the movement, in awareness that we are all inventing and reinventing ways to live as feminists.

The discussion at the AWID workshop focused on questions such as: 'How can I use feminism?'; 'What are the final or principal goals of feminism?'; and 'Who is feminist?' During the discussion we realised firstly that there are still strong prejudices against feminism, what it is and what it has been doing. These prejudices are often related to specific intentions to disqualify feminism and create confusion around it. Secondly, inside the movement there are notions about people's loyalties, and the essential identity of a feminist. Discussions need to be had about these notions. At present, they make access to the movement more difficult. This affects the nature and potential of activism, by limiting different, creative approaches to achieve our goals. It is important to keep in mind that the feminist approach is about respecting non-lineal processes, which are not restricted in terms of time or space. It is also important to remember that we are all syncretic women – that is, we are mixing traditional and modern ways of being women, and living out innovative ways of being. We are moving all the time, sometimes in a more contradictory way than at other times. As a global women's movement, our challenge in trying to move is to recognise that we are moving to the same beat, even if it is not at the same pace.

Evidence of this is the AWID Forum itself. It attracted more than one thousand women from all over the world, who wished to meet each other and share their actions, thoughts and concrete experiences with other women. This sharing was very intense work, While it did not result in – and was not intended to result in – any 'universal truths', it did enable us to challenge ourselves and each other to create global evaluations and strategies. These need to be based on acknowledgement of the diversity and complexity of the movement, and its current challenges.

What are some of the intergenerational tensions?

Generalising about older and younger women

Acknowledging that age is one aspect of diversity is useful for the women's movement; thinking of women of all ages as the same hinders our ability to move forward, in a number of ways. In this section, we are going to describe several of the main tensions that young and old women talked about during an inter-generational meeting. Of course, not all women of a particular generation think the same way, but as the panel discussion aimed to be a space in which all participants could focus on the tensions which divide us in order to ensure we could move forward, we will deal with these issues in a general way.

One of the first contributions from women in their forties and older was how uncomfortable they feel with the labelling of 'older' and 'younger' women. Many felt that old is considered less fashionable, as in beauty and fashion. These concerns were actually echoed by younger women who said that in meetings with older feminists they have doubts about how to refer to them. Although talking about younger persons generally does not present a problem, the term 'older' appears to be offensive, and most of the time is met by a range of comments, including: 'But I'm still young!' or, 'But I'm still young at heart!' We agreed at the panel that it is therefore important to keep in mind that all of these words represent vital cycles, and are not used to denigrate or devalue anyone.

We all need to be aware that there are stereotypes or prejudices which are based on an idea of youth and older age as dichotomous, so some qualities are attributed to one and excluded from the other. Generalising about people according to their age can have the effect of causing discomfort, without gaining anything. For example, older people are generally considered more experienced, knowing and wise, in relation to their longer life experience. However, this generalisation has resulted in some inter-generational tensions in the movement, since it leads to assumptions that young women don't have the experience and ability to make decisions or be leaders.

So, at present the existing tensions around age have some positive and negative aspects for each of the generations. In future, we need to keep the positive aspects, while rejecting what is negative. Firstly, we need to acknowledge that words give meaning which in turn leads to action. They are not politically neutral. It would be good to find a word which could be used instead of 'older', to avoid the negative connotations of that word. If we only talk of 'older' and 'younger' feminists, we forget that there are not just two generations. Individual women may not consider themselves as fitting into either of these categories.

Past struggles are unappreciated

Another big issue, which includes many variables, is the feeling that the struggles and achievements of older women are not appreciated by young women. Some veterans of the movement feel that younger women do not know much about the history and creation of feminism. As 'proof' of this they say younger women are less willing to call themselves feminists, and that there is no sharing of feminist values.

Creating a bridge between our own lives and past feminist action is a challenge for many young women. As we were born into an era in which the gains made by the earlier generation are a reality, if no one talks to us about the struggle and history of achieving those rights, we take them for granted and assume that they were always there. It is true that to approach feminism is still a matter of a personal desire, a decision to research, to read, to search. But women's history and feminism are not yet included in school curricula. Instead, as mentioned earlier, the term 'feminism' is often accompanied by ignorance, confusion and prejudice. Some young women stumble across feminism in their own search on their personal journey of making sense of the world we live in. Others are introduced to feminism by their own mothers, or through a teacher at school, a conference at university or a course of study they undertake. But although university-level courses on women, feminism and gender at university level are very important advances, these are not enough, and they are constantly under threat.

Should young women adopt the label of 'feminist'? We feel it is important to adopt the identity of 'feminists', in recognition of our history, and the fact that the struggle ahead is a political one. But our *diversity* as a movement should allow us to look for people with similar views for the purposes of building alliances, instead of resorting to the usual tendency of questioning the identity of a 'feminist' and thus creating points of difference and a means to cause divisions. Our discussion about these issues at AWID related the question to the ignorance and prejudices we have talked about. It does us harm to close our doors to collaborations with people who perhaps do not use our words or references, but are close enough to us in terms of feminist ideals.

Finally, it is important for young and older women to acknowledge that 'education' in feminism is also necessary for older women. Sometimes the impression is given that all the women in the older generation were supportive and part of the feminist movement, and that the gap appears only in later generations. But there are older women who are only now discovering or reconsidering feminism. Some of them are doing this because of young women close to them, who have integrated feminist activism into their daily lives. Others are doing it because they are working in institutions which require them to integrate a gender perspective or analysis into their work.

The movement is a 'reserved club'

One participant at the workshop recounted that she felt that the movement was like a reserved club to which she could not get access, even though she was keen to become part of it. The sensation of feeling like an intruder, and hearing criticisms about other people who are 'not feminist enough', has prompted us and others like us to run away many times. We feel that we might not measure up to the movement.

One challenge for all of us is to formulate and spread feminism in a positive way. In order to do this, it is important that the advances that we make as younger women, in our own lives, as well as the benefits of earlier feminist action, are seen as part of the history of the feminist movement. If this were the case, we would recover a sense of politics in our actions and lives. It is also important to acknowledge that there are different ways of being feminist. The act of criticising this different way of being or doing is a destructive one, which is contradictory to the objective of creating a movement of diverse energies and visions. Focusing on the issues and challenges that we face as young women does not mean that we do not care about the achievements of the last generation. Instead of criticising, everyone in the women's movement should be engaging with everyone else, building our individual and collective capacity to achieve change.

Perceptions about the way young women should work

There seems to be a perception that young women's contribution should continue what has already been started, but only in a prescribed way. But in fact young feminists are taking what has already been done or initiated, and continuing feminist action, even if it is not in the way that some older women would like. We are doing it in the way we understand it, with our possibilities and resources, and often we are doing it with older women. For example, in many countries now it is not so easy to organise mass marches of thousands of people, but in those places where it is possible and necessary, the young women are there, at the forefront. We are writing our songs, playing our guitars, painting our murals, and we are creating in very different ways of expression the same feminist horizons: some times out in the streets, at the congress, other times writing and studying, and at other times living and testing our freedom, travelling, or simply through the way we live our lives to the full.

As young women, our desire is not to take anyone's place. 'Older' women occupy some important spaces in the movement, and we have no intention of shutting them off. We should focus on the challenge of how to draw more women of all ages into the movement and to generate relations based in sisterhood, rather than on parent and child relationships. Sisterhood means the encounter of different and equal women characterised by friendship, who meet to accomplish objectives and in recognition of feminist principles. It also means listening to others, and being listened to, and taking criticism with respect, without remarking on the age differences, or the generation gap. Older women often behave as controlling mothers, seeing us as daughters, in need of guidance.

Sisterhood would mean older women introducing us to meetings and conferences where we can meet the women who made it possible for us to be where we are today, see how they live, learn our own history in flesh and blood, related to us. We want to read their books, watch them act, and support their proposals which inspire us. But, we are also writing, and we also have opinions on all of the goals of feminism, so we can also offer learning and inspiration to them. Because we are also adult women, and we are part of this movement.

Young women's skills are under-used

Returning to the issue of competition, one participant at AWID stated that: 'We do not want to just be photocopies of the movement.' It is not that younger women want to decide everything, or that we want to be 'the bosses', but some of us do feel that our capacities are not used to their best advantage by the movement.

Our sense of being on the margins is made more difficult to understand, since we often hear affirmations from older women that young women are the hope and new life of feminism. In fact, we think we are in the same boat as the older women. As young women we are not only interested in the future. We are going to continue with the feminist movement, and we are finding and experimenting with new ways of being in it right now, all together. But it sometimes seems difficult to recognise this when we are dealing with inter-generational issues.

The high cost of activism

Another issue young feminists have pointed out is the cost of activism in the movement, which has taken a toll on women who have preceded us, and is now taking a toll on us. Many of us experience illness, depression, poverty, anger and conflict. Many of us are struggling with addictions, not just to substances but also to obsessive work regimes which do not allow us time to reflect, or breathing space.

Being a feminist means we have many fascinating, complex experiences, trying to create a new culture, and re-create our own lives. But the destructive aspect of it, the guilt and sacrifice, at work and in our lives more generally, is a tremendous challenge. Young women are trying to pick up this challenge and do something about it. We want to find alternative ways of engaging that does not cause so much sacrifice and unnecessary pain. We know that if we are tired and burnt-out, we will be unable to continue doing the work we do, and will deprive the movement of valuable members and contributions. Secondly, the freedom and humanity that we are striving for should also bring us some autonomy and pleasure.

What strategies can we use for inter-generational organising?

In the end, to be true to the political ideals of the movement, and in the spirit of moving forward, it is imperative that we meet the internal challenges to become a movement relevant to women of all ages and generations. The AWID workshop gave some of us a chance to analyse this issue a little more, and identify what needs to be done. The challenge we face is to start talking, sharing and so forth with each other, for the achievement of an inclusive movement.

Having recognised the challenge to facilitate diversity and inclusiveness in the women's movement, some of the recommendations which came out of the AWID panel are:

- to recognise the diverse ways of being a feminist and engaging with feminism
- to intensify our efforts to form and spread feminism, including its vision and strategies, to ensure all generations gain from it
- to acknowledge the fact that the women's movement contains women from different generations, contexts and schools of thought. This diversity is fascinating in itself

- at the same time, to bear in mind that younger women are not the 'only hope' of the women's movement in future, and that the agenda is not already formed. In fact it is open to reflection and evaluation to ensure relevance and responsiveness to the needs of all women
- to confront openly, and challenge, notions of 'competition' between generations of feminists, and the spectre of the controlling parental figure
- to create opportunities for open and honest dialogue about the tensions that still cause divisions in the movement
- to promote the development of an agenda that can include the movement in all its diversity, and create an ideal of feminism which is non-essentialist (that is, which recognises many ways of being a feminist)
- to promote ways of being an activist which minimise sacrifice or damage to ourselves in our work and personal lives
- to share and continue the good inter-generational experiences and actions which already exist in the women's movement
- to recognize the role of pioneers at the beginning of the women's movement, but build alliances between the generations to ensure we achieve our goals in future
- to promote links with other movements.

In a movement that has accomplished so much for women globally, it is an appropriate time to reflect on where we are and where we are headed, and think about some of the barriers holding us back from achieving our goals.

Andrea Medina Rosas is a lawyer. She is Director of the Centre for Research and Attention to Women (CIAM) in Guadalajara, Mexico. andreagdl@infosel.net.mx

Shamillah Wilson is the Young Women and Leadership Programme Manager for the Association for Women's Rights in Development. Address: 221 Lawrence Road, Crawford, Athlone, Western Cape 7764, South Africa. swilson@awid.org

Notes

1 In this article, we use the terms women's and feminist movement interchangeably. When we refer to the movement, we are talking about the organisation of efforts (advocacy, mobilising, resistance and so on) toward achieving gender equality and social justice.

Reference

Marcela, L (1989) 'Enemistad y sororidad: hacia una nueva cultura feminista', *Memoria* 25, Centro de Estudios del Movimiento Obrero y socialista, México

Institutions, organisations and gender equality in an era of globalisation

Aruna Rao and David Kelleher

Development organisations can play a significant role in supporting women in the communities where they work to challenge unequal gender relations. The authors of this article argue that the majority of development organisations fail to do so because they pay insufficient attention to the importance of social institutions in perpetuating inequality. Two prominent approaches to gender mainstreaming emphasise organisational infrastructure and culture. Ideas in these approaches are necessary, but insufficient, to enable organisations to play a part in transforming the social institutions that perpetuate gender inequality. Gender at Work is a new global capacity-building and knowledge network aiming to promote institutional change through encouraging development organisations to analyse gender relations in the societies in which they work, and in the institutions they need to challenge. It reviews past efforts of development organisations to mainstream gender into their work, and develops programmes and processes to challenge institutional norms which work against women's interests.

Although much has been accomplished by now in the name of gender equality, it is still true that in no region of the world are women and men equal in legal, social or economic rights (World Bank, 2001). We believe that this is because the bulk of development and human rights work toward gender inequality ignores the role of the institutions (formal and informal) that maintain women's unequal position. There is a growing consensus among feminists across the world that to make a significant impact on gender inequity, we must change institutions. In India, for example, over one million women have been elected to local level governing bodies, as a result of a 1993 amendment to the Indian Constitution requiring that one-third of the elected seats to local governing bodies be reserved for women. This motion gives women a legitimate space to participate, and possibly a voice, but this does not guarantee their influence. That awaits the change of (largely informal) institutions that constrain women's political participation and influence in local decision-making.

To clarify, the terms 'institution' and 'organisation' are often used synonymously, but we find it useful to distinguish between the two. We understand institutions as the rules for achieving social or economic ends (Kabeer, 1996). They determine who gets what, who does what, and who decides. The rules that maintain women's position in societies may be stated or implicit. These rules would include values that maintain the gendered division of labour; prohibitions on women owning land; and restrictions on women's mobility. Perhaps the most fundamental is the devaluing of reproductive work.

Of course, changing institutions is far from easy and our global understanding of it is far from sophisticated. At the same time, there are changes in a promising direction. Women leaders around the world, whether they work on economic policy, legislation, education, organisational change or grassroots health care are initiating ideas and practices that have the potential to change institutions, but these innovations are not getting into the mainstream.

One clear understanding that has emerged is that institutions change (in large part) as a result of the actions of organisations. Whenever an organisation intervenes in the life of a community, it has the ongoing choice whether to challenge or support existing community gender-related norms. For example, BRAC (Bangladesh Rural Advancement Committee) is one of the world's largest indigenous rural development organisations, working with over two million poor rural and urban women in Bangladesh. When members of BRAC village organisations began to raise the issue of arbitrary divorces or unjust actions regarding inheritances, BRAC chose to start a para-legal programme which advised village women on their rights, thereby supporting them in challenging the authority of men in the village to act outside the law. This action, and others like it, requires challenging the power of those who benefit from the status quo. Most organisations have neither the inclination nor the capacity to challenge institutional norms. This is why organisational change work is so critical to the enterprise of achieving gender equality through development interventions.

To promote organisational change that will enable the organisation to challenge gender inequality, change agents must understand and link organisational change, institutional change and gender equality. A good deal of effort has gone into changing organisations themselves, in order to enhance their ability to challenge and change gender-biased rules in a variety of institutional arenas. In this paper, we look at approaches to changing organisations and institutional rules, and discuss the elements of a new approach. But first, let's look briefly inside organisations themselves.

Gender-biased organisations

Organisations are sites – like families, markets and the state – where institutional rules are played out. As mentioned above, these rules specify how resources are allocated, and how tasks, responsibilities and values are assigned. In other words, institutional rules determine who gets what, who does what, and who decides. Although institutions vary within and across cultures, and are constantly evolving and changing, they are embedded in relational hierarchies of gender, class, caste, and other critical fault lines, which define identities and distribute power – both symbolically and materially.

These institutional rules operate in organisations. They are often below the surface, but are nevertheless interwoven into the hierarchies, work practices and beliefs of organisations. And they constrain the ability of these organisations to challenge gender-biased institutional norms within the organisation and in communities.

There is good theoretical as well as empirical work on the gender-biased nature of organisations and how these constrain their functioning.[1] In our work, we focus on understanding the 'deep structure' of organisations, and how to uncover it (Rao, Stuart and Kelleher, 1999). By 'deep structure' we mean the collection of values, history, culture and practices that form the unquestioned, 'reasonable' way of work in organisations.

The most important of these is exclusionary power, and how it is used to keep women's interests and perspectives out. Very few organisations have mechanisms or ways of balancing or restraining the power of those at the top. Very few enforce accountability mechanisms. Although most organisations pride themselves on participation, this is almost always the type that keeps the authority structure of people, ideas and decision-making intact.

Power hides the fact that organisations are gendered at very deep levels. More specifically, women are prevented from challenging institutions by four inter-related factors:

Lack of political access: There are neither systems nor powerful actors who can bring women's perspectives and interests to the table;

Lack of appropriate accountability systems: Organisational resources are steered toward quantitative targets that are often only distantly related to institutional change for gender equality;

Cultural systems: The work–family divide perpetuated by most organisations prevents women from being full participants in those organisations as women continue to bear the responsibility for child and elderly care; and

Cognitive structures: Work itself is seen mostly within existing, gender-biased norms and understandings.

Gender and organisational change approaches

The table below highlights two prominent organisational approaches to working on gender equality: a gender infrastructure approach, and an organisational change approach, and delineates elements of a third approach, which we call 'gender and institutional change'.

Gender infrastructure approach

This involves putting into place a basic infrastructure, typically including an organisational gender policy, a gender unit of technically skilled change agents to work on organisational programmes, gender training and developing gender analysis tools, adopting family-friendly policies such as flexi-time and provision of

workplace childcare, increasing the number of women staff and managers, and increasing resources devoted to programming targeted at women.

What we call the gender infrastructure approach here is very close to what has been implemented in many development organisations under the rubric of 'gender mainstreaming'. Gender mainstreaming is a phrase popularised by the United Nations agencies. It was originally conceived as a way to bring about institutional transformation. It is seen as a means to achieve gender equality, in the equitable access to society's resources, opportunities, education, and equal participation in the shaping of decisions, influencing what is valued, and so on. There are many ways to work toward it, including integrating gender analysis into programme planning, implementation and evaluation; including women's voices as well as men's in decision-making; addressing women's interests; securing women's access to benefits, and making both women's and men's contributions to development visible.

However, while gender mainstreaming was transformatory in its conception, experience has shown that it has had limited success in its implementation. The track record of gender mainstreaming within development agencies (public and private) has been poor primarily because it has been reluctantly adopted by 'mainstream' development agencies, whose top leadership has not adequately supported this agenda. It has too often been an 'add women and stir' approach, which does not question basic assumptions, strategic objectives, or ways of working. Gender mainstreaming has been implemented in an organisational context of hierarchy and agenda-setting that has not prioritised women's rights. It has focused overwhelmingly on promoting women's perceived 'basic needs', and not on meeting the strategic concerns of women themselves in terms of supporting them to give voice to their interests, or to mobilise and change

Table 1: Gender and organisational change approaches

Approach	Outcomes	Change strategy	Notes
Gender infrastructure	• Gender policy, including family-friendly policy • Gender Unit • Increased female staff and managers • Increased resources for programme work targeting women	• Reference to international covenants and agreements • Management support • Internal constituency • External pressure from women's movement and/or donors	• This 'formal' architecture is necessary but far from sufficient • This approach may leave organisational attitudes intact, making overworked gender staff fight uphill battles • Unlikely to develop new programme oriented to changing institutions
Organisational change	• Changes in the 'deep structure,' such as power relations, work–family balance, instrumentality, etc. • Accountability to client constituency	• A mixture of organisational development, pressure from internal and external constituencies, management support, gender training	• This is the 'informal architecture' required to change institutions • This approach risks creating a black hole of organisational change processes in which gender equality work may be lost
Institutional change for gender equality	• Organisational ways of working to facilitate change in social institutions beyond the organisation itself (families, communities, markets and the state).	• Gender analysis of the institutions relevant to the organisation's programme, developing programmes and processes to challenge these institutional norms, changing reward structures, building organisational capacity	• This approach grounds the change effort in the work and maintains the focus where it should be • Difficult to sustain without strong external pressure and high commitment from within the organisation.

unequal gender power relations. Finally, in some cases, gender mainstreaming has got lost in traditional organisational development concerns, with inadequate analysis of the issues, context and power dynamics – both internal and external – that are perpetuating women's disempowerment.

On the positive side, many change agents see putting the infrastructure in place to support gender work as a necessary first step. In a range of organisations, it has opened up a space for gender inequality to be discussed and addressed, ensured resourcing, and granted greater legitimacy to gender equity concerns. In a few instances, change agents have been able to parlay these resources into systemic change. But in most cases, it is clearly not enough to challenge institutional norms.

Organisational change approach

This approach involves changes that build the organisation's capacity to challenge gender-biased institutional rules, including: democratising relationships between employees in the workplace; making women's voices more powerful in the organisation; finding ways to make the organisation more accountable to women clients, and more amenable to the participation of women staff in decision-making; and finding ways of building relationships with other organisations to further a gender-equality agenda.

Much of the work on organisational change for gender equality has adapted practices of organisational development and organisational learning, particularly with regard to the importance of the learning process and of participation. Organisational development typically focuses on ensuring that information collection, analysis and action planning are participatory; and there is a focus on issues of communications and relationships, and increasing the equality of managers and staff. But, unlike traditional organisational development, the organisational change for gender equality approach holds that a new political alignment, which ensures that new gender issues are put on the agenda, is as important to the change process as rational analysis. The challenge is to develop methods to bring about organisational change that combine politics and participation with an understanding of the part organisations can play in bringing about equality. For many practitioners, this means linking organisational and feminist theory.

The work of the Gender Team at BRAC is a good example of this.[2] Eight years ago, the BRAC gender team was charged with leading a long-term effort to improve gender equality, both within BRAC itself as an organisation, and in BRAC's provision of services to poor rural women in Bangladesh. (In contrast, many organisation development (OD) interventions focus solely on organisational processes.) To achieve its aims, the gender team's initiative aimed to change organisational norms, systems, and relationships. BRAC's initiative used a basic organisational development approach to change, as outlined earlier.

After two years, the most important outcomes were: a loosening of rigid power imbalances within the organisation; better communication across levels of the hierarchy; greater space to raise and discuss 'taboo' issues; more attention to women's voices and their needs; changes in relationships between women and men and across programming silos (non-integrated programmes); and a resultant improvement in the quality of the work environment, and in programme-related problem solving (ibid.).

However, the intervention did not specifically focus on BRAC's relation with communities, or on the organisation's potential as an agent for institutional change; that is, it did not connect BRAC to village women members in a way that could have transformed gender power relations between the organisation and village women, and within the community at large.

Institutional change for gender equality

If our organisations are to help transform social institutions to bring about gender equality, a new approach is needed. Serious questions are being asked about the efficacy and outcome of 'traditional' approaches to mainstream gender into organisations. Putting infrastructure in place to advance women's interests is not proving adequate. Increasingly, we are aware that efforts in private human rights and development or public sector agencies to change gender-biased institutional rules have proceeded (by and large) without connection to initiatives to support women to mobilise and give voice to their shared concerns. In other words, the 'supply' side of the institutional change equation has been divorced from the 'demand' side of the equation.[3]

Gender and organisational change efforts are also proving inadequate; many have become mired in the intricacies and dynamics of internal organisational change, and in the process, the real purpose of these changes has vanished from sight. In addition, many such initiatives remain unconnected to the larger contextual forces that are changing women's opportunities and threats, morphing unequal gender relations into new forms without challenging the underlying inequality, and eroding gains. We have seen that the entry of larger numbers of women into decision-making structures has not transformed either the nature of those structures (in terms of decision-making power, transparency, accountability, or accessibility), nor the policies emanating from them. Voice and representation do not necessarily translate into influence.

We can draw two important implications for our work from this analysis.[4] First, only those who work consciously to change social rules, and to redistribute power and privilege as well as resources, can make significant and sustainable advances toward gender and social justice. Second, to enable organisations to contribute towards this process of social change, they need a new approach to gender issues, which re-focuses our attention onto the big issue – that is, the need to ensure that our work helps change social institutions to support equality between women and men.

The 'Institutional Change for Gender Equality' approach is being developed in response to this. It has potential to help organisations play a part in challenging gender-biased norms and values throughout society, as well as within themselves. It links the 'supply' side of the equation (internal organisational commitment and actions relating to gender inequality) to the 'demand' side (the broad range of efforts aimed at women's mobilisation, citizenship and voice). It brings these two critical dimensions back together into the same

picture. Significant, sustainable advances toward gender and social justice can only be made by redistributing power and privilege, as well as resources. Adopting the approach would enable organisations to ensure their work contributes to upgrading women's position and voice, not only their material condition. Focusing on the wider picture of challenging unequal gender power relations in society will force attention (because of their importance to women's interests) on a variety of organisational forms including public systems, labour unions, and political parties, in addition to the set of more traditional governance, development and human rights actors.

Linking the 'supply' side of the institutional change equation more clearly to the 'demand' side requires that we go beyond asking how organisational values, power relations and practices need to change in order to actively take on, and respond to, the voice and perspectives of poor women. We need to ask a more profound question: that is, what are the key fulcrums and change processes that organisations can adopt, to enable them to interact with the wider environment in a way that results in positive outcomes which ensure justice for women? For example, accountability is a key fulcrum around which we can examine interactions between supply- and demand-oriented interventions, and analyse and change power systems.

Adopting this new approach requires organisations to ask some key questions:

- Are programme strategies consciously designed to change the way resources, power, and privilege are distributed between men and women in their societies?

- Are programme strategies changing gender-biased social rules and the institutions that enforce them, overtly or even covertly?

- Are organisations accountable to their constituencies for equity and gender justice outcomes; do women have a means of recourse if they are not?

Addressing only one of these basic changes through a programme is insufficient. For example, the easiest kind of programme to instigate and fund is one that promotes changes in the access to and distribution of resources. Yet strategies that address the need for changes in power and social rules are more critical in promoting positive change in gender relations. In the absence of a clear focus on gender relations and the institutions that shape them, programmes can end up either reinforcing existing social arrangements, or creating new male élites. Work that does not address women's interests and gendered power relations will not achieve transformative social change. To turn to organisations themselves, only moderate gains in gender equality have been achieved because of the resistance of male managers, organisational culture, and lack of accountability including monitoring mechanisms and mechanisms to prevent gradual backsliding. We believe that organisations that intend to change power structures and biased gender and social relations have to put their money where their mouth is. They have to mirror these principles in their own structure and functioning in order to be effective.

Conclusion

To conclude with a critical question: how can we all develop better understandings of how to transform power hierarchies and institutional biases embedded in our organisations, and enable them to become more effective engines of social change? For Gender at Work – a new global knowledge and capacity building network on gender and institutional change – this is the driving question.

Gender at Work is currently working in India, South Africa and Latin America, in partnership with a variety of social change organisations to build new knowledge for practice (the strategic 'hows'), specifically highlighting key aspects of strategic interventions that challenge and change power relations and promote better accountability to women's interests. This work involves analysing past efforts to effect organisational change to bring about gender equality. It also involves developing ideas about how to do this work more effectively, in a way that is relevant to developing country contexts, and social change organisations. We will examine the assumptions at the heart of 'feminist' organisations, particularly with regard to leadership and decision-making processes, and ask 'what happened?' We will look for stories of innovation, as well as challenges, ruptures, and contradictions at the nexus of gender equality, organisational effectiveness and institutional change. We plan to initiate action-learning processes, to change gender-biased institutional rules and change organisations. Through these processes, we hope to develop a collective voice, rooted in successful on-the-ground experience, to change international thinking and work for gender equality.

Aruna Rao is Convenor of Gender at Work. She is a gender and institutional change expert with over 20 years' experience of addressing gender issues in a variety of development organisations, primarily in Asia. Address: 3/23 Shanti Niketan, New Delhi 110021, India. Arao@kvam.net; www.genderatwork.org

David Kelleher is Convenor of Gender at Work. David is an independent organisational consultant. For more than 30 years, he has worked with numerous non-governmental and public organisations helping them build their capacity to further their social mandates. He is currently the Afghanistan, Pakistan and Bangladesh Co-ordinator for Amnesty International (Canada). Contact information: Box 467, Maxville, Ontario, Canada. kelleher@glen-net.ca; www.genderatwork.org

Notes

1 See, for example, the work of Naila Kabeer, Anne Marie Goetz, and Joan Acker.
2 For a more complete description of principles, concepts, strategy, and tools, see Rao, Stuart and Kelleher, 1999.
3 This disconnection is obvious in other fields as well – citizen voice initiatives around the world, for example, are often considered quite separately from efforts to deal with public-sector efficiency problems. See, for example, Goetz, 2001.
4 This analysis draws on work done with Srilatha Batliwala in 2002 on women's leadership for social change.

References

Goetz, A.M., J. Gaventa, et al. (2001), 'Bringing citizen voice and client focus into service delivery', *IDS Working Paper* 138, Brighton: IDS

Kabeer, N. (1994) *Reversed Realities: Gender Hierarchies in Development Thought*, London: Verso

Rao A., R. Stuart and D. Kelleher (1999) *Gender at Work*, West Hartford, Conn., USA: Kumarian Press

World Bank, *Engendering Development, Through Gender Equity in Rights, Resources and Voice*, Washington: World Bank, 2001

Resources

Compiled by Ruth Evans

Publications

Marketisation of Governance: Critical Feminist Perspectives from the South (2000), Viviene Taylor, DAWN Secretariat, The University of the South Pacific, Suva, Fiji Islands.
www.dawn.org.fj/publications/index.html
This analysis strongly criticises global financial and trade institutions for re-modelling the state to support global economic, financial, and trade liberal-isation. Based on the findings of regional research and consultations, the analysis highlights the challenges and dilemmas for social movements pursuing economic and gender justice in the era of globalisation. It sets out a number of key recommendations. An accompanying 30-minute video, *Marketisation of Governance*, is also available from DAWN.

Engendering the Political Agenda: The Role of the State, Women's Organizations and the International Community (2000), INSTRAW, César Nicolás Penson 102-A, Santo Domingo, República Dominicana.
www.un-instraw.org;
instraw@un-instraw.org
This publication from the United Nations International Research and Training Institute for the Advancement of Women (UN-INSTRAW) assesses the impact of inter-national activities on gender at local and national levels. The report discusses how this interplay shapes the introduction and

sustainability of gender issues on the political agendas of individual countries, based on case studies from the Dominican Republic, Romania, and South Africa. The effects of international legal instruments such as Convention on Elimination of Discrimination Against Women (CEDAW) and donor funding for gender equality are examined.

Globalization, Gender Equality and State Modernization (2001), Noleen Heyzer, Gender Series No. 2, Third World Network, 121-S, Jalan Utama, 10450 Penang, Malaysia.
www.twnside.org.sg/title/gender2.htm
This paper authored by the Executive Director of the UN Development Fund for Women (UNIFEM) examines the links between processes of globalisation and gender equality. It discusses key questions such as the relationship between economic growth, poverty, and gender equality, the role of government and market liberal-isation. The paper also assesses the progress of women in reshaping globalisation.

Globalization and its impacts on indigenous women: the Philippine experience (2001, Victoria Tauli-Corpuz, Gender Series No. 1, Third World Network, Malaysia.
www.twnside.org.sg/title/gender1.htm
Written by the director of an indigenous people's international NGO based in the Philippines, this paper examines globalisation

and its impacts on indigenous women, with examples from the Philippines, Mexico, and Colombia. It examines issues such as the feminisation of labour in industry and services, the liberalisation of agriculture, the social, health, environmental, and economic impacts on indigenous women, and dilemmas in tackling the globalisation agenda.

Gender, Globalization, and Democratization (2001), R.M. Kelly, J.H. Bayes, M.E. Hawkesworth, B.Young (eds.), Rowman and Littlefield Publishers Inc., 4720 Boston Way, Lanham, Maryland 20706, USA. www.rowmanlittlefield.com

Taking an historical approach, this book shows how the impact of globalisation on women throughout the world has been as negative and undemocratic as it has been positive and liberating. Drawing on the perspectives of contributors from around the world, this book discusses the prospects for democratisation and gender equality, and studies the successes and failures of mobilising efforts to achieve change.

Gender and Global Restructuring: Sightings, Sites, and Resistances (2000), M.H. Marchand and A.S. Runyan, Routledge, 11 New Fetter Lane, London EC4P 4EE. www.routledge.com

This book provides a theoretical analysis of globalisation and its relationship to gender. Feminist experts from a range of disciplines show the complexities and contradictions of ongoing global transformations (or global restructuring). They criticise the gender-blindness of neo-liberal and critical accounts of globalisation, and offer feminist approaches which stress women's agency. The book reveals how states, markets, civil society, households, and gender identities are simultaneously being restructured in different ways in various regional and national contexts. It also shows how women's resistances connect the global and the local, the public and the private.

An Alternative View of Gender and Globalisation (2002), ILRIG Globalisation Series No.6, International Labour Resource and Information Group, PO Box 1213, Woodstock 7925, South Africa. http://aidc.org.za/ilrig

This introductory booklet raises important questions about how globalisation processes are gendered and in particular, how they affect women in Africa and women workers in South Africa. It provides an introduction to the key concepts of gender and globalisation, and then examines the relationship between gender and globalisation in three areas – the changing role of the state, feminisation of manufacturing industries, and the gendered implications of the World Trade Organisation's Trade-Related Intellectual Property Rights (TRIPS) regulations. It concludes by exploring the gendered challenges to globalisation.

Feminist Futures: Re-imagining Women, Culture and Development (2003), Kum-Kum Bhavnani, John Foran and Priya Kurian (eds.), Zed Books Ltd., 7 Cynthia Street, London N1 9JF / Room 400, 175 Fifth Avenue, New York, NY 10010, USA. www.zedbooks.demon.co.uk

Feminist Futures challenges established approaches to development, and argues for a new paradigm, Women, Culture, and Development (WCD), that places women and gender at the centre. New theoretical, feminist perspectives are brought to chapters covering sexuality and the gendered body, the environment, science, and technology, and the cultural politics of representation.

Gender Justice, Development, and Rights (2002), Maxine Molyneux and Shahra Razavi (eds.), United Nations Research Institute for Social Development/Oxford University Press, Great Clarendon Street, Oxford OX2 6DP, UK. www.oup.co.uk

This book reflects on the global shift towards greater emphasis on rights and democracy. It discusses why many of the positive changes in women's rights and political representation have not been matched by increases in social justice. Through theoretical reflections and regional case studies, contributors address issues such as neo-liberal economic and social policies, democracy, and multiculturalism from a gender perspective.

Women, Globalization and Fragmentation in the Developing World (1999), Haleh Afshar and Stephanie Barrientos (eds.), Macmillan Press Ltd., Houndmills, Basingstoke, Hampshire RG 21 6XS, UK. www.palgrave.com

This book explores the gendered implications of globalisation at the grass-roots level in the South. It discusses the conflicting interactions between the global and local political economies, cultures, and faiths. Drawing on case studies from Asia, Africa, and Latin America, it demonstrates the contradictory and fragmented impact of globalisation at the local level, and its impact on the lives of women in the developing world.

Trade Myths and Gender Reality – Trade Liberalisation and Women's Lives (1999), Angela Hale (ed.) Global Publications Foundation, Box 1221, 75142 Uppsala, Sweden. www.globalpublications.org

This booklet examines the gendered impacts of trade liberalisation, drawing on case studies from Asia, Africa and Latin America. The reports demonstrate that poverty associated with trade liberalisation is threatening the livelihoods of some women and involving others in new and highly exploitative forms of employment. Providing an overview of conceptual and policy links between trade and gender, this publication also gives recommendations to integrate a gender perspective into the trade liberalisation process.

World Survey on the Role of Women in Development – Globalization, Gender and Work, (1999), UN Division for the Advancement of Women, Department of Economic and Social Affairs, New York. www.un-instraw.org

This UN World Survey reflects on recent labour market trends within the context of globalisation, and also on how the world of work is being transformed from a gender point of view. It discusses the globalisation of trade, capital, and finance, and the effects on employment and displacement from a gender perspective. It also analyses the re-organisation of work and 'flexi-bilisation' of labour, changing patterns of rural women's work, and gender dimensions in the public policy environment. The report concludes with recommendations and suggestions for developing a gender-aware policy framework throughout economic policy design and implement-ation.

Electronic Resources

Trade Liberalisation, Poverty, and Livelihoods: Understanding the Linkages (2002), Nazneen Kanji and Stephanie Barrientos, Institute of Development Studies (IDS), Working Paper 159, University of Sussex, Brighton, UK. www.ids.ac.uk

This paper (which is also available in print) reviews and assesses key analytical approaches that are used to understand the linkages between trade, poverty, and livelihoods, and their relevance in the context of sub-Saharan Africa. The paper discusses two theoretical approaches to poverty analysis within the context of sub-Saharan Africa, and examines different perspectives which assist researchers to integrate social, economic, market and non-market forces into an analysis of trade and poverty.

Globalisation and Gender-Development Perspectives and Interventions (1996), A. Keller-Herzog, Canadian International Development Agency (CIDA). Available to download from:
www2.ids.ac.uk/genie/search

This discussion paper explores the complexity of the concepts of globalisation and gender, and the dynamics of their interaction, including the uneven distribution of costs and benefits according to gender. The paper argues that both governmental and non-governmental institutions can play a key role in mediating between vulnerable groups and the risks from globalisation.

Trade, Sustainable Development and Gender (1999), papers presented at the Pre-UNCTAD (United Nations Conference on Trade and Development) Expert Workshop on 'Trade, Sustainable Development, and Gender', 12–13 July 1999, Geneva, Switzerland. Available to download from: www2.ids.ac.uk/genie/search

The Pre-UNCTAD Expert Workshop on 'Trade, Sustainable Development, and Gender' focused on the role of employment in the eradication of poverty and on women's empowerment. Experts from a range of organisations and institutions bring a gender perspective to three main areas of concern: globalisation, trade-related issues, and specific problems faced by low-income countries.

Engendering International Trade: Concepts, Policy and Action (1995), L. Beneria and A. Lind, Gender, Science, and Development Programme, Women in Global Science and Technology (WIGSAT). Available to download from:
www2.ids.ac.uk/genie/search

This paper maps out the relevant issues for future policy research on gender and trade by identifying the gaps in mainstream trade policy research. The paper argues for a new conceptual approach in theory and practice, which recognises the differential

impact on women compared to men. The authors call for policy and action-oriented organisations to document the ways in which women and men in different regions are affected by trade liberalisation and set research priorities for issues and case study sectors.

Global Trade Expansion and Liberalisation: Gender Issues and Impacts (1998) M. Fontana, S. Joekes, and R. Masika, BRIDGE Report No. 42, IDS, Brighton, UK.
bridge@ids.ac.uk; www.ids.ac.uk/bridge. Print copy also available.

Commissioned by the UK Department for International Development (DFID), this report argues that gender analysis is important in understanding why some countries, sectors or regions are unable to capitalise on potential trading opportunities. The report shows how the benefits of trade expansion differ between women and men, as well as between different groups of women, with implications for both gender equality and poverty reduction goals. Based on evidence from Asia, Latin America, the Caribbean, and sub-Saharan Africa, the report offers recommendations to achieve greater gender equality in the labour market.

Gender and Economic Globalisation: An Annotated Bibliography (2002), Emma Bell with Paola Brambilla, Bibliography No. 12, BRIDGE, IDS, Brighton.
bridge@ids.ac.uk; www.ids.ac.uk/bridge. Print copy also available.

This bibliography focuses on the economic aspects of globalisation and their impact on gender relations. The key texts cover the impact of globalisation; trade agreements, policy and financial institutions; and responses to globalisation. The overview discusses the impacts of globalisation, trade agreements, policy and financial institutions and the different responses by the women's movement. Ways to incorporate gender into theory, policy, and practice concerning globalisation are explored, with suggestions for future research.

Briefing kits

Women Challenging Globalization: A gender perspective on the United Nations International Conference on Financing for Development, March 18–22, 2002, Monterrey, Mexico, (2002) Joan Ross Frankson (ed.), UNIFEM and Women's Environment & Development Organization (WEDO), 355 Lexington Avenue, 3rd Floor, New York, NY 10017-6603, USA. Available to download: www.wedo.org/ffd/ffdreport.htm

Based on the 2002 UN International Conference on 'Financing for Development', Mexico, this accessible report discusses the conference from a gender perspective. Contributors discuss issues, process and outcomes of the 'Financing for Development' conference. They analyse the roles and situation of women in the global economy and suggest advocacy action at country and global levels.

Financing for Development Gender Policy Briefing Kit (2002), United Nations Development Programme and Women's Environment & Development Organization (WEDO), 355 Lexington Avenue, 3rd Floor, New York, NY 10017-6603, USA. wedo@wedo.org www.wedo/org/ffd/kit.htm

This toolkit is a practical guide to gender and financing for development. It covers issues such as gender analyses of macro-economic policies, gender and economic decision-making, gender budgets and further resources.

Local Action/Global Change, Learning about the human rights of women and girls (1999), Mallika Dutt, Julie Mertus, and Nancy Flowers, UNIFEM and Center for Women's Global Leadership. Available from Women, Ink., 777 United Nations Plaza, New York NY 10017, USA. www.womenink.org

This accessible training manual provides tools for women and men to critically examine the framework of human rights. It includes information about the human rights of women in the areas of violence, health, reproduction and sexuality, education, the global economy, the workplace, and family life in relation to international women's human rights agreements. Suggested training activities include discussion, role-play, storytelling, expression through art and music, to relate human rights principles to women's personal experience.

Journals

Feminist Economics Journal, Carfax Publishing, Taylor and Francis Ltd., Rankine Road, Basingstoke, Hants. RG24 8PR, UK. www.tandf.co.uk/journals

Feminist Economics is a leading academic journal that attempts to develop an inter-disciplinary approach to feminist perspectives on economics and the economy. Articles cover analysis of macro-economic policy, micro-finance, gender budgets and globalisation from a gender perspective.

Agenda, PO Box 61163, Bishopsgate, 4008, South Africa. Tel: (+27 31) 304 7001; Fax: (+27 31) 304 7018; editor@agenda.org.za; subs@agenda.org.za; www.agenda.org.za

Agenda is a quarterly feminist journal published by a women's media project in South Africa since 1987. Selected articles are available online. Of particular relevance is issue 48, 'Globalisation: Challenging Dominant Discourses', June 2001.

Lola Press, Greifswaler Str.4, 10405, Berlin, Germany; San José 1436–11.200, Montevideo, Uruguay; PO Box 1057, Lenasia 1820, Johannesburg, South Africa.
www.lolapress.org

Lola Press is a bilingual (English/ Spanish) international feminist magazine published three times a year (two printed issues and an electronic issue). November 2002 issue contains several articles based on the 'Re-inventing Globalization' AWID 2002 Forum, Mexico.

Organisations

Association for Women's Rights in Development (AWID) 96 Spadina Ave., Suite 401, Toronto, Ont., Canada M5V 2J6.
Tel: (416) 594 3773; Fax: (416) 594 0330; awid@awid.org; www.awid.org

The Association of Women's Rights in Development (AWID) is an international membership organisation connecting, informing, and mobilising people and organisations committed to achieving gender equality, sustainable development, and women's human rights. AWID's 9th International Conference, 'Re-inventing Globalisation', held in October 2002 focused on the key question: 'How can we re-invent globalisation to further the rights of all women?' Papers explored the economic, political, social, ecological and cultural implications of globalisation and proposed alternatives promoting gender equality. AWID also launched the 'Globalize This! Women's Rights in Development Campaign'.

Gender at Work, Aruna Rao, Convenor, 3/23, Shanti Niketan, New Delhi, India.
Tel: (91-11) 2410-8322;
www.genderatwork.org; arao@kvam.net.

Gender at Work is a new knowledge and capacity building network focused on gender and institutional change. It was created in June 2001 by AWID (Association for Women's Rights in Development), WLP (Women's Learning Partnership), CIVICUS (World Alliance for Citizen Participation), and UNIFEM (United Nations Fund for Women). The organisation works with development and human rights practitioners, researchers, and policy makers. It aims to develop new theory and practice on how organisations can change gender-biased institutional rules, values, and practices. It also aims to change the political, accountability, cultural and knowledge systems of organisations to challenge social norms and gender inequality. The website contains an up-to-date collection of resources on Institutional Change for Gender Equality.

Development Alternatives with Women for a New Era (DAWN) DAWN Secretariat, PO Box 13124, Suva, Fiji Tel/Fax: (679) 314770; admin@dawn.org.fj; www.dawn.org.fj

DAWN is a network of Southern feminists and activists working for economic and gender justice and political transformation at the global level. One of DAWN's key research and advocacy themes is the 'Political Economy of Globalisation'. The website provides a range of publications and resources on trade, globalisation, and gender.

Women's Environment & Development Organization (WEDO), 355 Lexington Avenue, 3rd Floor, New York, NY 10017-6603, USA.
wedo@wedo.org; www.wedo.org

WEDO is an international advocacy network that seeks to advocate for women's equality in decision-making in governance and in policy-making institutions, forums and processes, at all levels, to achieve economic and social justice. Key programme areas include 'gender and governance', and 'economic and social justice', and WEDO participates in the UN 'Financing for Development' initiative.

European Women's Lobby, 18 Rue Hydraulique, B-1210 Bruxelles, Tel (+32 2) 217 90 20, Fax (+32 2) 219 84 51; ewl@womenlobby.org; www.womenlobby.org

The European Women's Lobby (EWL) aims to achieve equality of women and men in Europe and to serve as a link between political decision-makers and women's organisations at EU level. The bilingual website (English/ French) contains a range of resources, including position papers, policy documents, and publications. A key focus of Policy and Campaigns is 'Women and Globalisation', which provides a range of papers on engendering international trade and the impacts of trade liberalisation and globalisation on women's lives.

WIDE (Network Women in Development Europe), Rue du Commerce 40, 1040 Brussels, Belgium. Tel: (+32 2) 545 90 70; Fax: (+32 2) 512 73 42; wide@gn.apc.org; www.eurosur.org/wide.

WIDE is a European network of gender specialists, women active in non-govern-mental organisations, and human rights activists. A key focus of their advocacy and lobbying work is on International Financial Institutions (World Bank, IMF etc.), the World Trade Organisation, and Liberal-isation and Globalisation. Recent publications include the WIDE bulletins, 'Instruments for gender equality in trade agreements' (2001), available in English and Spanish, and 'Globalisation, develop-ment and sustainability: A WIDEr view' (2002), which discusses the UN Conference on Financing for Development (FfD), March 2002, Monterrey, Mexico and the World Summit on Sustainable Develop-ment (WSSD), August 2002, Johannesburg, South Africa.

UN-INSTRAW (United Nations Inter-national Research and Training Institute for the Advancement of Women), César Nicolás Penson 102-A, Santo Domingo, República Dominicana Tel: +1 (809) 685 2111 Fax: +1 (809) 685 2117 www.un-instraw.org (English/ Spanish/ French) instraw@un-instraw.org

INSTRAW aims to promote gender equality and women's advancement worldwide through research, training and the collection and dissemination of information. Website contains information about many publi-cations on gender and globalisation issues (some available in a range of languages) available to order through INSTRAW.

Videos

Life (2000), Robert Lamb (series editor), Television Trust for the Environment. Available from Bullfrog Films, PO Box 149, Oley, PA19547, USA. www.bullfrogfilms.com; info@bullfrogfilms.com

This 30-part series looks at the effect of globalisation on individuals and commun-ities around the world. It looks at progress since the 1995 Copenhagen Social Summit when world leaders promised action on poverty, employment, and social inte-gration. The series examines how people's lives are affected by globalisation in Africa, Asia, North and South America, the Middle East, and the Pacific Islands.

Who's counting? Marilyn Waring on sex, lies and global economics (1996), Terre Nash, National Film Board of Canada. Available from Bullfrog Films.

In this film, Marilyn Waring, one of the leading voices in the field of feminist economics, demystifies global economics from a feminist perspective. She challenges the myths of economics, which ignore the unpaid work of women and damage to the environment, and offers new approaches to political action. Accompanying study guide is available.

Remote Sensing (2001), Ursula Biemann. Available from Women Make Movies, 462 Broadway, Suite 500 L, New York, NY 10013, USA or Ursula Biemann, Schrennengasse 21, 8003 Zürich, Switzerland. www.wmm.com (N. America) www.geobodies.org (rest of world)

This video essay traces the routes of women who travel across the globe for work in the sex industry. The film investigates the consequences of the US military presence in South East Asia as well as European migration politics. It links processes of globalisation and new technologies to the sexualisation and displacement of women on a global scale.

Conferences

2003 Conference on Feminist Economics, International Association for Feminist Economics (IAFFE), June 27–29, University of the West Indies, Barbados. www.iaffe.org

The conference themes include: gender dimensions of macro-economic policies; globalisation; work; women's human rights; and women's international feminist alliances for social and economic change. Conference papers may be available from individual presenters after conference. Contact: IAFFE, 100 D. Roberts Hall, Bucknell University, Lewisburg, PA 17837. Fax to: 570-577-3451. iaffe@bucknell.edu